Dedication

I dedicate this work to those who love the people, animals and natural elements about them. Folks who live from the heart hold the key for successful evolution and survival of all that is earthly.

I0094434

HUMAN STELLAR VOYAGERS

Preparing Homo Sapiens to Survive Apocalypse And Colonize The Universe.

ROBERTO SYLVAN DELMAR Ph.D.

Purple Bosque
Voyager Media

Copyright © 2018 by Roberto Sylvan Delmar Ph.D.

All rights reserved. A reviewer may quote brief passages. This publication may not be reproduced in whole or in part, stored in a retrieval system, or transmitted in any form or by any means, without written permission from the author or his representatives.

This book is for the education of the individual and group. The suggestions and recommendation herein cannot be guaranteed to produce positive results. Hence, the author assumes no liability. Those wishing to set a course for growth and development are advised to seek qualified mentors for guidance and support.

Cover design and interior art work by EMMA TROY DESIGN.

Acknowledgements

The original source of these ideas and concepts is questionable. Family, friends, clients, culture, nature and the entire universe have had a say in the creation of who I am and what I do. I am thankful for their contribution to my essence.

Maria Gunn provided the initial manuscript assessment and structural edit. I appreciated her patience with my poor literary skills. I learned a great deal from her.

In the final revisions of the work; I am indebted to Joel Welsh for his comprehensive review and copy edit. As an English teacher, he has a masterful ability to design text into a seamless, smooth flow of grammar. We share an interest in the philosophical; this allowed him to identify with the concepts of the book, which made for a dynamic interchange between us and better writing on my part.

Author's Details

After receiving my Ph.D. in clinical psychology, I became research director for a private community mental health centre (CMHC) in the rocky - mountains, and eventually its' director of the alcohol and drug abuse program. My next position was director of a CMHC in a Midwest state capital. Additionally, I served on a National Institute of Mental Health (NIMH) review team conducting on site reviews of CMHCs, and served as the clinical board member of a National Alcoholism Abuse (NAA) local chapter.

Next, I set up a private practise specialized in group therapy, hypnosis, interpersonal relationships, marriage and family counselling, children's problems, alternative life styles and gifted people. I have conducted research in and written articles on interpersonal relationships, alcohol and drug education and presented extensive workshops on sex, marriage, child rearing, personal development, career path and time management. In my spare time I taught university courses in personality theory and developmental psychology.

I have lived in 5 different cultures on 3 continents, travelled in over 50 countries and speak several languages. I am an ardent outdoorsman, boater, animal lover, musician, cook, and jack of all trades, and have designed and built my house.

I eat too many chocolate chip cookies, doughnuts, tend to be impatient and get bored easily.

Human Stellar Voyagers
Table of Contents

Human Stellar Voyagers

Human Stellar Voyagers

Preface

I sit in my corner-study bathed in warm sunlight; the summer air, scented with pine and wildflower, enfolds me. Outside, the brook gurgles over rocks and through reeds on its way to the lake; dew drops glisten on the maple leaves. I often sit enraptured gazing out the window, as the chipmunks scamper beneath the trees in search of seeds and nuts. Since childhood, natural settings have always impelled my mind to wander and to wonder; what is going on, what is life all about, why does it exist? Some say the purpose of life is to experience the joy of living. It's fun to think about these things; but as far as answers go, I haven't got a clue and sometimes feel presumptuous asking such questions. If thousands of philosophers haven't figured it out, it's not likely I will; but I enjoy trying.

My interest in space began as a teenager reading science fiction and following NASA's activities. Like countless others, I have often wondered what it would be like to live on the moon. I frequently visited the aerospace museum at nearby Wright Patterson air force base. The study of psychology and world travel further increased my interest in the universe.

For several years now, I have lived in the clear air of rural Australia. I often sit at night gazing through my telescope and wonder how we will successfully travel into the heavens and colonize them?

Preface

Before such an event can take place, we have a number of hurdles to overcome. Our destruction of the natural biosphere must cease, and we must remove the threat of violence that hangs over the head of too many people. More of our contemporary problems will be detailed in chapter two. Einstein and other notables suggest we must change our perception of ourselves, our neighbours, and the entire world if the human race is to survive. In this second decade of the century, many experts are indeed forecasting an imminent crisis threatening extinction of human life.

Many of the publicized predictions of a coming chaos are from the lips of highly educated people in the middle or upper classes. It seems to me they are behind the times, and out of touch with contemporary life. I wonder what other people think of these chaos forecasts? Such as one of the billion Asians living in poverty, or the indigenous Amazonian who after 15 thousand years of life in the jungle is having his land stolen by corrupt governments and corporations. Then there are the centuries old Syrian towns that now lie in rubble. It is October 2018, authorities claim there are 68 million refugees fleeing-Africa, Burma, Afghanistan…; chaos is not coming, it is here.

How will we survive a world crisis, successfully undertake planetary colonization? These issues prodded me into a great deal of thinking and literature research. From these activities I have distilled suggestions, concepts and methods to help prepare humans for survival on earth and the journey into space. Some human body elements originated aeons ago in space. I suggest our evolutionary goal may be to return to the stellar regions.

To do so is a matter of reclaiming Homo sapiens' full genetic endowments, maximizing his potentials, shedding his harmful behaviours and creating a learning environment to achieve these goals; that is the content of this book.

Human ingenuity and hard work have created awesome advances, yet we remain a destroyer species hell bent on exterminating other life forms, denuding the landscape and killing each other. Technology may devise an awesome spaceship, magnificent housing structures for a spatial colony and impeccable infrastructure, but this will all be to no avail if the inhabitants are unable to coexist happily and productively. Future life on Earth and planetary colonization requires exemplary integrated groups of, what I call 'stellar personalities', people with superlative mastery of their natural capacities.

I have become intimately familiar with the multitude of cultural and societal factors instrumental in creating mental, emotional, physical and spiritual disequilibrium. Much research has been conducted on these issues and the endless list of brain functions operating as coping mechanisms. As a psychotherapist I assisted individuals and groups to more accurately perceive these influences, to modify their self-perception, and establish a more stable and balanced pattern of living.

Preface

I will detail some brain functions which impact on a persons' ability to achieve their potential. Unfortunately, these functions receive little attention from the public or the professional community. I make no claim to be an expert on the complex functioning of the brain. However, my professional training, combined with experience and ongoing knowledge acquisition, allows me to present these ideas and methods to recover our full capacities. This will enhance our ability to tailor make a successful life here on earth, as well as, in the cosmos. I'll limit the amount of research data, and professional jargon. I will write in a memoir style, including personal anecdotes to illustrate the issues.

Understanding the past helps one to take command of the present. Hence, the introductory chapter provides autobiographical information inviting the reader to walk a bit in my shoes and possibly see how and why I view the world as I do. The first chapter contains historical data pertinent to the issues, followed by a chapter on the contemporary status of society.

The chapters will follow chronologically from past to present. The concepts I present have been around a long time. My hope is to re-generate interest in them, encouraging people to debate them, find their flaws and strengths and possibly benefit from their kernels of wisdom. Some items are conjecture - the best educated guess possible at the time and open to debate.

Preface

The program of action I offer requires diligent work: a great deal of thought, patience, and joining hands with others. These efforts will assist the continued survival of Homo sapiens and his exploration of the universe. I suggest the traditional communal (Hub) family structure with its breadth of skills and its focus on the psychosocial facets of life needs to be reinstated. I believe living in such a community is necessary for us to find the vitality and resilience to meet and overcome obstacles.

We will look at controversial issues, for example, how self-deception and pretending can threaten life, will space exploration result in the annihilation of humanity. Some of the concepts herein may seem offensive or shocking and not fit into your perception of the world. Yet the contemporary progressive collapse of world society and the eventual harsh realities of space travel are far more confronting. I suggest you read with a sense of charity, to maximize the truth and rationality of the propositions. When confronted with ideas that conflict with your own view; take it as an opportunity to engage with the evidence and formulate your own response.

My words come with sincerity from my innermost being, yet they are not the words of an individual. There is no individual. All beings of all species are interconnected with, and reliant on, their fellow kind and all other life forms, as well as inanimate elements. When I speak, it is also you speaking, for we share hopes and fears, dreams and wishes. Each beat of my heart resonates in the beat of your heart. The thoughts of my mind flow amidst the thoughts of your own mind. In the centre of each of our cells and in the very depths of our souls we are kin.

My words are not those of a stranger; but of family. You and I may not look alike, and it is likely we have contrasting opinions; but we are family. As family, you and I must honour, love and support each other. We must work together, to make sure our children and children's children have a viable future. You and I cannot join the families of plants or fishes or birds. We could spend our entire lives traveling into the infinity of the universe and while we might encounter other families, we would never find our own family. Our family is here on earth. It's just you, me and all our other family members. All any of us have is each other, our family. I hope my words will help benefit our family.

Chipmunk Fun.

'The chipmunk frolics & runs around
Up the pine tree, down in the ground.
They sit up chirping, tails a quivering
Wary of hawk and fox their life would be ending

It was time for lunch, so I ate a bit
Got in the tent, laid down for my kip
As I dozed off, I felt something soft
run across my knee

15

Sat up looked around,
There on the ground
a chipmunk looked back at me.

I waved my arms about,
hollered and shouted "get out."
He ran for the door, I shouted more
Terrible words including "bleep".

I laid back down, and with no sound
I slipped back into reverie.
The little bugger came back,
sat on my back
and ate my afternoon tea

Human Stellar Voyagers
Introduction

I squeal, laugh and holler 'giddy-up' as I ride grandpa's galloping knee on Christmas eve of 1943. I rode till both of us were worn out, then climbed into his lap and snuggled against the warm, soft plaid shirt. I'm enthralled with the Christmas tree in the corner. It is festooned with colourful bulbs, shiny tinsel, strings of popcorn and little unlit candles. Grandma puts a big 78 record of Christmas music on the RCA turn table with its megaphone that has a listening dog pictured on it. Grandpa tells me a story about a baby deer following its mother through the forest and how they met other creatures and discovered beautiful waterfalls, magical lakes and ancient trees. Wisps of sweet smoke drift upward from his pipe. I've heard the story before, but I never tire of it and never seem to make it to the ending.

Hours later, in the chilly half-light of morning I hear grandma tell Mopsy, their English sheep dog, to go upstairs and wake me. He bounds up the stairs, down the hallway, into my room and leaps up onto the high four poster bed with its canopy of lace. I try to hide in the quilts, but he nuzzles me out. Filled with the excitement and joy of Christmas morning I remove my stocking hat and my mittens as my parents pass down the hallway, telling me not to come downstairs till they call me. Mopsy and I play hide and seek in the bedding.

Grandpa carries me down the stairs and into the living room where the Christmas tree is now aglow with lit candles, it is an awesome spectacle. He won't let me touch the tree, but instead places me in his big easy chair. The adults toast Christmas with their whiskey laced eggnog and give sips to me and my older sister. Then the candles are blown out.

Grandpa was always smiling and pleasant. I loved that we shared the same first and middle names. I felt I belonged to him. His presence gave me a sense of security and happiness and no doubt was a positive influence on the building of my personality.

***

The core of a human resides in the brain's gelatinous protein mass, with its genetic (G) material containing the potential for the personality, intelligence, memory system, mechanisms governing physical functioning, and so on. Coupled with this, life episodes form environmental learning (EL) experiences which are instrumental in the building of personality. I hope to assist the reader in understanding the formation of their own personality and those of other people.

I'll examine methods of strengthening potentials. Astrophysicist Bernard Haisch (*The God Theory*) points out that esoteric wisdom believes the origin of creation lies in God's desire to actualize potential, to experience itself in material reality. In this sense maximizing one's potentials could be seen as a religious endeavour.

You are familiar with maximization; such as trying to get the most mileage from a tank of fuel; cramming in the most fun on your annual holidays and so on. I use the process with my yacht; I strive to streamline the hull, reduce its whetted surface, tune the rigging tension, fit strong well-shaped sails, all in an attempt to achieve maximum speed.

We will investigate the brain's filtering system (gate theory); which determines what we allow into consciousness and what we ignore. The process is akin to the vacuum cleaner training I received from my mother at an early age. She taught me to point the nozzle at dust, small pieces of dirt or trash, and to avoid sucking up newspapers or food scraps.

An efficient filtering system is necessary for the maximum development of potentials; both are required for success in life. They help build self-confidence, and they are essential for social interaction. They also guide our interaction with the environment. Achieving these goals requires a living environment conducive to growth,

I'll devote a chapter to the criteria involved in establishing the 'golden ambience,' the ideal environment conducive to human flourishing These settings exist in families who have fashioned the people we admire: easy going, happy individuals who are successful in most areas of life. Growing up, I had the good fortune of being around families like this and I learned a great deal from them. I had the misfortune of a damaging home life and multitudes of dysfunctional people around me serving as models of what not to be. Regrettably I absorbed some of their bad habits.

I do not know which had the most detrimental impact on me: genetics, family or culture. Genetics had given me small eyes and bi-lateral amblyopia - poor vision. In my American Midwest blue-collar family

19

Introduction

of four children, I had a sister nine years older than me and two brothers several years younger. Dad was a brutal authoritarian with a streak of paranoia and mom was standoffish and cold. They were the black sheep of their respective families. Warmth, affection and security were not a part of my upbringing.

During the early years, my brain filters were calibrated to accept the families' unwholesome conditions as ok, as reality, as the norm. I had little contact with grandpa as he lived in another town and I had no contact with other relatives. By age five my perception was beginning to change due to contact with others in the neighbourhood and church. Also, some home events began to strike me as wrong.

I was assigned a lot of work: vacuuming, mopping the kitchen floor with a rag, setting the table for meals, feeding the dog and chickens, cleaning out the chicken coop, digging up an unwanted shrub. That shrub got the best of me. I was seven at the time, and I remember it took me several days to dig around these roots. The hole ended up being as deep as I was tall. A neighbour man spent hours helping me, muttering occasionally how crazy it was to expect a child to do this. Similar happenings left no doubt in my mind that dad was not quite right. He dealt out harsh criticism or a beating if I failed to do things correctly. Dad severely beat my sister for the littlest provocation. Not only did these beatings provoke my fear, they gradually instilled in me a deep sense of loathing for my father. My sister escaped via marriage immediately upon high school graduation. This left me as the target.

Introduction

As the years rolled by, I continued to receive incessant physical and emotional abuse at home, and I often went without food many days in a row. The treatment I received from the wider community wasn't much better. In school I was constantly ridiculed for my 'coke-bottle-bottom glasses', and for getting poor grades. No one taught me how to study or that it was important to do so.

After school hours and weekends, I scrounged food from friends and church; it wasn't enough to survive, I needed money. I got a newspaper route, mowed lawns, walked alleys searching for pop bottles and old newspapers, shovelled snow and in the spring, went door to door selling chocolate Easter eggs. By age twelve I bought all my clothes, school supplies and most of my food.

Getting away from the house was the prime joy of my childhood. Friends would invite me over, sometimes for the night and I would revel in the happiness of the family and the plentiful food. Church youth fellowship weekend retreats and the summer week at Boy Scout camp were fantastic. At the age of eleven I saved up enough money from cutting lawns, to take a day trip. My neighbourhood buddy and I took a special steam train, 80 miles to the state fair. A fun trip, which the authorities in today's insecure world would never allow. I was having such a good time, I contemplated not returning home. We could sleep in the cow barns and snitch food wherever. Jules wasn't keen on the idea.

I read plenty of astronomy books which led me to spend hours sitting in the dark at Princeton Park looking at the night sky through a pair of

21

cheap binoculars. Book and flashlight in hand, I could spot a few of the 88 constellations. I was rapt with the two bears-Ursa Major and Ursa Minor, although it was easiest for me to see the big dipper. But, as a child I was most excited about Draco the dragon, queen Cassiopeia and king Cepheus.

Age fifteen I got a job as a bag boy at a super market. It not only provided more money (65 cents an hour), but a feast of food as well. Being a teenager, I had the usual worries of pimples, worrying what people thought of me, and girls. Sometimes I had anxious feelings for no apparent reason. Worse yet, I would impulsively do things that I knew were wrong. For the life of me I had no idea why I did such things. My preoccupation with asking 'why, what, and how' provoked a sense of being lost, and gave me doubts about the wisdom of my elders, our leaders and human intelligence. It was some consolation when I realized my friends and a lot of adults were in the same predicament.

For a year I saved most of my store wages and when I turned 16, spent $500 for a 1951 V8, stick shift Ford Coupe with twin Hollywood pipes. Roaring around at high speeds, I eventually got nabbed by the cops. They escorted me home to my family who were furious with me. I had to attend counseling sessions at juvenile court. On the good side, the car gave me the mobility to go places. I regularly visited the air and space museum at Wright Patterson Air Force Base. I was excited to watch their films and model displays of rockets firing into space. Living in the Dayton Ohio area, one grew accustomed to large numbers of interesting aircraft passing overhead. I wanted to get a pilots' license, but my eyes were too weak.

The car helped the dating game, and although I was a bit ugly with my thick glasses, I still had plenty of dates. Sometimes they took precedence when they probably should not have. Elvis came to town for a concert. An older photographer friend had two passes to the press conference and invited me to join him. Being a rock and roll fan, I would have loved to meet Elvis, but I opted instead to go on a hot date with a cute blond in Brookville.

I was third from the bottom of four hundred plus classmates when I graduated from high school and I didn't have the faintest idea where the hell my life was going. The economy was in a recession and jobs were difficult to find. I walked from 8 a.m. to 4 p.m. five days a week through industrial estates. After three months I found a job in a ware house unloading trucks. Four months later I was laid off.

My brother-in-law got me a job in the aeronautical lab where he was a model technician. He built all kinds of aeronautical models and would be gone for weeks at a time testing the models in wind tunnels. My most interesting task was the partial assemble of a mechanism which prevented the machine guns of a fighter jet, from shooting itself down.

March 1960, I attended the week-long national convention of Baptist youth fellowships in New York City and Washington D. C. Visiting the Smithsonian further spurred my interest in space exploration. The many displays of great human achievements impressed me. I was part of a small group of 40 who had an hour chat with a young presidential candidate in his office. He was gracious and shook all our hands. Everyone liked him but said there was no way a Catholic could be elected president.

When the lab job petered out I went to work at the world's largest printing plant, where my father was a printer. At the beginning level of flyboy, I scooped up the twenty-five kilo packets of printed pages coming off the press, compressed and aerated them on a table to form neat uniform bundles and stacked them on a pallet. Each bundle took three minutes. I often worked twelve-hour shifts, seven days a week, usually in 38C heat.

A young physically fit guy could handle the task for a couple years till he moved up in seniority and got the easier job of paper roller and ink man, eventually to become the head press operator. I was barred from that route by my poor vision. I was unable to see the tiny defects in the printing plates or the printed page. I was in a job that would destroy my health and paid the lowest wages of all the industry groups.

In my free time I questioned people, took college evening classes and read many books on astronomy, psychology, and philosophy among other things. The more I learnt, the more I realized that my perceptions and beliefs about the world were askew. My family and culture had instilled in me a defective operational system; allowing the brain filters to accept harmful input, and disregard important input. In November, the Catholic was elected president.

Introduction

In one of my evening psychology courses, I had a professor whose daytime job was with the air force aeromedical lab at Wright-Patterson air force base. He had slides and film clips of their work preparing chimps for space travel. In one hilarious clip, a chimp was easily suited up and then placed onto a rocket powered sled. The sled was then fired down a set of tracks, only to be water-braked at the end. In a day or two the researchers wished to repeat the experiment. The chimp was suited up, but when they tried to get him back onto the sled, he went berserk. It took half a dozen big men almost an hour to get the chimp back onto the sled.

I felt myself a real part of sending the chimp 'Ham' into space in 1961. I had similar feelings in 1962 when my fellow Ohio resident John Glenn orbited earth three times. Kennedy's vow to reach the moon gave me a new appreciation for human capabilities.

During my early twenties, I endeavored to bring my ideas and behavior into harmony with what I was learning. Some days I did well; other times I screwed up. I was puzzled why I, and others made so many mistakes and why I felt discontented. I was like a rudderless ship lost at sea, erratically thrown about by wind and wave. I needed direction, I needed role models, and I couldn't find either.

My initial solution was to leave the world behind-and become a hermit monk. I did some reading and talked with a Catholic priest. But I decided that there was no way I could accept celibacy; I gratefully dropped the hermit idea. In upcoming chapters I'll discuss various sexual issues, including the possibility of teaching young children to have sex.

I obtained a group leader position in the Montgomery County Juvenile Detention Centre. I supervised group 3; a dozen boys aged 14 to 16, for their on-unit time, meal trips to the cafeteria and sporting events in the gym. Most of the delinquents lacked motivation to do anything constructive in life and possessed questionable values. They had limited ability for systematic logical thinking, and the ease with which they would guiltlessly act out depraved behavior was depressing.

On the afternoon of November 22, 1963, some of the boys were reading, two were playing ping pong, others at checkers, and a few were in front of the TV. The TV show was interrupted by a newscast; President Kennedy had been assassinated.

In the following months I became acutely aware that I was not using my potential. I don't know if the assassination had anything to do with this new insight. I did not even know what my potential was. Some of my thinking and behavior was crazy, but not as crazy as the world about me. What is the point in living, if great potential is to be over ridden by sub-human degeneracy? I was lost. Being an evening college student gave me access to the counseling department so I sought help.

***

After giving the counselor a list of my work experience, I said -
'I've come in for vocational counselling.'

Introduction

'You have a diverse work background. What is your overall life plan?'

'I haven't got any plan; I'm just trying to survive.'

'If you are content to spend the rest of your life 'trying to survive'; then you won't need a plan. Otherwise, you need a plan.' He explained to me with a note of seriousness.

'So how do I make a plan?'

'First you have to know what you have to work with; how much money you have, what are your strengths and weaknesses, and what kind of assistance is available from those around you...'

'Well I have no money, nor people to help me. My parents are a drag. My wife has started work as a secretary; it helps pay some of the bills. As far as strength goes I'm physically strong and fit, except for bad eyesight. The high school counsellor tested my IQ and said it was high; he obviously was wrong as I graduated at the bottom of my class.'

'The IQ assessment may have been right. You can't expect to succeed in school or anything else without good plans.'

* * *

He asked for a list of the books I had read the previous year. Thankfully, I had kept a record of the books I had read for the last three years. He set up more testing and the results irritated me. The IQ test gave high results - the same as the battery in high school. The vocational interest test revealed exceptionally high scores in the social sciences, psychology in particular. I tabulated my file card system of the books I

27

Introduction

had read; 70% had to do with psychology and the social sciences. The counselors' talk and the test evidence pointed me towards the study of psychology at university - a ludicrous idea.

The counselor guided me in setting up a plan to attend university, I was excited on the one hand, but frightened and depressed on the other. I doubted I was capable of doing this. According to my family and friends, it was a crazy and irresponsible idea. I was poor, married with an infant daughter, had graduated at the bottom of my high school class, had incredibly poor eyesight, and no study skills. If I flunked out, it would also prove I had low intelligence—a depressing thought. Despite dissension, doubt, and terror, I applied and was accepted into university.

* * *

I lose control of the grocery cart on the snow and rough ice, it tips over, spilling our groceries onto the supermarket parking lot. Laughing, the three of us gather up everything. Christmas is a week away and we are in great spirits. Gingerly pushing the cart, we trundle up the road to the Christmas tree lot which is ablaze with strings of lights. Five years old, Anna is a babble of excitement - she wants all the trees, but finally agrees on just one. We place it on top of the cart and head for our rented duplex in Whitehall a half mile away.

I return the cart to the supermarket and get lost in thought as I take a shortcut home through deep snow. I should be feeling happy, first term of university is over, I haven't flunked out. My one foot is wet and damn cold from the snow in my boot. My ear lobes are numb and tingly. At

28

times like this, when I'm alone, the doubts creep in. I don't try to avoid them, but I don't think about them either - they are just there, like the blemish on my chin. Maybe I'll fail next semester? If I failed, I would always be known as a flunked out uni student by my friends, family, wife, daughter and grandkids. Would I ever have anyone's respect? Would I respect myself? Would it be the beginning of many failures?

I continued my studies. Biology and botany courses confronted me with the fact that I had always had a plan: it was in my genetic code. This impressed upon me the importance of devising detailed plans for all those aspects of life not covered by my genetic blue print.

As I worked my way through one semester after another, my gruesome doubts faded further and further into the background. In two-years I reached the halfway point to a Bachelor of Science degree. I was jubilant with my success. I was beginning to entertain the possibility of not being a factory rat. If I succeeded in my studies, I would be the only university graduate in my family; I would be a psychologist in some form or another, which appealed to me, even though I didn't know its full implications.

***

The black robe swished around me as I walked down the aisle. I received my B.S. degree in my left hand, shook with my right, and passed the cap tassel from one side to the other. I continued towards the exit with a grin as broad as a barn door. I did not know whether to cry or

Introduction

laugh. To top off my euphoria, a few days later the lunar module 'EAGLE' set down on the moon's Mare Tranquillitatis plateau.

***

Graduate school was much more to my liking since most of the course work was in psychology However, statistics made me shudder. My classmates and I were required to undergo individual and group therapy. This helped recalibrate my brain filters, resulting in less neurotic thinking and behavior.

I continued to follow happenings within NASA and learned a great deal from neighbors; some worked out in the Utah desert for the rocket fuel producer Thiokol. Others were in the Idaho desert at the *'WESTINGHOUSE'* unit or the *U. S. NAVY NUCLEAR SUBMARINE HEADQUARTERS.*

After 10 years of university training, I received my doctorate. The student loan debt kept me poor for a long time. The years of study and internships gave me a vast knowledge and understanding of human beings, yet ironically, it made me more aware of how much I didn't know about the human brain and the complexity of personality. One thing for sure, I learned the importance of a plan.

Now I plan most areas of my life. It is necessary if I am to be successful and sometimes my survival depends on it. Before going to sea in my yacht, I study the charts and plot a course to take advantage of the prevailing winds. Sailing into the wind is slow and uncomfortable. I know I must use the tides wisely otherwise they will wreck me on the

Introduction

reefs of life. My charted route circumvents pirate areas. I set a course through deep waters rich with life; there is nothing worse than running aground in shallow stagnant water where muck mires you down into a meaningless monotony and hopes of ever going anywhere are lost.

I can understand how people without a plan end up in the wrong career, with a disagreeable spouse, in poor health, living in an inhospitable location and investing assets unwisely. Achievements in life are more likely to occur with a plan - setting goals with respective time tables for the week, month, year, and long-term goals.

I learned early on that a plan was useless if it was not put into action. If there is no action, it is like thunder that brings no rain, nothing can grow. I have met many people who become bogged down in reading, thinking, writing and discussing the deepest issues of existence, and yet fail to take sensible actions in the ongoing pattern of their lives. I try to avoid this pitfall by writing down strategies and a time table for implementation. I also try to accept the responsibility that my plans and actions have an important impact on family, friends and the future of my children.

Regrettably, plans and actions are not the end of troubles. Fear and confusion have been an ever-present element in my life journey. I felt it when I processed the numerical data for my doctoral dissertation, where I had to choose a variety of statistical formulas to analyse the data. I had always struggled with mathematics, but I managed to get through the year of required math for my Bachelor of Science degree and the year of

31

statistics/probability theory during my doctorate. Nonetheless, I had little faith in my statistical formulae choices and had to forge ahead in spite of my fears.

The data was punched onto IBM cards and taken to the university computer lab to administer my specified statistical methods. Several days later they telephoned, my results were ready to be picked up. Walking across campus I felt sick in my stomach, my nerves were a jangle.

> 'Hi! I got a call my run was completed?'
> 'Right! Here's the cards and print out.'
> 'Anything else?'
> 'No.'
> 'Any problems?' I enquired, with a sense of trepidation.
> 'Nope, your program ran fine. I checked the print out summaries, they look like they should.' He responded quizzically.

I headed home with a sense of relief, but I was angry that I had allowed myself to get so upset. I reviewed the results; they were formatted correctly and made sense. I was shocked – I had designed an intricately complex statistical program that worked! Sometimes we know more than we think we do,

In our present western cultural milieu, I guess ten to twenty per cent of people are in the know and have viable maps and run their lives accordingly. I hope my writing encourages others to consider plan making. Planning and the concepts I present may be most acceptable to students of life; those who marvel at the milky way, the earth's forests, mountains, deserts, oceans and the numerous species of life. Those captivated by the complexity of human beings, and their capacity for creativity, love and great achievements.

Life for me has been and continues to be a scenario of ups and downs, wins and losses, experiences of loneliness, and experiences of social exhaustion. I have experienced moments of utter confusion when confronted with preposterous information and affronting situations. Like everyone, I struggle to keep pace with the constantly changing nature of the universe. Within this fluidity, I often have to force myself to pause and acknowledge the support and strength surrounding me, the creative force of the universe, mother earth's energy. Sometimes it has been family, friends or my ancestors. Let us take a closer look at this latter group, humanity's earliest members.

Chapter 1   Intelligent Apes

Two days ago, we sailed out of Luganville, Vanuatu's most northern town on the island of Espiritu Santo. There was little wind, and yesterday it decreased further. I put the spinnaker up alongside the 140% genoa and motor sailed across a flat sea. This morning a twenty-knot breeze set in, I killed the engine. Silently clipping along at six knots is more satisfying than doing three in the doldrums. Not having a cup of tea is annoying. We should arrive in Bundaberg on Australia's east coast in about seven days. I occasionally refer to the 'Pilot Book' for this area of the Pacific Ocean. Pilot books compile information from mariners who have previously traversed an area and gives details on the preparation and care needed for navigation in a given area. This makes the journey more efficient, enjoyable and safe, but doesn't rule out human error.

This morning I discovered I not only forgot to buy more tea, I did not install the larger fuse in the radar as recommended by the electrician. I also left my sunglasses at the pub. No big deal, I can drink water and be extra careful not to drop my spare sunnies overboard. I'll install the fuse shortly. All this made me realise I need to improve my 'before setting sail' to do list.

* * *

History and social science writings are like a 'Pilot's Book' for life's journey. They provide insight into historical perspectives which facilitate present day life and offer glimpses of what lie ahead. Such reading is important for everyone, and particularly for small families sailing off into the universe. Families isolated on Mars cannot afford to make the mistakes of Earth's inhabitants. Let us look at our planet's history, starting about four million years ago when the first human bipeds emerged on the scene.

***

The rainforest trees rang with howls, screeches and chattering as little primates ran along the limbs; the brachiators swung from branch to branch, and the large hairy knuckle walkers sat on the ground munching celery. Smaller red-buttocked, dagger-toothed tricksters ambled about searching for food on the savannah bordering the forest. Then the new kid on the block showed up, also a member of the primate group; the 'ape-man', a sparsely haired humanoid walking upright.

***

In my early twenties I often visited the Lincoln Park Zoo in Chicago. I would sit enthralled for hours observing the primates. Later, as an undergraduate at Ohio State University, I frequently visited the gorilla compound at the Columbus Zoo. This was the first zoo to successfully breed gorillas. As a psychology student I visited other primate enclosures and read the studies of the Yerkes Primate Centre and other research units. It was easier to gather info about my 'sparsely haired' ancestor. I simply visited public places, such as the mall, train station sports stadium...

Professor Barbara King points out that our ancestors, like many species of apes, were highly social animals living their entire lives in social groups of fifty or less, characterized by long term social bonds. They worked, ate, played, and slept together. They eventually intermingled with other humanoid species. Interbreeding took place (check out professor Svante Paabo's studies of Neanderthal Man), expanding human social, emotional, physical and intellectual capabilities.

Human survival required their brain filters to be tuned to the complexity of their environment. Their intelligence empowered them to locate food and water, outwit large predators and develop multiple skills. Skill acquisition was neither easy nor efficient by modern day standards; however, it provided an interesting and fulfilling life style, further improving human performance.

This group life style was so successful it went on for 99% of human history. Since all human life and action emanated from this group, I refer to such a group as the Hub of life. History reveals that a human adapts best to challenging environments and life circumstances when living in groups, and when they mingle with a mixture of life forms. Hubs are humanities most likely means of surviving the planet's worsening chaos, as well as, the dangers of extra-terrestrial environments.

Environmental Control and Life Support Systems (ECLSS) are crucial factors on all long-term Stellar voyages, and for alien planet colonies. The Hub offers the most salient approach for grappling with the psychosocial aspects in these situations. The ECLSS is of grave concern given we presently are unable to provide a satisfactory ECLSS for a village on earth.

Eight Hubs in close proximity form a Circle/village containing less than four hundred individuals. Research suggests social cohesion collapses, and general dysfunction begins when a community exceeds this sum. A constellation/town then could be formed from two or more neighbouring circles, located far enough apart geographically to avoid the problems associated with large populations. Chapter 18 will spell out the key elements of the Hub.

Humans are an inquisitive species. We are forever digging in the earth, tearing logs apart, investigating the habits of wildlife, noting the life cycle of plants, and planning how to cross oceans, rivers, mountain ranges and now outer space. We like being on the move, exploring. About 1.7million years ago, the first of at least 3 migrations left Africa. 50,000 years-ago some humans migrated from Asia back to Africa and some travelled south to Australia. Around 15,000 years ago indigenous clans left northern Asia/Siberia and traversed across the Bearing straits land bridge to populate the Americas.

I wonder how many of these migrations were the result of over-crowding with its inherent depletion of resources, and how many were simply the result of curiosity, wanderlust?

37

Travel is an essential facet of my personality, it is as fundamental as eating and sleeping. I can appreciate where I am: the landscape, animals, people, my job. I can live contentedly day to day for about a year. But then I get a twinge. I gaze upon the local creek and wonder where this water originates from and whether it makes it to the sea. I find it hard to sit still if I spot a V formation of winged waterfowl. The twinge becomes a gnawing at my mind, a sense of dissonance, as if my heart is reaching out for something. An inner voice questions, cajoles, calls me. I have to go.

I set out and meander, like a stream, leaving behind home and friends, the known, the familiar. It does not matter if I don't know where I'm going - flowing onward is the only concern. I like to feel the adrenalin of the unexpected, to hear the whispers of the folk along the shores of life. I need to experience my freedom, to know I'm alive, searching for new experiences, new connections around the next bend in the mountain trail, or the next forest meadow, or the next island...

It is exhilarating to set off on an adventure, to drift through an ever-changing world; yet with time, the stream of scenery and acquaintances blurs into a montage of sameness. Home, like a magnet, begins to tug at me. Weary of the journey, nostalgic thoughts and memories flood in. I begin to yearn for the security of the known, for familiar foods, my recliner, the sense of belonging, support and love, the warmth and contentment of home.

One winter my wife and I left the freezing cold of February behind and spent a month in the jungles of Costa Rica and the islands off Honduras. My love, a sun worshiper, was in her element. I enjoyed the humid warmth, but the itching insect bites were terrible. In this natural setting I, like my ancestors, learned new skills. A local native taught me to spot half a dozen edible plants. Early in the mornings I sat beneath the forest canopy and mimicked the chatter of monkeys, bringing them close for an inquisitive look. Forty feet down on a reef, I used a small dowel rod with a loop of string to snare a green lobster, a cool experience. I never ate so many sweet tasting bananas in my life. A ten-foot python lived below our thatched hut; I was told he kept the rats in check.

Several weeks after arriving back home we held a dinner party. Our friends were there along with one of my wife's workmates. He was an accountant, although I didn't hold it against him. His wife, as well as our friends, enjoyed the slides of our trip. He seemed offended by the photographs. All he could talk about was the craziness of wasting money on travel. 'You could have bought a good used car!'

Buying and owning things does not feel important, nor does it excite me. Travel on the other hand makes me smile, dance a jig; each time I return from a journey, I am a different person, I have changed. I tried to explain to him I would always have the learning's and memories of my trip, but the car would be a rusted pile of junk in ten years. 'Yes, but you would have had ten years use of the car. If you want to learn you go to uni or read. Memories are of no use.' Maybe he's right? I wouldn't want to be trapped in a space module with him, I might do something dastardly.

I have benefitted from my travels and believe the ancient peoples did as well. They learned from each of the new environments they inhabited. When they stumbled upon another clan, the exchange of items and knowledge led to the evolutionary growth of both groups. This growth continued back home, as they had the free time to wonder, play, create, question and experiment. When they sat around the fire, knowledge and skills were pooled and available to all present via demonstrations, activities and talk. The oral transmission of knowledge played a major role in helping the individual and group to succeed on a daily basis. Such a life style resulted in enormous growth of the brains neural connections, creating ever greater capabilities and potential.

Since there are no living survivors or written texts from the majority of human existence, we have to rely on anthropology to determine what prehistoric life was like. Contemporary research publications (*Current Anthropology, Nature, Science...*) provide insight. *Guns, Germs, and Steel* by Jared Diamond, *The Ancestors Tale* by Richard Dawkins, and similar books are rich with the details of ancient times, migrations and peoples. Jean Auel's *Children of the Earth* novels are fascinating reading, and professional anthropologists claim they are very accurate in their depiction of stone age life.

Our hunter-gatherer ancestors lived an organic life style. They wandered about foraging for vegetables and fruits, much as present day baboons do. Meat protein came from seafood and small animals they could club, catch or trap. They learned to run some herd animals off cliffs. Being relatively small and frail, hominids were no match for the large cats, bears, rhinos, and crocodiles. Human cognitive superiority led to the invention of the knife, the spear and the bow, and this gave them greater predatory skills and reduced the danger of daily life.

Helen Wambach (*Reliving Past Lives*) reviewed New York City death statistics in the 70's and concluded life was more dangerous in New York City than it was in the jungle in 2000 B.C.

Professor Scott Lacy ('Anthropology and the Study of Humanity') depicts the ancient environment as having plentiful resources. The physical necessities of food, water, clothing and shelter were readily available. Malnutrition, homelessness, and poverty did not exist. The social bonds of group membership enhanced self-identity, self-worth and a sense of belonging. They shared food, housing, tools and each other. They lived long, healthy and prosperous lifestyles. Their diets were more diverse and balanced than the farming people of the recent agricultural revolution.

In primeval groups each person had important roles and responsibilities. Out of necessity, the group would have been dedicated to the resolution of difficulties and the promotion of progressive growth.

Direct reciprocity/helping one another was a fundamental element of life. The brain's need for stimulation and intellectual-social-emotional growth was met. I suspect ancient Hub life was more social, fun, stress free and satisfying, than our contemporary western life. It is this mode of existence that our future space pioneers would aim to replicate.

Human brain size more than doubled over time until it reached an average of 1,450 cc. This helped our ancestors to create weapons, tools, better shelter, clothing, healthier diets, and dramatic artistic expression. They initiated scientific investigation into astronomy, geology and the use of flora and fauna for medicine. Ethical principles were established to guide emotional/interpersonal interaction within their group. All of this culminated in what I believe may have been the high point of human existence sometime prior to 15,000 years ago. It forms the base line against which you may compare your current quality of life.

Were we to bring an ancient person to our present-day society, would they willingly relinquish their life style for a modern one? Would they conduct their activities in accordance with artificial time, work at a boring job - eight hours a day, live in a polluted unnatural environment, have only one intimate partner, and play with their children for less than an hour a day? I doubt it.

Their reluctance to join contemporary life could in part be due to greater intelligence than current day humans. But it is more likely to be the result of habituation. They were accustomed to their way of life; they accepted it as the norm. In the same fashion, present day humans are adapted to their unnatural lifestyle and would not be able to comprehend the superior aspects of the primitive lifestyle.

The ancient Hubs were nomadic, therefore they did not accumulate objects or cling to ideas of private property - the usual causes of war. Small family groups by necessity have reconciliation mechanisms to resolve conflicts which might impair their social cohesion and therefore their ability to survive. I suggest we consider the natural human as similar to the bonobo ape; a peaceful character more interested in fun social interaction and cooperation than aggression. Maslow, among others, felt the human being to be a peaceful, caring creature.

Humanity's departure from a progressive evolutionary course may have started when clan numbers exceeded a hundred or so. This led to the loss of traditional knowledge and a reduction in coping abilities. More and more clans containing more and more members made it impossible for the nearby environment to satisfy a group's resource needs for more than a short period of time. Groups were forced to repeatedly move about in search of food. As troupes encountered one another, foraging conflicts ensued. But outright war did not exist. Archaeological evidence suggests that war did not become a reality until the agricultural revolution and the rise of urban centres.

Our ancestors ship got lost in the sea of life and forgot how to see beyond day-to-day existence. To this day, human society is unable to plot a course that will ensure a bright future for our offspring. By now we should have replaced our land faring ship with a space ship and be cruising amongst the stars. But, we have been too busy playing war games, building megalomaniac structures, tinkering with toys, and placing our faith in fairy tales. It has become a ship of fools; humanity's evolution has stalled.

***

LADY MORNING DOVE

The bright full moon shone through the chilly night air, softly illuminating the settlement on the banks of the European stream. 'Morning-Dove' stepped from the hut; her lustrous hair falling in waves to her waist. She made her way to the trench amongst the trees, squatted and gazed over the fifteen dwellings on the streams edge. Ten huts occupied the opposite bank and eight more were on the bluff downstream.

A lot had changed in her forty years; as a youngster there were only a dozen dwellings in her group, less than a hundred people. It had been a ten day walk to the nearest neighbouring troupe. Her family had lived in one spot for a year before wild game depletion forced them to move to a new area.

As a child she had good relationships with all her troupe members. Now there were so many she could not remember all their names. Most of those across the stream and down on the bluff were like strangers. She did not feel at ease amongst them and she refrained from visiting them as they had some strange customs.

She remembered how in the past, objects of daily life, including food and tools were shared. Now it was not uncommon for a hunting party to return and not share the meat. Formerly, decisions had been made by consensus; now, a few aggressive types would often force their will upon others. Honesty, openness and fairness were not the same. Her brow furrowed, she contemplated her future.

***

In large tribes, the individuals' identity with the group suffered; identity became attached to smaller groups of blood relationships presently called the extended family. In these tribes, multi skilling was unnecessary; a few practitioners in each skill met the needs of the group, specialization began.

A few of the hunters perfected their predatory skills to slaughter rival bands. In this process, some would have honed their destroyer traits by attacking the opposing groups' dwellings. Non-human predators primarily kill to eat, to survive. I surmise some of these destroyer type personalities became entranced with the power they wielded and learned to kill for an idea, or for the sheer joy of carnage, of breaking bones, spilling blood and guts.

Some hunter gatherer groups were dysfunctional, showing little concern for the environment; this resulted in the extinction of many animal species and natural foods. About 12,000 years ago the agricultural revolution set in and humans settled in one spot to raise livestock and grow crops. Many continued their abusive ways, tending to overuse the land and destroy its ability to produce crops and support livestock.

Villages and towns sprang up. Urbanization made it easier to meet the material and security needs of children, maintain the objects required in daily life and store a surplus of food and other supplies. The larger number of people in settlements provided more physical safety and facilitated the pooling of knowledge and skills. There were significant downsides.

Settled life decimated Hub solidarity, breaking it down into extended families. In the traditional Hub, women had been specialists in child rearing and food gathering. Their tender nurturing and caring cemented the group together. The numerous women in a Hub guaranteed the provision of love, support, recognition, and guidance - for all the children and adults as well. These benefits dwindled in the extended family. Yet the extended family offers far more benefits than our current nuclear family. Psychologist Gordon Neufeld (*Hold on to Your Children*) champions a return to what he calls 'the attachment village', a village of extended families supporting each other.

Today's overpopulated western cultures have seen the demise of the extended family and as a consequence basic human needs are not being met. Self-governance, social cohesion and individual freedom are diminishing. This has resulted in fear, confusion, frustration, and anger; people are haunted by the feeling that they are not important and do not belong anywhere. The number of diseases has increased, brain size has decreased, general health has plummeted and longevity shortened. Innate human potentials have withered.

The effects of urban high-density populations have been studied extensively. Calhoun's (1962) animal research found crowding brought about a decline in normal behaviour and reproductive rates, with a subsequent rise in aggressive behaviour. In human societies crowding has been found to increase blood pressure, secretion of stress hormones, aggressive and withdrawal behaviour and a decrease in task performance and altruistic behaviour. K. Brown and N. Gruenberg, in an issue of *Physiology & Behaviour* look at crowding effects and point out that crime rates are the highest in cities, lower in the suburbs, and lowest in rural areas.

Studies of high-density populations, makes it easier to understand why our crowded planet has repeatedly erupted into violent confrontation. The situation has been exacerbated by the proliferation of the power, and destroyer types invading every area of life. Their antagonistic, adversarial and dishonest manner lowers human existence to a juvenile level.

Society's childish behaviour turns off more genes. People struggle to think for themselves and take responsibility for their lives. Perhaps most of all, they fail to grasp the significance of the world about them. Ruth Anshen refers to these types of stunted people as *'social dinosaurs'* who are unable to live in an evolving universe. You can read her thoughts on this, in *On Caring* by Milton Mayeroff. Nietzsche termed the masses 'herd animals.'

From a developmental perspective, humanity has some characteristics commonly associated with five-year old children (belief in fairy tales, obsession with toys and games...). Although, on-the-whole, teen behaviour predominates. This is termed 'patho-adolescent' by Bill Plotkin in his book *Nature and the Human Soul.* The most common being, attention seeking, over sensitivity, emotional instability, bull headed, cliquish, obsessed with appearance-food-drink-sex, and the lack of mature judgment. Let's look at some examples.

Attention Seeking – Society loves to talk and boast about its great literature, architecture, technology and high ideals. Yet it tends to flounder in confusion about its potential, its limitations and its responsibilities.

Oversensitivity – It has difficulty admitting its mistakes. Thus, it is often unwilling to take risks. No one wants to take on the largest problem facing the planet - overpopulation. To make things worse, those who want to experiment and think outside the norm are often marginalised and silenced.

Emotional Instability – One moment doing the right thing and the next impulsively doing the wrong thing. Capable of loving, caring behavior one day, and then harboring grudges, and violently lashing out the next.

Bull Headed –Wanting their own way and showing no restraint in using force to obtain what they want, usually ignoring the possible consequences of their actions, acting as if nothing bad could happen to them.

Cliquish – Society possesses the teen agers' herd-mentality, the out sider is viewed with suspicion or contempt. There is gross egocentricity in the wealthy ruling elite of society who have little regard for other people and often look with disdain on the working class. Powerful nations will bully those countries not part of the in group.

Obsessed - with forms of escapism. Physical appearance is a major cause of anxiety for many. Government funds are devoted to architectural monstrosities while the tourist is shunted away from the dark side of town. The population is fat, overindulges in alcohol and other drugs and has ignorant sexual attitudes and practices.

Lack of Mature Judgment – When an infant, probes an electric wall socket with a fork, we have one trial learning. The child will no longer have to cope with the difficulties of life. In a similar way, contemporary world leaders show a perverse determination to incite war.

Mother earth has become a planet of disturbed children; youngsters who have lost the exuberance, curiosity and creativity of healthy kids. Their personalities becoming sub-human, more akin to herd animals like sheep; their daily life is boring, full of tedious work, lacks meaning and direction. All about them they witness societal leaders who show little foresight or discernment, pander to vested interests, ignore vital concerns in the community and refuse counsel from scientists, historians, philosophers…

Today most western citizens have had little or no contact with mature people who are physically fit, emotionally strong and stable, mentally adept, flexible, creative, who have good relationships with themselves, others, animals and nature. The lack of familiarity with these attributes results in the individual having no interest or concern with them.

Yet intimate familiarity with these factors is necessary if one is to live up to the accomplishments of our organic ancestors and continue evolutionary progress, to survive, to travel into outer space. The seed of humanity, so full of potential, has only just sprouted; it is struggling to blossom, but is held back by the immature child mind stalled on its evolutionary course. Brain filter tuning is a step towards getting the human ship back on course; we will shortly investigate it.

Perhaps humans are incapable of maturity; things are just as they should be? This is exactly what John Gribbin and Jeremy Cherfas propose in their book *The 1st Chimpanzee*. They theorize the current human is a sexually mature juvenile ape; kind of a teenage chimp, that hasn't grown up. The adult human face doesn't look at all like an adult ape face; but rather like the face of a baby chimp.

Perhaps achieving full potential is the wrong goal? I should be out gambolling around the pasture climbing the trees and most importantly doing what the bonobos do to settle conflicts (have sex). As I look at pictures of my grandkids, it is not too difficult to imagine my great, great, great… grandkids becoming hairy adult apes bouncing around on all fours in low gravity. A planet of the apes may come to be.

Our ancient organic Hubs had minimal impact on their surroundings. Todays' society engenders massive changes; within the tiniest molecule, through all life forms, including the mighty force of the planets oceans. The changes we wrought now confront and change us. We are surrounded by people who do not care; humans have lost respect, trust and faith in their species. Mother earth has shouldered our disrespect and now strikes back with increasingly hostile weather, new diseases and violent geological events. She will not provide more clean air and water; we will have to live in our own filth. Our abuse of other life forms is beginning to be countered by food crops that refuse to grow, infestation of pests, virulent virus and bacteria... I believe these factors have embedded a deep sense of fear and insecurity in the human psyche.

In fifteen thousand years or so, humanity has gone from living a glorious life harmonious with nature and the cosmos, to a stunted imbecile unable to occupy his place in nature, nor devise a meaningful ongoing life style. I theorize human immaturity, dysfunction and societal entropy were well established by 10,000 BC. Are humans on the path to extinction? Aberrant functioning has certainly carried on into recent history with the likes of Pharaohs, Attila the Hun, Ghengis Kan, Kings and others. Today one can witness it in the antics of oligarchies, politicians, corporations and organizations. They distort the fabric of day-to-day existence, mislead brain filtration and block human potential development.

If it has taken us approximately 3.4 million years to reach the age of 13; at this rate we should reach the mature age of 25 in another 3 million years. Will we make it? Statistics reveal foolish behaviour claims the lives of many teenagers every year.

It might help our understanding of the baffling evolutionary process if we examine epigenetics.

EPIGENETICS

Epigenetics investigates the inherited changes in gene expression. Environmental circumstances can bring about these changes in the foetus and the adult throughout their lifespan. Humans were originally lactose tolerant only for the first several years of childhood. Those groups that became pastoralists developed life-long lactose tolerance. Studies found poor care during infancy may initiate epigenetic changes resulting in long term impairment. This has links with the appearance of psychosis, personality disorders and maladaptive behaviour. *'The Imprinted Brain'* *by C. R. Badcock* delves into this process.

An article in *'Biological Psychiatry' by Rachel Yehuda,* reports on a study of Holocaust victims and their children. A gene which regulates stress hormones, thus playing a role in coping with the environment; was found to be defective (turned off) in the parents and their offspring. The parent's lived in the Nazi death camps where coping was virtually impossible, thus the gene shut down. This dysfunction was passed on to offspring. Researchers label this as a clear sign that a person's life experiences can affect subsequent generations.

Another study found a higher than normal rate of schizophrenia amongst girls whose mothers had been pregnant during a famine. Similarly, one investigation found that men who began smoking prior to puberty, begat heavier than normal sons.

Animal studies have shown learned experiences to be passed down through generations. The team of K. Ressler and B. Dias at Emory University trained mice to fear cherry blossoms. The fear turned up in succeeding generations. A similar study conducted by by Dr. J.

Hettema, of twins in the Swedish Twin Registry, suggested up to one half of the fear conditioning process is inherited. A recent 'Scientific American' article by UCLA professor W. R. Clark, suggests some fear, depression and anxiety have a clear genetic component.

Fighting for survival here on mother earth or on another planet is bound to alter genetic makeup; how much change and in what directions are unknown. NASAs' twin studies found hundreds of mutations in both twins not attributable to being in space.

The majority of DNA information in human genes has been there for millions of years; geared to help one survive life in small closely bonded social groups within natural settings. Human DNA is not designed to deal effectively with isolation from the social group, such as the nuclear family, space capsules or cities. Nor are we primed to cope with the daily bombardment of emotional stress and infinite hours of boredom.

During the building of civilizations, the increasing number of power and destroyer type personalities may have played a role in turning off the human genes for peace and cooperation, dulling the intuitive faculties, distorting brain filters and retarding the usage of potentials. This halt in maturation is a stunting process similar to the bodies reaction to inadequate nutrients; the system atrophies, weakens, becomes disabled. Our brain, our whole being so capable of creating an optimal existence, is relegated to a declining status of minimal functioning; only focusing on the basic lower levels of survival. Over time this poor level of functioning has been handed down to offspring; each succeeding generation increasing the population of marginally functioning humans, who have become accustomed to their dysfunction, unable to perceive it.

Today those few citizens who have not inherited immaturity are surrounded by those that have. Thus, mature people are the outcasts, always under threat, and over time likely to sink into the dysfunction of those around them. Research shows those around us have a major impact on our personality, mental and physical health and virtually every aspect of our life. The 2013 book '*Friendfluence*' by Carlin Flora details some of the influence others have upon us.

When we consider the genetic basis for group living; people living alone or in a nuclear family have sunken below the functioning level of chimpanzees and gorillas. Our atavistic characteristics may still exist deep within us, but the original Homo sapien has essentially gone extinct. Today the etiolated Homo sapiens comprise the majority of the population. Einstein referred to the masses as dull in their ability to think and feel; in a stupor they think is normal and ok.

I find the epigenetic literature dis-heartening as it hints at a continuing trend in the shutting down of gene functions resulting from our fractured social structure and the obliteration of the natural environment. It appears the human personalities' ability to operate at higher levels has shrivelled. Since the mind and body work together; I cannot help but wonder if the stunted mental, social and emotional behaviour also lead to stunted physical functioning? Is this a reason we do not live to 120 as researchers say we should? Does this mean the findings of our mass population based social and medical research are inaccurate?

Historically there have always been a few who refused to follow the flock into sub-human performance. These sages/seers have sought to help individuals and society stay on their evolutionary course. There have been many successes. About 3,000 BC the Sumerians had an organized society that contributed writing, the wheel, and bricks among other things. Halfway around the world the Chinese had their share of inventions like paper and bronze.

Plato lectured on the pros and cons of specialization. Years later his student Aristotle stressed the importance of sensory knowledge and posited the need to flourish, to function well, as his central value. He saw balance and the use of all abilities as necessary to attain happiness. Three forms of happiness must be present at the same time to achieve fulfilment.

1 – A life of pleasure and enjoyment
2 – Life as a free and responsible citizen.
3 – Life as a thinker and philosopher.

He advocated the 'Golden Mean' similar to the Buddhist concept of moderation; neither too much nor too little courage, liberalness, food and so forth. Some of the concepts he advocated were every day practises in Morning Dove's time.

A renewal in the importance of full functioning and balance occurred during the 14th to 16th century renaissance. The term 'renaissance man' (polymath) described the ideal of excelling in many fields of work, knowledge and physical skills. Such an individual might paint artistically, speak several languages, play a musical instrument, have prowess as an athlete and write poetry. He was open to new ideas, new ways of doing things. During this era the Polish astronomer Copernicus put forth his heliocentric model of the universe. Galileo perfected the telescope; allowing him to view lunar craters, Jupiter's satellites and solar spots.

During the 19-hundreds self - actualisation and other movements, attempted to keep 'renaissance' ideals alive. It appears to be a losing battle; as the modern worlds prevailing societal and cultural values are mired in lower level concerns such as specialization, economics and materialism. Today, the importance of maturational growth, of diversification and balance remains in few cultures.

In the 1930's an article '*The anatomy of Tolerance*' was published in the Michigan Alumnus magazine; warning that specialization may support bigotry and pedantry.

State Governor Adlai Stevenson's 1955 commencement address at the all-female Smith College; voiced concerns about the deleterious effect of specialization on men and hence society. He feared the demands of specialization deigned men unable to achieve a wholeness of mind and breadth of outlook, thus incapable of socially functioning as complete human beings

In 1958 the English publication *'Bulletin of the Atomic Scientists'* questioned the English grammar school's curriculum concentration on science and math. It may give the student a "narrowness of vision" that does not prepare them for successful relationships with others and may render them unable to appreciate the compassionate and aesthetic side of life.

The book *"Environmental Economics and International Trade."* by *T.R. Jain, O.P. Khanna, Vir Sen;* details how specialization in the production of some goods, leaves other industries floundering and restricts the employment opportunities of the citizens.

In 1961, the French documentary *'The sky above-The Mud below'* tracked a seven-month French-Dutch expedition into the wilds of New Guinea. They investigated the life and customs of cannibals and head-hunters. In one film clip, a native is chopping out a tree trunk to make a canoe. The French explorer, via an interpreter, explained to the busy native how canoes could be made more efficiently if one man specialized in canoe construction, while another tribe member specialized in making something else. The native continues working and calmly says how boring a life that would be. The Frenchman was speechless; boredom is a major complaint of workers in the western world.

Einstein lamented how the study of science can evolve into a narrow area of knowledge, creating a specialist unable to perceive the big picture or understand the world of the average citizen.

Prior to attending university, I was employed in a broad range of jobs. At university I first studied business and then transferred to the psychology program; where I enrolled in a host of courses outside my psychology major. Although, I am professionally a specialist, a clinical psychologist; my varied work history and diverse interests label me more as a 'generalist; than a 'specialist.' This focus on the general has been further enlisted in my writing.

My writing background has been primarily devoted to theories, hypothesizes and research findings in the social sciences; a narrow focus. My desire to write for the general public has necessitated acquiring broad based writing skills; to do so, I have over the years enrolled in writing courses and read numerous 'how to write books.' A book on non-fiction writing, published by the 'American Society of Journalists and Authors'; has a chapter devoted to the pros and cons of specialization. The chapter starts with saying that one of the best ways of getting published is to specialize, to become an expert in a specific area, such as education, sports, the economy. The specialization concept is deeply entrenched in modern culture.

Specialization, whether it be at the personal or national level, creates high functioning in a specific realm at the cost of limited overall development; very similar to natures creation of an 'idiot savant' This retardation stunts the life of the individual; this is readily observable in the field of sports.

***

Listless twenty-year old Carol sat unblinking, her face dull, expressionless. She was beyond crying. She had been spending fifteen hours a day in bed, rarely bathed or brushed her hair. Lacking social-skills she had no friends. Nor did she have any interests or hobbies.

'Carol can you describe for me how you feel?'
'Nothing.'
'Do you have times when you feel something?'
'Sometimes a terrible ache of loneliness, no point in living.'
'Any other feelings?'
'No, just numb.'
'What interests do you have?'
'None.'
'Over a period of days is there anything that interests you?'
'Yes… I want it to be over.'
'Have you planned it?' She reached in her backpack, pulled out enough sedatives to kill a horse. Until I've had time to work with her I'll have to set things up so she is never alone.

* * *

At age four she began ice skating every day; focused on becoming a professional skater. By age six, she was spending several hours a day on the ice, this doubled by the time she was in high school. There was no time to develop other interests or social skills. She was an excellent ice skater, but not a great one, placing in many competitions, but never first place. As an adult she repeatedly failed to obtain a position in the commercial ice-skating shows. With her poor interpersonal skills, teaching skating was out of the question. It is not hard to understand that in her view life was over.

She refused hospitalisation; but accepted mother moving in with her. I saw her an hour a day for two weeks, then less frequently for over a year. She worked hard at her therapy assignments and eventually came good, going on to lead a happy successful life.

Professional athletes often have short careers due to aging and injuries. When the time comes for the athlete to make a transition into another career; they often have a difficult time, as they have not developed other brain functions, nor learned other skills. Specialist technicians suffer a similar fate, as technological advances eliminate their jobs. New ideas and professions displace older academics.

Before embarking on a path of specialization, it would be wise to collect statistical data. What is the percentage of aspirants that achieve the top? How many of them live happy lives, commit suicide? What happens to all those that don't make the grade? Happiness and success are elusive states of existence; particularly when you place all your hopes on two thin blades.

Lin Yutang decries the usage of scientific thinking and specialization that has failed to incorporate intuition, insight and plain common sense in the integration and application of knowledge to the problems of living.

In graduate school I ran afoul of our societies' belief in specialization; one of my professors requested I meet with him. I had no idea why he wanted to see me?

'Roberto, I have called you in because I am concerned about your study habits.'

'Oh! I wasn't aware there was a problem?'

'I think you are either studying incorrectly or simply not spending enough time on it.'

'What made you think that?'

'Your grades are not what I would expect of you. You obtain B's rather than A's, when It's obvious you have the wherewithal to get A's?'

'I don't believe in striving for A's, as the only difference between A's and B's is learning a lot of trivial details. If I learn the real meat of the subject it will give me a strong B, which I am happy with.'

With a look of horrified exasperation, he lurched forward in his chair and launched into a lengthy tirade.

I finally got a chance to explain how the time and effort saved from studying trivia I spent on studying other books or research in the same subject, thus giving myself an even wider base of knowledge. He didn't buy it. I felt disappointed that he could not see any merit in my argument. Fortunately, I obtained enough A's (without studying trivia) to be a viable student in the graduate program. It was times like these, when the sympathetic support of Reid, one of my professors, was much appreciated.

There have always been individuals and groups stressing the importance of more wide-ranging concerns like emotion, theology, power, and other potentials; but it has not been a balanced nor consistent effort. The people voicing these concerns have often been viewed as threats by the power holders. Some were tolerated as long as they had little impact; others were shunted off to the side and many were exterminated. Some people were able to escape stultifying cultures via migrating to less populated areas. Today, in our crowded world there is no place to escape.

Bear in mind the severe problems associated with specialization, as they foretell of possible tragedy in a survival situation, space flight or planetary colonization. The answer lies in the multiply skilled members of a diversely talented Hub group.

The importance of groups like a Hub is not surprising given groups of cells make up the human body and the body of all animals. Groups of firing neural cells within the human brain make possible the countless actions of the human. The botanical world; as well as the rock and soil of mother earth, are each composed of cell groups. Groups of water droplets comprise the ocean, upon which I sail as overhead the Milky Way of planetary cells shines down upon me.

Hominids have lived a group life style for millions of years; making them a social animal. A human has a deeply entrenched genetic need for extensive social participation and bonding. Maslow lists social needs on the third level of his pyramid. Family, intimates and friends play a crucial role in fulfilling the need for love and belonging and a sense of connection.

An article titled '*The Social Cure*' in the Sept./Oct 2009 issue of *Scientific American Mind;* is adamant that our need for close social involvement which evolved over millions of years of living in groups, remains a necessary requirement for a successful life.

The family group I call a Hub, can be compared to the hub of a wagon wheel which radiates spokes outward supporting the rim. A family Hub is the centre of human life radiating the spokes of existence which support the rim (life) as it flows thru time and space. A Hub is a family of up to fifty adults and children of all ages, not all being biologically related; who may be from various ethnic and cultural backgrounds. They live together, sharing all aspects of life; with a common goal to safeguard and enhance the well-being and success of the Hub and its members. The groups helping relationships, shared goals, extensive knowledge, experience and wisdom form an internal solidarity that gives it a strong voice capable of dynamic action to protect and further its interests. Such a lifestyle reduces health problems and increases life span.

The 'how to' development of Hubs and their human inhabitants will be detailed throughout the coming pages. This concludes our historical review; now let's scrutinise what is going on today.

Human Stellar Voyagers
Chapter 2 Planet of the Children

The Down Hill Slide

In 1964 Carl Jung (*Man and his Symbols*) said he was fascinated by the number of dysfunctional people. He observed that many do not use their minds, and an equal number use their minds in an amazingly stupid manner. Others fail to use their senses, and thus are not really aware of themselves or the world around them. Some people are rigidly fixated in their day to day functioning, bereft of all imagination. Oscar Wilde lamented that most people don't live, they just exist.

In the half century since Jung's comments, human potential has diminished more and more. It is not necessary to travel to another star system to find aliens. Many of our planet occupants are alienated from themselves and their true genetic endowments, from each other and mother earths' natural environment. Over the past 15,000 or more years, vitally important genes have been turned off, thinking ability has been dulled, self-sufficiency has been castrated and the genetic blue print for collaborative, cooperative, communal, natural existence has been thwarted. This is not life, but rather a precursor to death, to extinction.

Current society is deceitful. It fosters economic exploitation and social manipulation. Its nuclear family places impossible demands on parents, and cannot meet a child's need for emotional, social, psychological, mental and intellectual guidance. This culminates in insecure, immature ego-centric adults obsessed with objects and violent power.

The coming civil disorder, and space travel, will require physical strength and stamina to withstand severe deprivation of food, water, shelter, sleep… Survival in these situations demands a fully functioning fluid intelligence that possesses the mental clarity and agility to create successful coping strategies. Likewise, superb social skills and emotional fortitude will be needed to unite people into calm, decisive, proactive groups who are able to overcome the violent societal upheaval, the trauma of bloodshed and the hostilities of space travel. Humans need to reclaim their primate attributes and reconnect with nature. These actions require a training program.

The journey of growth I outline is a daunting task, challenging your most precious beliefs about how you and the world should be. I have repeatedly asked myself 'is there an easier way?' It would be nice if we could pop a pill or indulge in ice cream. I'm not aware of a quick fix. If someone comes up with one tomorrow, it would take a lifetime to validate. There is the chance a blow to your head or some other brain calamity could give you superior abilities (acquired savant syndrome).

One morning I sat with a fifty-year old man referred in by the medical community. He was an accountant who had started painting portraits and landscapes two years ago. He didn't understand why, he just felt he had to do it. With no prior training or interest in visual arts, he produced many works, had exhibitions and generally astounded everyone. Then one day, he physically collapsed.

Surgeons removed a cancerous tumour from his brain. Though he survived the operation, the cancer was throughout his body, forecasting his imminent death. His quality of life was poor in part due to the large amount of medications used to subdue his pain. Using a variety of psychotherapies, I successfully reduced his discomforts, allowing a reduction in drugs. This gave an improvement in life quality.

I viewed his paintings and was duly impressed. After surgery, he no longer had an interest in painting; I encouraged him to give it a try again. The results were far below the quality of his former paintings and were more typical of the average non-artistic person. It seems that the pressure of the tumour or related neurochemistry in the brain were responsible for his former noteworthy artistic productions.

Similarly, Daniel Tammet, an 'autistic savant,' is a whiz at various forms of mathematical and linguistic manipulation. He suffers from two brain anomalies, high-functioning autism and epilepsy. In his books he suggests his highly creative actions are the result of 'hyper connectivity' wherein normally separate functioning brain areas work together. Daniel and the accountant's cases hint at great human capability. Abnormal brains may account for historical cases of genius such as Mozart.

We are stuck with the need for intensive training. First let's identify barricades we must overcome.

PERSONAL, FAMILY, SOCIETY, ECONOMICS, GOVERNMENT, ENVIRONMENT

Personal - Maintenance of the physical body is under threat by our sedate life style, excessive food intake, harmful food additives, polluted environment, and dangerous activities. Add to this our history of self-destructive warfare and a brain that easily falls into a rut, it is easy to entertain the idea that our enfeebled Homo-sapiens species may disappear. Zoologists tell us 90% of earth's life forms have gone extinct.

Many of us struggle with negative personality traits such as being pretentious, pompous, ignorant, selfish, self-pitying, deceitful... Some of these features are the result of immature emotionality. The media supplies us with plenty of evidence of our emotional instability - high rates of depression and neuroticism, anger leading to violence, hate leading to racism, fear leading to escapism, anxiety attacks... The failure to meet genetic needs may be involved; I encountered this problem when I mishandled a newly purchased thoroughbred mare.

* * *

I have two docile riding nags in our 20meter square corral. Occasionally, I hobble and stake them in the unfenced pasture and they have never been a problem. I wanted a more spirited riding horse, and finally located a magnificent thoroughbred mare that was sixteen hands high. The owner Roy saddled her and I took her for a trot around his ten-hectare pasture. She responded well, and showed no hesitation getting into the trailer. I paid Roy, trailered her home, and put her in the corral. Within a couple hours the three steeds had their pecking order worked out.

The next day I went out rubbed her down and cleaned her hoofs – and she was fine. I was looking forward to the weekend when I would have time to ride her into the foothills. The next day she was jittery, fractious and wouldn't settle down no matter what I did.

This morning loud banging woke me up. I jumped up and ran out to the corral. She was kicking the corral beams and trying to climb over them. I considered distracting her with some grain, but that would put more fire in her belly. I wasn't game to try and ride her, so with a handful of alfalfa I managed to snap a rope on her bridle and coax her into running in circles within the corral. After an hour she finally settled down. I went in the house and telephoned Roy.

'Good morning Roy, I have a problem with Delta. Yesterday she was high strung and nervous all day. This morning she was trying to kick down or climb over the corral. What's going on?'

'Have you ridden her?'
'Nope, plan to do that tomorrow.'
'How big is her pasture?'
'I haven't put her in a pasture yet; she's in the corral.'
'I reckon that's your problem. You can't keep a thoroughbred in a small corral; she's bred to run. You pen up a thoroughbred so it can't run and it'll go whacko onya.'

* * *

The human, like other animals, is physically and genetically pre-set to exist in a narrow range of circumstances. The human body perishes under water, in too much heat or cold, with too little food or water, by loss of blood, and so on. The human ability to adapt will be severely tested by the coming chaos and stellar travel.

In one of Leo Buscaglias' books there is an amusing story of animals attempting to step outside their preordained slot in the scheme of things. Leo is dubious about the viability of liberal education and describes how the forest animals start a school based on the liberal idea. The rabbit enrols in a flight training class given by a robin. He does well in the classroom but has a real problem with practical application. He needed help to climb to the take-off limb high in a tree. His first attempted flight ends in a nasty fall and serious brain damage. You can imagine some of the catastrophes experienced by the other animals.

Much of modern western life distorts reality and teaches inappropriate values, which turns off genes. The misguided individual is burdened with excessive expectations and stress. With too many coping genes turned off and lacking a supportive communal family; we have difficulty obtaining control over significant elements of our life. We are unable to develop a stable sense of personal identity, of where we fit in, what is important and what is not important, what we should do and not do. Consequently, our self-confidence plummets. This may leave us with a feeling of emptiness, a yearning to belong, to be valued, to have control over our lives. Many, live in fear, not of death but of life; various forms of compensatory behaviour may take over.

Some people cloister themselves in a lifestyle they hope will hide them from the terrors of life. This accounts for not a few scientists and engineers, which are the major groups in space programs. Others resort to an 'if only' solution - I'll be right 'if' I can-lose weight, save enough money, find the right partner, purchase the most fashionable (car, house, clothes). Many drown themselves in the pursuit of pleasure.

Hordes have few life experiences, they are life observers rather than participants. They watch movie and television actors play out make-believe experiences, they swarm to sporting events and concerts, visit the paintings, sculpture, and architecture of the specialist visual creator, listen to the music of the specialist, rather than using their own creative PELGAM to develop their musical potential. Instead of developing their naturalistic – physical – emotional PELGAMs, they seek stimulation with cars, boats, amusement parks and so on. Some seek crowds trying to fulfil the need for human contact, rather than develop their relationship

72

potential. Instead of wielding power over oneself to destroy ineffective thinking and behaviour, many people allow power mongers to guide their lives.

Universities do an excellent job of training specialist scientists for NASA and other space programs: engineers, mathematicians, biological and physical scientists. However, this university instruction includes little or no involvement in the social sciences. Likewise, NASA's early schooling programs ignored the social sciences. One NASA administrator depicts a good astronaut candidate as being a socially adept introvert who doesn't need others to be happy. A spokesperson in another space program has said the key to picking space venturers is to choose people without personalities, dull people.

It is not surprising that an organization dominated by engineers and scientists would disregard psychosocial issues and sexuality. Research has shown both career groups tend to be socially conservative, have poor interpersonal skills, be dogmatic, authoritarian and have difficulty dealing with ambiguity or change. Consequently, many of them have trouble getting along with work colleagues and spouse in their personal lives. They are often at a complete loss in the rearing of their children.

Space exploration attracts adrenalin junkies, escapists and dreamers. I wonder how many astronauts become like narcissistic rock stars and movie idols who succumb to the glory of the bright lights? Grandiose self-importance and a sense of entitlement are not conducive of the cooperation needed to survive societal collapse and visit alien planets.

Survivalist groups face a similar problem in that they attract problematic personality types. Their fascination with weapons and military type procedures provides a comfortable home for power wielders and destroyer types. Some survivalists have passive-aggressive personalities, tending to resist the demands and expectations of others by being sulky, irritable and argumentative. Some are more subtle, wreaking havoc by procrastinating or simply saying 'I forgot'. There are bound to be paranoid personalities incapable of trusting people or organizations, who assume everyone is out to take advantage of them. They are easily slighted and often angrily erupt.

Antisocial personalities can be expected to go against the norms of the survival group (or any group), harass members, be deceptive, steal… Avoidant personalities are more sedate on the surface but underneath they fear criticism, hence they keep their thoughts and feelings to themselves.

Success in life's endeavours relies on closely bonded cooperative relationships. Such relationships are impossible for dysfunctional people. Inchoate personalities are the nemesis of any venture: sports, the arts, business or space programs. In leadership positions it results in reduced productivity and decreased staff morale. NASA, after many years of ignoring the psychosocial issues, is now admitting that its major problems are with people, not the environment.

Research data from sequestered groups (e.g. underground workers, Antarctic polar stations, submarine enclosures, astronauts) clearly demonstrates being away from family as the major hardship for the individual in these isolated situations. How is today's family?

Family - Change is not always progressive. It was catastrophic when the ancient Hub/clan structure was swallowed up in large tribes, and the smallest family structure became the extended family of blood relatives. In time this was followed with another step backwards: the invention of the nuclear family consisting of two parents and offspring. Currently, we have an increasing number of single parent families - the last step in the dissolution of human unity. This progression of family breakdown is a strange phenomenon, given we are genetically programmed to live in groups.

The mainstream nuclear family is incapable of developing and supporting the human animal. Two young people cannot possibly have enough knowledge and life skills to support each other or rear their young into viable adults capable of realizing their potential, and creating a meaningful life and sustainable society. The nuclear unit results in isolation, loneliness, need deprivation, incomprehension, low self-esteem, poor relationship skills, high stress levels and low learning accomplishments. It is worse if a father's job keeps him away from the family for long periods (military, oil rigs, mining…); the children do not learn how to relate to males.

Even if the nuclear family adults possess adequate child rearing knowledge, their full-time employment does not allow adequate hours to train and guide their offspring. The parent's isolation results in negligence and mistakes. Hence, children grow into immature, ego-centric, emotionally insecure and unstable adults. These adults go on to be teachers, politicians, policemen, scientists, astronauts… It is truly a miracle that society functions at all.

Choosing to lead an unbalanced life for a short time can appear to be a wise choice. I have counselled many couples who both worked long hours. Their goal was to pay off their house, car and so on by age 35 or 40. This often brings about a shattering death of the family. The intimacy of the couple and family is lost, and the children are neglected. All the while the adults scream, 'but I was doing it for the family!'

They were victims of the commonly held myth that material possessions enrich life; they do not, retail therapy does not work. Consumerism may be an attempt to fill the emptiness resulting from the demise of the communal family.

Families are the foundation stone for building a personality and a successful society, whether that society is in a mountain valley, metropolis or on Mars. Success requires setting aside old laws and customs which are not working, such as second class citizenship to women, minor ethnic groups, the disabled... , and governmental regulations that violate innate natural morality.

Society - Our ship of humans has been drifting rudderless for thousands of years on a sea of misperceptions and untruths. Culture tells us we can win recognition and become wealthy if we focus on our singular task and work hard. The tale is supposed to end with our hero achieving the goals and living happily ever after. Sociological research and my contacts within the community have rarely revealed specialists achieving happiness even if they were successful in their pursuits.

A recent TV newscast interviewed a female teenage swimmer in training for an international competition. During the past year she has ignored schooling and social life, focusing on her training schedule. This will have disastrous negative effects throughout the remainder of her life. It is a hellish price to pay for the transitory moment of winning a trophy. Where are her wise parents and mentors?

Development of ones' potential as outlined herein is out of the cultural mainstream and therefore likely to incite condemnation. Neighbours could pose a threat. Beneath a thin veneer of civilization lies a population of immature humans living in ignorance and fear. Most are good hearted souls struggling to survive day to day and pose no threat. Others are boiling over with pent up frustrations seeking a vent. These people can lower their frustration by making others suffer; it would be one of the few joys they get in life.

Protection from societal dangers requires keeping abreast of current trends and attitudes, without becoming embroiled in them. This entails participation in the activities of the local community, and some, but not too much, coverage of the national and international news. A significant portion of the daily news comes from governments, corporations and organizations intent on grooming you to become a supporter of their cause. When you ingest the news, you do not know which bits are news and which are mind controllers.

Do a thorough study of history; then you can forgo the daily news. According to Thoreau, the news is always the same except for the names, date, time and place. The saved time might be more meaningfully spent visiting neighbours, finding out what is going on in their lives, and how you can be supportive of them. When you help others lead a happy and successful life, it reduces the likelihood they could be a problem to you.

Western society has numerous divisive and counter-productive attitudes and practices; sex is one of them and will be examined in the 'Physical PELGAM' chapter. Legislation of law has at times been a roadblock to societies attaining an accommodating and agreeable lifestyle. Often this is a manipulation to keep the population divided and thus easier to control. Another issue is private ownership fostered by the capitalistic system which thwarts the human need for cooperative communality. Let's take a closer look at this.

Economics - The capitalistic economic system is not a viable method for the development and maintenance of a functioning society. It places too much assets/power in too few hands, resulting in a wealthy minority, a modicum of moderately well off and masses who struggle to meet basic needs. Capitalism creates poverty, crime and destroys the community's social cohesion.

Financial institutions squander money on poor investments and exorbitant salaries (14 million dollars) for CEO salaries. This depletes funds needed by businesses, home buyers, education... Banks over charge for their services and strive to keep the common man in debt. The banks are owned by the wealthy. Neither pay their share of taxes, which places further fiscal hardship on the average citizen.

A nation's monetary basis rests upon the common worker's shoulders. Their labour provides support for the individual, Hub, government and the wealthy. Yet the government offers minimal career training programs, minimal financial help for the poor, disabled, and elderly, and chooses instead to support a large intake of migrants. This is designed to keep a high unemployment rate, thus keeping worker pay rates low, and greater profits for the corporate owners.

We cannot blame all social financial woes on governments and greedy business owners. How many schools offer courses in financial management? Furthermore, there are plenty of people who desire bigger and better things than their wallet will permit. Nonetheless, the recent prediction that 30% of Australians will be unable to afford their own home is a clear sign that the society is heading backwards towards mediaeval times when only the aristocrats possessed land.

Government - Generally speaking, governments do not occupy a nation's seat of power nor do they represent the masses. Usually the national seat of power is jointly held by factions from corporations, the wealthy, military, religious groups, organized crime and self-interest groups. The government's first obligation is to serve and protect those factions occupying the throne of power. Thus, the government brokers international trade agreements, creates tax loopholes, limits business regulatory laws, sells public assets, draws in foreign students, underfunds education, undermines unions, maintains a counterfeit justice system and employs brutal police tactics…

The second concern of politicians is themselves. Most thrive on the wielding of power, and many have a destroyer mentality, resulting in intellectually and emotionally unbalanced leadership. Governments bent on controlling the masses are apt to view filter training and maximization of potential as a threat to the inventory of current values and a disruption of 'business as usual' (BAU). Communal living increases the strength and solidarity of the local community, making Hubs more resistant to governmental control. The state can be expected to oppose group living endeavours.

Government tertiary institutions tend to focus on specialization and creating an income for the school. In general, they will eschew balanced development efforts. Professors in the sciences and professions are specialists of the first order; they are unlikely to appreciate the relevance of broad-based learning, viewing it as a frivolous detractor and threat to their financial support. The major impetus for tertiary education to participate in balanced development may have to come from the students.

Governmental policies only serve the public when it will not negatively impact the power sharing group or the politicians. This disables the government's ability to react appropriately.
In a crisis they are unable to quickly make use of new knowledge or to make any progress.

The recent documentary *The Coming War with China* by John Pilger, interviewed an individual who claimed the Chinese government is the real power in China because it is above and beyond the interfering tentacles of vested interests. He went on to explain that this is the reason why China is able to initiate rapid policy changes, which may in part account for China's spectacularly fast modernization? If it is true, it will allow China to successfully move into the future, outpacing those nations crippled by antiquated practices and vested interests.

Environments - Humans traditionally lived and thrived in natural settings but today this is impossible. Few natural environments remain; cities have taken over the landscape. Towns of several hundred thousand are like a cancer, creating uncontrollable- disease and dysfunction. Urban crowding breeds violence and dictatorial policing governments. Urbanites view natural settings as primitive and frightening. I view huge cities as a threat to the survival of the human species. I am obviously out of step with the Chinese; on the first of May 2010, China opened World Expo in Shanghai, a town of twenty million, with the theme 'cities are the future'. In a later chapter we will examine more closely the ideal earth living environment.

If an individual does not get caught up in the negatives, the conflicts and stress of metropolitan life can help create personal strength and adaptability. Some questionable cultural facets also have good attributes, for example competitive sports breeds adversarial thinking, but it also brings people together. Any event may have a bad or a good outcome or no outcome at all.

Living in a space station or on another planet has both positives (to be addressed later and negatives. Previous space capsule crews and current residents of the crowded, smelly, stressful International Space

Station, face issues similar to inhabitants of other sequestered groups. Problem personality quirks come out quickly in isolated environments. Many men and women living for a winter in an Antarctic research station were diagnosed with a variety of disorders. The most common were related to mood and adjustment, and there were cases of sleep related issues, personality problems and, as you might expect, substance abuse.

Currently, the International Space Station houses the individual for six months or more. There have been cases of interpersonal antagonism and hostility leading to a member being ostracized or socially isolated. Anxiety, moodiness, depression, insomnia, and muddled thinking are common features of living aboard. These factors can break down social cohesiveness which further stresses the crew, lowers task productivity and leads to human errors.

On one NASA mission, engineers confused metric with imperial measurements; a probe was sent off on the wrong course, resulting in its premature destruction in the Martian atmosphere. In 2007, a female astronaut physically attacked another female astronaut, apparently the result of a love triangle. This latter event is an example of chaos resulting from ignoring psychosocial issues which in turn is the result of negative societal factors.

Societal entropy seems to be continuing. Prominent people and organizations are predicting a near term scenario in which artificial intelligence, robots, computerized manufacturing... will decimate employment opportunities. Food and water shortages are forecast as imminent. History reveals that corrupt business practices, governmental tyranny, crime, police brutality... have been around a long time. We don't need the Buddhists to tell us life is full of suffering.

K. S. Robinson's Mars trilogy predicted the present global chaos of refugees, mass starvation, the lack of medical and educational services and so on. He describes many of the colonizing population of Mars as carrying forth similar earthly policies, resulting in a fragmented Martian culture in which people have difficulty overcoming differences and uniting.

Contemporary earthlings are not ignorant. From the wealthy to the poor, the professional to the garbage man, the prime minister to the political party volunteer, people are aware society is broken, yet they each believe they can carve out their career within their private circle of security and get on with their life without attending to the larger picture. Current world society is like an empty fragile egg shell - given the slightest of pressures it will collapse.

Successfully coping with adversities is beyond the capability of a single person or a couple. Many earthlings will not survive the impending cataclysmic destruction of our dysfunctional society. Likewise, stellar voyagers imbued with our society's foibles stands little chance of successfully colonizing another planet. When we find other life in space, we can only hope it will be a lower form than our own. We have failed to integrate within our planet's life forms or develop a society of internal integrity. We would be no match for an extra-terrestrial society of similar abilities who were free of our foibles. One wonders how aliens will respond to our history of self-destruction?

We can see the four horsemen on the horizon, some coming in a thunderous roar, others with sophistry. The galloping hooves of the corporation slash deep wounds into mother earth's surface. The government's heavy hand oppresses the people. The soldier strews the dead over the land. Those of the cloth destroy the integrity of the human soul. Pestilence, famine, war and death are upon us. Yet on any given evening or weekend, western culture people go about their lives eating, doing chores, relaxing, playing, socializing... weaving an illusion of stability, that all is well; against the background of catastrophic world chaos that is about to engulf them.

In the scheme of the universe, the demise of the Homo sapiens may be the best thing. There are doubtless dozens of planets in the universe inhabited by well-functioning sentient beings. The extinction of our species could be seen as a natural and beneficial cleansing of the heavens. Arthur C Clarke stated he was sure the universe was full of intelligent life, too intelligent to come to mother earth.

I have not given a complete list of the negative factors hindering human development, just a starting point. Saving humanity from extinction is the responsibility of everyone. If people form communal groups, and a few of the wealthy power wielders join forces with the masses; the situation can be turned around.

While living in various cultures, I have met many people who demonstrate good intellect and plain common sense, in spite of having little formal education. Often leading more meaningful lives than many university graduates. It has given me faith in human tenacity. Our species has the capability to overcome the obstacles, develop our maturity, and become stellar beings. Tuning brain filters and maximizing potentials are potent steps towards stellar functioning of the individual and the society.

You are the captain of your journey into the future. The following pages will offer ideas, concepts, insights and methods to help you navigate the hazards, select the best routes, devise winning strategies and take positive actions.

Chapter 3 Captain of The Ship

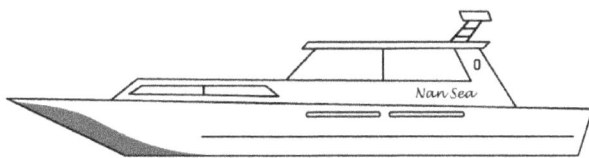

A fifteen knot north-westerly helps push our twin diesel Princess 37' south along Italy's west coast. The sun warms my skin and the cool breeze brings the scent of olives from the orchard covered hills. Screeching gulls swoop back and forth over the vessels wash, searching for fish. I periodically refer to the chart clamped on the chart table; through the binoculars, I scan ahead to spot rocks and beacons listed on the chart. The coast is well beaconed and relatively safe. With the auto-pilot doing the steering, I sit back, sip my tea and enjoy the day.

***

That particular day was brought back to my memory a few years ago, when an Italian cruise ship traversing the area ran aground and rolled over, killing people. Making such a mistake with state-of-the-art navigational equipment and in a well-marked area is incomprehensible.

As a ship's captain I am legally responsible for the operation and maintenance of the vessel and this entails a multitude of tasks. My treasure chest brain overflows with task capabilities, such as preserving the integrity and beauty of the physical structure, guiding her through all manner of waters and weather conditions, upholding the proper relationship to other vessels, keeping the power running steady, and so on.

Similarly, a human is the captain responsible for the operation and maintenance of their personal existence. This also is accomplished via the brain's resources, which performs a host of jobs: physical actions, emotions, thoughts, sense perceptions...

The majority of the brain's physical structure is a sticky paste (glia cells) that holds everything together. Neuron cells compose 10% of the brains mass. They carry electrical chemical signals via axon branches away from the neuron's nucleus and bring signals in from other areas via dendrite branches. These branches join up with thousands of adjoining cells. A single simple human thought requires the simultaneous electrical firing of millions of cells. Undeniably, the brain is a marvel.

But here we are not concerned with the composite structure of the brain, rather our focus is on the functions and tasks performed by the brain, and their genesis in genetics, ancient memories and environmental learning.

Numerous needs have to be met for the brain to efficiently perform its tasks. Those needs include: stimulation, a sense of order, completion of tasks, challenges, learning, and understanding new concepts. The brain demands interaction with other humans, animals, plants and life's unending experiences; these stimuli initiate changes in the neural pathways and the firing sequences of the brain, leading to efficient learning. *'All life is an experiment, the more experiments you make the better.' Ralph Waldo Emerson.* Throughout life we expand our brains ability to receive, transmit and function. The acquiring of new knowledge is most efficient when the student is rested, relaxed and limits study periods to an hour or less

An energy field connects and brings order to all things in the universe including the brain. The Asian Indians call this energy 'Akasha'; they view it as the source from which all matter and force evolves. The Chinese label this 'ChI'; some scientists name it 'bioplasma.' Erwin Laszlo refers to it as the 'cosmic plenum'; Barbara Brennan tags it the 'universal energy field'(UEF), and contemporary physics titles it the 'zero point field' (ZPF).

In 2006 Lynne McTaggart published *The Field*, a book based on ZPF research conducted by universities, government and business organizations around the world. The zero-point field is a subatomic field of energy existing in what we normally call 'empty space.' Within this field, all known existence lies interconnected via quantum waves. The ability to tap into this field and to be in touch with all that exists may explain ESP activities, the feats of remote viewers and people who can influence random number machines. Theoretical physics suggests that light in the form of an electromagnetic field within the ZPF is what creates and sustains the world of matter that fills space and time.

The brain reads the phase, amplitude and frequency of energy waves coming from the 'ZPF,' and from objects (we will look more broadly at object waves in the 'oceanic sense' section). When we synchronise our personal waves with the surrounding wave energy patterns, it enables us to perceive the objects about us. The brain tends to identify with its surroundings and usually will adopt the functioning level of the background. Hence, when two people get together, their brain wave patterns tend to synchronize; the higher functioning, more coherent brain will pull up the functioning of the less coherent brain. It's a good hint on how to pick friends. The brain waves of a group of people tend to become somewhat similar. We daily live amidst this interconnected web of contact and transmit our photons (light), and bosons (force), and all the info about ourselves to everyone else.

The interaction of waves from the ZPF and the environment results in wave interference patterns. Stanley Pilbram suggests these patterns are the language of the ZPF and the brain; our brain may use these patterns as our memory banks. Perhaps human consciousness arises from the interaction of 'EL,' 'G,', 'AM' and the ZPF. Is it also the case that this linkage is the source of intuitive awareness - the inner voice and intrinsic power of the person's innate personality and inherent world truths? Is it the force coupling the wildness of the natural world with the wildness of the human genome *('in wildness is the preservation of the world'*

90

Thoreau)? Does it direct the individual's life journey along specific seaways while avoiding other routes? In floats the galactic ghost.

The bringing together of innumerable facets to spawn the actions of life remains a mystery to science. We cannot see, hear nor touch this force, but we feel its presence, it guides our life. These attributes along with the possibility it is part of the ZPF leads me to label it the galactic ghost. In each and every situation in your life this wispy character knows which of your experiences to draw upon, which memory banks to tap into, what of your knowledge is applicable... You get on with daily life thinking you are consciously in control; but, lurking in the background, perhaps in the unconscious, the galactic ghost is helping you along.

The 'romanticists' of the 18th century viewed human consciousness and action as an unfolding (flowering) or growing process similar to that of a plant. More recently William E. Channing stated a person had a responsibility to grow (like a plant) -their mind, powers and potentials, to become a 'well-proportioned person' (balanced). In line with this, tuning brain filters and maximizing potentials will result in an expanded consciousness, as well as, providing greater access to the vastness of the unconscious realm. According to George Bernard Shaw, finding yourself is not your life task, your goal is to create yourself.

The brain absorbs experiences which assist our survival and evolutionary growth, and also takes in some elements that are detrimental to our well-being. Your ancestors (not all) avoided being eaten by predators or bitten by poisonous snakes, spiders and other harmful creatures. They learned to climb up in the trees for food and safety. Before they discovered fire, they had to cope with the fear of the unknown when darkness fell. They accumulated a wealth of knowledge, emotional responses, behaviour and cognitive patterns from aeons of life experiences; these became imbedded in the DNA structure, and thus were inherited by succeeding generations. I label this prehistoric neurological circuitry 'ancient memories' (AM); it assisted and guided the life of humans in the past and continues to do so in the present day.

Ancient memories, intuitions and knowledge are sometimes referred to by the Freudian term 'instincts.' Freud's student Jung gave the label 'collective unconscious' to ancient memories and expanded the concept to include the religious and mythological experiences shared by the species. In his work with holotropic states of consciousness, Stanislav Grof found evidence of ancestral memories and memories from animals that preceded the hominid chain of life.

AM may spontaneously appear; like when you have a sense of familiarity in a new location or with a new acquaintance. Certain fears (poisonous snakes, spiders, loud noise, the dark… are examples of 'AM.' An article by Anjana Ahuja in the September 12, 2014 issue of *The Telegraph* discusses these common ancient human fears.

Research has validated the presence of genetic (G) functions in the brain that carry out specific tasks; these functions may be labelled: an ability, aptitude (inherent ability), intelligence, and potential. Some of the 'zero-point field' theorists suggest intelligence and memory exist in the ZPF, not the brain; the brain serving simply as a transfer mechanism.

The concept 'intelligence' remains a slippery eel that is difficult to grasp. High in the ivory tower the robed scholars continue the fierce debate about how to define the word; what constitutes an intellectual faculty? Some say it is a set of processes, others posit intelligence as a skill or ability measured on intelligence tests. I was interested in Hebb's idea of an innate and learned intelligence, and Spearman's general and specific factors involved in each mental task. Scholars have suggested numerous intelligences exist and created tests to measure them (mathematics, spatial ability, reasoning...). A small cross-section of these tests became the known 'Intelligence Quotient' (IQ) test; supposedly underlain by a general intellectual ability. Wechsler's intelligence tests for adults and children are prominent examples.

Since learning begins shortly after conception, a test purporting to measure innate intelligence would have to be administered immediately upon conception. Otherwise we would not know if the test performance was genetic, learned, or a mixture of both. Current tests in part measure an innate ability; but for the most part, I suggest they measure the learning of cultural norms.

Speed of learning and reasoning are sometimes referred to as examples of genetic cognitive intelligence. Both can be measured via reaction time. Studies have shown speed can be accelerated via training. Moreover, many individuals who have scored high on a particular function fail to achieve success in that function in their day-to-day life. Success requires more than intelligence.

I label intelligence a potential, a partially latent ability, with many dormant aspects which may flounder or succeed, depending on linkage with relevant ancient memories (AM) and environmental learning (EL). Environmental learning helps to bring out a person's innate personality and assists them to intuit transcendental truths from the ancient memories. The 'G' (potential), 'AM' and 'EL' factors working together in a mental-physical-emotional process, produce action we call a successful function or intelligent behaviour. If we are to understand the various intelligences, I suggest it is this process we must study.

I am in debt to Hebb, Spearman, Cattel, Wechsler and the multitude of other researchers who have contributed to our understanding of brain functioning. In particular, my writing has been impacted by the 'multiple intelligences' work of Howard Gardner of Harvard University; he focused on seven intelligences: linguistic, musical, logical-mathematical, spatial, body kinaesthetic, intra-personal and inter-personal. I draw upon and supplement Gardner's work in this writing.

I conduct a partial functional analysis of brain filters and eleven intelligences (potentials), investigating their aspects, role and manner of integrated operation. Information to maximize their efficacy will be offered. All have been studied by researchers, and recognized as strategic factors in daily life. The positioning of the eleven potentials and the grouping of other functions within each has been somewhat arbitrary, bowing to my personal preferences.

1) Brain Filters

2) 'Physical' Gardner's 'body kinaesthetic' and the range of possible physical actions.

3) 'Spatial' remains as researchers define it.

4) 'Emotion' is included due to its' impact on life.

5) 'Creative' I limit my discussion to the musical, linguistic and visual.

6) 'Intrapersonal Relations' Relationship with oneself.

7) 'Natural Relations' with the world of nature.

8) 'Interpersonal Relations' relationship with others.

9) 'Spiritual Relations' with Gods and/or spirits.

10) 'Philosophical' the cognitive processes, including logic, ethics and math.

11) 'Destroyer' destruction (innate and learned) initiated by the brain.

12) 'Power' command over one's life and others.

These potentials, and others exist in everyone, although some may be unused. Non-swimmers are an example of an unused potential. Since we have evolved from water, we have an aqueous potential, a proclivity to interact with water, to swim. Memory is another universal function.

When a genetic potential (G) is combined with ancient memories (AM) and environmental learning (EL), sequential neural firing patterns commence, action occurs. It might be the mental construing of a plan, physically kicking a ball, bestowing love, painting a picture, and so on. I label potentials that are put into action 'PELGAMs.' 'P' stands for PELGAM. EL represents environmental learning; which includes the learning from interaction with the surroundings, and learning from cognition (thinking processes), G stands for genetic potential and AM for ancient memories. P+EL+G+AM.

Memory – is an essential element of living matter. S. Grof in *Higher Wisdom* notes the memory processes of the sea slug, and the 'protoplasmic memory' found in single cell organisms. In humans, brain filter tuning and PELGAM development involve learning, and learning requires memory. The brain registers memory traces from conception onward. Both genetic and learned attending behaviour must be imprinted in the brain circuitry so it can be used in future situations. This is memory. It plays a major role in all PELGAMs.

Memory allows you to remember the body movements and energy needed to throw the baseball, to recognize the facial features of your best friend, the formulae for an algebraic equation and so on. An eight-year old can remember the past, imagine the future, and therefore can lay plans for her life. Her memory will improve till age thirty, when it will level off, and by fifty it slowly begins to deteriorate. Elders often can learn and remember as well as younger people if they are given ten percent more time to study the material.

When I try to learn a foreign language or math formula, I study the material the hour before bedtime. Sleep can strengthen memories by enhancing and stabilizing them. While we sleep our brain finds patterns within studied material. Research has pinpointed lack of sleep as interfering with memory and cognitive functioning. An article in *Scientific American MIND Vol. 19, #4, August 2008*, suggests some aspects of memory consolidation only happen with six or more hours of sleep.

Be cautious about trusting your memory; each time you remember a past event there is a chance you will alter the memory depending on your current emotional state and surroundings. Consequentially, your recollections become distorted and inaccurate over time; memory is fallible. This malleability of memory is put to use in psychotherapy to reduce the stressful effects of traumatic experiences.

When I sit down to play the guitar, I am amazed at what happens. It is as if I were two people. I begin to play, not being aware of remembering anything. My right-hand strums and picks with the correct beat, while my left hand seems to be doing its own thing, as it whizzes up and down the fret board finding the correct notes.

Prior to the invention of the written word, pictorial displays (like aboriginal cave paintings) and oral transmissions were our books for untold time. Humans relied on their memories to draw upon the learnings of others.

Contemporary science considers memory traces to be repeatedly spread over many areas of the brain. However, some theorists studying the 'zero-point field' (ZPF) suggest the brain may not be the memory reservoir. They use the example of 3D hologram images, which are the result of laser light photography. They suggest that the light of the ZPF may capture all our life experiences, recording it in a hologram within the ZPF. If this is true, we might achieve astounding memories by learning how to access the ZPF.

If we are able to access the hologram memory in the zero-point-field, we may tap into the memory bank of all existence, all humanity. Perhaps we could recover viable economic, political, spiritual, and relationship practices that were destroyed during the era of evolutionary stalling. It could facilitate choosing the correct geographical location for communities, crop fields, and in making better use of hunting and fishing areas.

The human and the possible ZPF memory bank are a rich resource of information and insight supplementing cognitive processes. This results in what is usually referred to as 'common sense.' It is a form of instinctive native intelligence, giving the individual the ability: to integrate diverse information, analyse it from various angles, arrive at meaningful deductions, make rapid - good judgments, devise appropriate plans and initiate effective action.

Presently, we do not know how to utilize the ZPF. In the meantime, consider using memorizing techniques. Each month memorize a saying or short poem that illustrates an important value in your life. Regularly recite this, incorporating mental images, memory traces of all the senses and emotional feelings. As the years go by you will have more and more you can recite at will. This increases the likelihood of applying these bits of wisdom to your life. The Web has games, exercises and other commercially available products for improving your memory. A study of world-class memory performers, found that most attributed their skills to learned strategies. *Trends in Cognitive Sciences. June 2003*

It is near the end of 2018 and I know there are young people fooling around with memory improvement and all manner of activities to expand their over-all functioning. A few of these, don't know it now, but they are going to be our first representatives to visit Mars and other heavenly bodies. It might be the kid next door, or perhaps one of your offspring.

* * *

The bow noses into the petite Italian harbour with its backdrop of pastel houses climbing up the hillside. An uomo in a broad rim hat, motions us toward an open spot on the stone quay. My love slowly spins the boat about, slips the engines into reverse, and eases backwards as I toss the lines to the fella. Once secure, I give him a few coins for his assistance, a common practise here.

Now comes the hard part of the day, do we make lunch on board or seek a village cafe? Assailed by a raft of tantalizing aromas coming from who knows where, the decision is made; we traipse off to the village square.

Chapter 4   The Gate of Life

What you let in and what you keep out
determines the flow of your life.

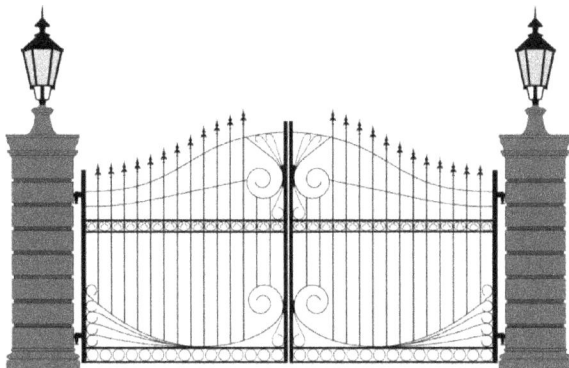

A week ago, we moored in the port on the Italian island of Capri as a fierce early winter storm swept in. It raged for five days and only slacked off yesterday. It's October, time to get on the move. We want to get down and around the toe of Italy, and over to Corfu for our winter anchorage. This morning I reckoned the seas would be manageable; I was wrong.

We are in peril off the bay of Salerno, repeatedly sliding down six-meter waves into dark holes and struggling to climb up the next mountain of debris strewn water. The starboard engine stops. With only one engine, I fight the wheel to keep even with the rolling waves pushing us from behind. I repeatedly press the starter button. Finally, very hesitatingly, she coughs into life. The rough seas are stirring up sediment in the bottom of the fuel tanks which is beginning to clog the furl filters - a dangerous situation.

Nanc takes the helm as I attach the sea anchor rode to the bow; if we lose both engines, I can throw it overboard to keep the bow pointing into the waves, hopefully keeping us from being rolled upside down. The engine dies again and will not restart.

'Take the helm Nanc. One hand on the throttle, the other on the wheel.'

As she takes over, I lift the floor board revealing the engines below.

'What if I do something wrong?' She asks, as a tear rolled down her cheek.

'You know how to keep the bow going straight with the flow of the sea.'

'It's hard to do that with only one engine.'

'Yeah, I know, but you must! Allow her to go sideways and we'll be rolled. It will be the end of us.'

'Oh my God!' She screams. 'Look at the size of this wave.'

Wrenches and new fuel filter in hand, I lower myself down between the two diesel beasts. It is difficult to find a way to wedge myself so I can safely work. The heat is oppressive, and the careening boat threatens to throw me into the running engine. My knuckles get bashed and cut.

'Aaaaaah!' Nanc shrieks, 'a cross wave.'

The boat violently lurches sideways, slamming me into the bulkhead. I grab the cross beam. I see stars, feel faint, hang on. As my vision clears, blood drips, off my forehead. The hull levels up, so I move back to the filter and turn the feed valve off. Then painstakingly remove it. The new filter slowly screws up tight. I bleed the fuel line and open the valve. 'Nanc, hit the starter button.' She cranks over a couple times but will not start. I bleed the fuel line again. 'Nanc, hit the starter again!' The engine roars to life.

We struggle on afraid that at any moment an engine might stop. Off to the southeast I see a mountain top above the mists and clouds, but other than that, no land is visible, just an endless expanse of huge, frothy windswept seas. Over the next two hours the seas calm a bit. Finally, a coast line appears. At a distance of 5 nautical miles, we come abeam of Acciaroli, Hemingway's favourite Italian village.

The port engine is overheating which means the raw water intake filter is probably clogged. I shut her down. Nanc takes over the helm and circles while I drop into the bilge and remove bits of plastic, wood and seaweed from the water intake. The engine restarts without trouble and we continue east towards the port.

The binoculars reveal a scary scene; monstrous waves are breaking across the entrance sand bar which lies west of the north-south running entrance channel. I am having a devil of a time trying to spot the entrance through the stone walls. I cannot find the red marker. I see what appears to be two entrance towers, but they are both white? There is a group of people on the stone quay inside the port, watching us. The port engine is in trouble again, slightly overheating.

If I try to cross the bar close to the entrance, I might bottom out, ripping the hull open. A straight approach inside and parallel to the bar would require perfect timing, otherwise the cross waves would roll us. I must get to the other side of the channel where I can face the waves head on. Nursing the port engine and using the starboard as my main thrust, I swing wide away from the entrance and head for the beach. It is terribly rough and foamy as I turn around and nose back towards the entrance channel.

We pause 15 meters from the channel and hover, counting the seconds between waves. The timing pattern figured out, I ease up closer. Each wave rises up on the outside bar, drops into the channel, then rises again on the inside bar only to hit us face on and slip under us. Just as a wave dumps into the channel I gun both engines and shoot into the channel. We swerve to starboard and rocket through the entrance just as the next wave crashes behind us. We made it.

At the quay the locals grab our lines and help us secure, all the time admonishing us for being out in those seas.

'Senor it is crazy to be out there.'
'Yeah! I know it was crazy.'
'Why are both entrance towers white?' I ask the port captain.
'One is supposed to be red.' He told me they had run out of red

paint. I reckon that's good Italian logic, make do with what you've got.

***

In a yacht, fuel and water filters can be a matter of life and death. It is the same for human brain filters. If the brain's gates allow too much stimulus to enter consciousness, then mental confusion can lead to paralysis, the inability to act. When the gate denies entry to important data, one may be run over by a Mack truck. E. Sherman likens this to a 'stimulus-reduction system.' The gates allow our brain to focus on incoming information that is vital to our survival, and dismiss irrelevant data.

Just as our eyes are unable to spot a mouse from a mile away, and our ears cannot hear the entire range of sound frequencies; our brain is incapable of taking in the infinity of the world. Of the amount it does receive, researchers estimate filters reject as much as 99%. Hence, it is farcical to think we are in touch with reality.

Our immediate surroundings play a significant role in training the filters. If I'm from an extended, musical, agnostic farming family in the north of the country; and you are from a nuclear, race-car enthusiast, religious, urban family living in the south of the country, we do not perceive the same world. Matters get worse when you add in the impact of turned off genes, neuroticism… I think I'm correct in my assessment of the world and what should be done. You are likely to have quite different opinions and are sure you have it right. The guy down the block doesn't agree with either one of us.

Aldous Huxley explains in his book *The Doors of Perception* that the brain's gates (filters) normally only allow into consciousness immediate reality that is relevant to our current situation. At times this normal process may be pre-empted by brain damage, drugs or unusual experiences which act like a grain of sand that gets stuck in the filter, wedging it open. The reality of the unknown can seep in with a swirl of strands, of flotsam and debris, or purity, clarity and cleanliness. We are shocked to perceive ourselves as love, hate, depravity, holiness, fire, calmness... We may be horrified at confronting our pandering to self-interest or how we mentally live out the fantasies we don't have the courage to embark upon in real life.

Sensory gating continues to receive research attention. In 2009 scientists at *The Norwegian University of Science and Technology* discovered a brain mechanism that screens out unwanted thoughts. Studies have shown people who have a large volume working memory are able to filter out irrelevant stimuli more successfully than people with a small volume working memory. This filtering process appears to be a cooperative effort of two brain areas, the basal ganglia and the prefrontal cortex. In 2011 J.M. Trujillo of McGill University reported on prefrontal cortex neurons that play a role in suppressing unwanted information. Efficient filtering enables greater reasoning and problem-solving abilities. Some relevant filtering studies are covered in the June 2008 issue of *Scientific American Mind; by A. McCollough and E. Vogel.*

I envisage the brain filtration system as a vacuum cleaner with many nozzles. One group of nozzles attends to stimulus coming from people, another group attends to stimuli from the inner world, such as physical/mental states, emotions and whatever pops out of the unconscious. Other nozzle groups attend to other animals, elements in the landscape, and so on. I imagine a censor sitting atop each nozzle, selecting what gets sucked up into conscious awareness and what gets pushed aside. His decisions are based on genetic cues (G), ancient memories (AM) and the person's environmental learning (EL) experiences.

The 'G' guidelines have existed since the ancient creation of life. Visual and auditory detection of movement are examples of 'G' cues. The 'AM' data is developed from millions of years of life experiences being encoded within the DNA. It includes wariness when smelling smoke or hearing loud noises. This is why we have an innate fear of certain animals. The 'EL' component comes from the current life span. It includes learning that has taken place in the womb and the external environment. Information from people or written material is likely to be let in, while the feel of sand on the feet, traffic noise and the smell of pollution might be denied entrance. These are all examples of 'EL'. Many 'G', 'AM' and 'EL' factors are unique to an individual; hence, filtering systems differ from person to person, thus everyone has a different view on reality.

Problematic Filtering - is the result of faulty filter training in the womb or at any time during the life span. The filters either take in too much, too little, the wrong stimuli, or they distort the incoming material. These errors can occur at the external level (data from the surrounding environment), or at the internal level (thoughts, memories, unconscious revelations).

Too Much – The 'Hyper-Markets' mass stimuli or the central business district pandemonium can be nauseating, overwhelming. A flood of internal data - thoughts, emotions, and memories may result in confusion, fear, panic, physical distress, rapid heart rate, and high blood pressure. Under such circumstances, people tend to make the wrong decisions and fail to take care of important life issues.

During waking hours, human consciousness is awash with bucket loads of thoughts, memories and unconscious retrievals, a huge proportion of which are unimportant and unusable. If the filters allow this barrage to continue, or permits the same thought or memory to repeatedly fill conscious awareness, then the individual can become preoccupied and unable to tend to important matters. The worry-wart fusses about or sits in a daze. The obsessive-compulsive brushes and flosses teeth every hour, urinates in every toilet in the mall. The hypochondriac has obsessive concerns about their physical health. Filters taking in too much, is commonly seen in people with depression, hyperactivity, excessive anger...

When an excessive number of hoses are delegated to one area of functioning, such as in specialization or an obsession, there are not enough hoses left for important areas; hence, it acts as a learning disability, the person is unable to function adequately in these crucial areas.

Too Little – intake at the external level makes it difficult to interact with the surrounding world. This could involve ignoring a fallen power line, the warnings on a bottle of medication, or the complaints of the boss. All of which can result in dire consequences. City dwellers screen out enormous amounts of auditory and visual stimulation. This could prove fatal in a world crisis environment where hyper alertness is needed. Likewise, stellar voyagers and colonists must keep filters open to their new planetary environments and the communication from aliens.

Examples of too little intake can be seen in the local neighbourhood. Henry buys a racy vehicle that looks the way he wants to feel, oblivious to the fact he cannot afford its thirst for fuel. Chubby Glenda fills the shopping cart with sweets and fat, in the bliss of denial. Think about those people you know who only hear what they want to hear or see what they want to see.

Excessive Filtering of Internal Data - Ignoring the body's feeling of physical strain or pain has led people to repeatedly injure themselves: muscles strains, broken bones, excess weight and so on. Filtering out too many thoughts, ideas, or memory bank data can interfere with the ability to benefit from previous learning. This may impair problem solving and productivity. When too many emotional feelings are filtered out, it produces a cold indifferent personality.

Deleterious personality and cultural influences may instigate too much screening. A narrow-minded accountant may be insensitive to the outdoor natural realm and social etiquette. There are blatant optimists unaware of the negatives. In some cultures, the members do not recognize input from women, or other ethnic groups which are deemed unimportant second-class citizens. People lacking stable beliefs and values may filter out too much as a means of coping with their fears.

Wrong Stimuli – Imagine a mountain hiker rapt with the splendours of the weather who fails to notice the hazards of the trail. Or consider the house buyer who likes the name of the street, the flowers in the yard and the colour of the house, but pays no attention to the crumbling walls, sagging floor and leaking roof. The love-struck female accepts a date with the trendy dressed handsome fellow in the flash car, oblivious to the reek of alcohol, nicotine and the local gossip he is a criminal.

Distort Incoming Data - I have seen employees who interpreted the friendliness of their supervisor as an ok to fart around and not work. I pretend doughnuts have few calories.

Religious organizations, cults, pyramid selling schemes, elderly housing estates, time share resorts, stock share offers, and so on, exaggerate the positives and ignore the negative details of their proposals. They exhort you to have faith, to consider what you might gain, think of the benefits. These destructive societal forces warp the brain filtering and cognitive processes of citizens. This results in irrational and irresponsible behaviour, rampant consumerism and excessive debt.

RESULTS OF POOR FILTERING

Filter training begins in the womb as the foetus senses time, sound, waves, action and emotions of the mother, via their shared blood stream and the mother's neurological-chemical-electrical system. The mother's good and/or negative patterns may duplicate themselves in the foetus, and be revealed when the infant is born.

I remember an obsessive compulsive mother who continually arranged the linen, tableware, clothing and furniture in colour coded neat symmetrical fashion while ignoring human interactions. She brought in her three-year old daughter who was exhibiting the same behaviour. The realization her daughter would end up like her motivated her to go successfully through psychotherapy. After that, changing the behaviours of the daughter was relatively easy.

How many children grow up in sparse restrictive regimented surroundings teaching them it is ok to hate, to disregard the well-being of others, that school is not important... This mal-adaptive training of filters and behaviour regimens continues twenty-four hours a day, seven days a week, year after year, becoming firmly entrenched in the child's behavioural repertoire. Early childhood enrichment programs designed to eradicate these destructive systems only run four hours a day, five days a week; this is insufficient time to dig out problematic filter and behaviour patterns and establish fruitful, long lasting changes.

Children in western culture receive filtration training emphasizing physical appearance and being popular. Self-interest and personal economic gain are viewed as prime goals. Conformity to the status quo is expected. Empathy, caring and love are regarded as exaggerated sentimentality. This results in inconsistent physical, cognitive and emotional behaviour. Consequently, family, career, and social life are in shambles - it is a case of arrested development. These under-developed people form the majority of the population and create dysfunctional societies in which poverty, ignorance, injustice, and human abuse are the norm.

BUILDING EFFICIENT FILTERS

Four components. 1 - Allow more data in. 2 – Allow less data in. 3 - Be accurately selective. 4 - Don't distort. All four must deal with issues the family (Hub) deems crucial to the well-being of the family. Local cultural norms must be considered; likewise, planetary patterns of thinking and behaving must be factored in.

More/New Data – Stepping out of one's comfort zone may allow more and possibly new data to enter conscious awareness, but, it requires courage. For this reason, it is most likely to happen by accident, when circumstances force one into a new space. Unfamiliar terrain, cultures, experiences, and people are apt to initiate new awareness. Unitarian Universalist Sunday school and adult services routinely have guest speakers from other religions, cultures and diverse interest groups, thus providing the congregation with more information and data than they would otherwise experience.

During the 'mid-life-crisis' people often lower filter restrictions to investigate taboo areas and do the unexpected. During the senior years, prefrontal cortex controls loosen allowing modification and adjustment of the filtration system. It provides an opportunity for elders to open up to more of life's offerings and allow a shift in attitudes, beliefs, values and also a resurgence in creativity. The golden years can offer a sense of freedom not possible in youth.

Throughout the flow of daily life, the conscious mind may experience brief glimpses of thoughts, ideas, memories, emotions and revelations from the unconscious and ancient memories. Meditation, introspection, arm chair cogitation may facilitate this process, permitting these titbits to be grasped and closely examined.

Loafing and daydreaming may goad the censor to open the door of the unconscious and dredge things out. Searching for these unique bits of mental life is the goal of brain storming and lateral thinking where the censor is inhibited or turned off, allowing the creative mind to open and provide solutions, create works of art, build objects and do unimaginable things.

Less Data - Reduction of incoming external data is the goal of sensory deprivation research. The subject is encapsulated in soft foam on a soft bed in a sound proof room, with opaque goggles and earphones playing white sound. I have had clients experiment with sensory deprivation by floating in their bath tub of body temperature water, in a dark bathroom with the hum of a fan in the background. Others put in earplugs and sat in the closet. Athletes and performers learn to ignore the cacophony of the stadium.

Taking in less data at the internal level requires suppression of the conscious stream of thoughts, including unconscious revelations. You may accomplish this by involving yourself in activities that require high concentration: singing in a choir, playing a musical instrument, reading a captivating book, constructing a complicated object.

Meditation or hypnosis that strives to empty the conscious mind or focus on a single item may effectively limit awareness of internal and external stimuli.

More Accurate Data - Improving censor accuracy is to a large extent dependent on the degree to which the person becomes experientially involved in the mental realm and the physical sphere: thinking different thoughts, expressing various emotions with varying intensity, brain storming ideas and solutions, probing the unconscious, introspection of beliefs/values, travel, social activities, hobbies, sports, education....

Mindfulness practices may assist the censors to have a more accurate awareness of the incoming flow of both internal and external data. Professor R.D. Siegel of Harvard Medical School has researched, taught and written extensively on 'mindfulness' benefits.

Distortion Free - Only accept appropriate undistorted data - neither too much nor too little for what is required in the context of the current situation. You can aid this process by using a notepad when you think about issues of concern. List what the relevant points are and discard the irrelevant. Then you will be able to focus on initiating appropriate responses which leads to a successful pattern of behaviour.

An emotionally stable mother with proficient filters is apt to give birth to an infant with filters primed to facilitate the same successful behaviour. When the baby leaves the intrauterine realm of even temperature and constant physical contact it enters a domain of fluctuating temperature and sporadic physical contact, forcing the filters to broaden their range of acceptable input. Over time, childhood experiences provide more filter calibration. Parents can act out appropriate behaviour and their child will mimic their behaviour. This filter training forms the basis for the child's future understanding of, and interaction with, the world.

Good filter training produces an adult who has a thorough familiarity with the major facets of their mind, the environment and their cultural milieu. Their sensors select the fundamental internal and external data for the existing situation and time. They utilize the information to plan accordingly and to initiate the required actions. Thus, they solve immediate problems and plan a productive future. Their success across the broad spectrum of life is indicative of viable, accurate filtration. These stellar traits could assist a beleaguered survivor through the firestorm of chaos and an isolated space colony through galactic perils.

Synthesis - The accurate tuning of filters begins in the womb, proceeds through the family and friend network and culminates in community organisations. At birth children are like sponges, readily soaking up things. Teach the child to expect stability and his life will be a stream of frustrating confrontations. Teach him to anticipate changing unstable situations and he will learn to appreciate changes and flow with them. Encouraging a child to keep their mind open to various possibilities will assist his learning: math, reading, thinking, creativity, music, relationship skills, and all the other important issues in life.

Those who rear children need to be alert for the idiosyncrasies of each child. Within each child lies millions of years' worth of memories, emotions, knowledge, talents, dreams… that sensitize their filters. One child's ancestral history may have involved successful endeavours in horticulture. Therefore, providing this child with early training in botany, farming and so on, is likely to produce a happy individual of great horticultural skill. Another infant may have had a long line of ancestors who were traumatized by military type vicious physical conflict. This child will need comprehensive assurance and support from the Hub and Circle.

Human touch is vital for all children and must be maintained with the child the first eighteen months and to a lesser degree up to the age of four. In some cultures, the child is carried in a sling or papoose board till the age of two or three. Children should sleep with adults till age four or five and then with other children or animals. Humans should never live or sleep alone as this fails to meet human needs and cripples the filters' ability to receive data from other people.

117

A family group (Hub) must define the characteristics of the ideal family member and then design filter training programs for infants, children and adults to achieve the optimal person. These programs will highlight the importance of: plans, dreams, relationships, and maintenance of stable daily life issues. At present, western culture focuses on physical needs (food, water, sleep, evacuation…), but ignores intangible needs. I suggest the infant's filters be set to motivate the child to daily show respect, caring, cooperation... The creation of efficient and accurate filters in a child is the single most important responsibility of family adults after all food, shelter and safety needs have been met.

An article in the August, 2003 issue of the *'Journal of Clinical and Experimental Neuropsychology,'* suggests the neural wiring involved in thinking processes (and brain filtering) may become more efficient via recreational activities and social participation. Hence, adults need to partake in these pastimes and encourage their children to do the same.

The network of family and friends play a vital role in the development of optimal filters, by providing a diverse range of experiences without too many do's and don'ts. A group living environment containing grandparents, uncles and aunts, numerous mothers, fathers and siblings provides the necessary models for the child's growth and instils a sense of love and security within the child. When social, cognitive, and behaviour skill training are lavished on a youngster, the child is able to develop its genetic endowment for cooperation, caring and respect.

118

The impact of modelling on young ones can be witnessed by watching your friend's children and noticing how much the child imitates the parents. Other examples can be seen when you observe young animals.

A baby raccoon follows its mother along a stream and mimics her behaviour. It searches for shell shaped objects and wriggly movements in the water, ignoring seeds and nuts. A baby squirrel similarly follows mother along a tree limb searching for seeds and nuts, ignoring the stream below. If you swap the babies at birth, their brains learn a filtering system that will not work when they return to their species.

Juvenile prairie dogs and ground squirrels mimic adult surveillance of the sky - birds of prey are a major threat. It is the opposite for deer in the forest; as a fawn they learn danger is on the ground not up in the air, they will ignore hunters sitting in trees. This is much like the kangaroos feeding on the lawn beneath my second story veranda, showing no fear of the people above them.

Several years ago, the wildlife department trapped some kangaroos on a coastal island. These kangaroos were accustomed to swimming in the islands fresh water lakes and shallow streams; their brain filters allowed water into the safe category. The rangers hauled the captured roos on a barge to a nearby island devoid of roo life. Over a period of days, the homesick roos attempted to swim the mile gap back to their home island. They are great swimmers, but only a few made it home. The sharks had a feast.

The well-being of human children requires them to learn to avoid the ego centric, aggressive, highly competitive, emotionally cold, hyperactive, and materialistic type of people. To accomplish this, the youngsters need good models, people who are open, well balanced, and highly functioning. Such models help the child construct a prioritised list of what to pay attention to.

Unfortunately, human filters prefer to suck up information that supports their currently held view of reality and ignore things which do not agree with these presuppositions. The majority of humans in western culture have bizarre filter systems that are not viable in todays' world.

Society also needs good models to achieve meaningful progress in the balanced functioning of the populace. Currently there are too many models of specialization, power wielding, egocentricity, and so on. Human ingenuity has taken us to the bottom of the ocean, to the moon, mapped the human genome, cloned life and countless other accomplishments. Yet it has failed to produce clear, concise, consistent, straightforward directions for training the brain filters, raising children, and living life.

There are organisations helping people learn to filter out harmful and irrelevant data, and focus on important material. Universities and high schools provide evening adult education classes. Church and hobby groups have much to offer. Our local U3A (university of the third age) group offers a broad curriculum of courses: philosophy, computers, writing, painting and more. All these efforts can help unify filter training and eliminate disparate censor systems. If the viable values of various cultures were pulled together, surely it would it make for a more efficient filter system?

I setup the OCIP "Organization for Culturally Independent People" to test such a hypothesis. Fifty members from half a dozen nationalities socialized once a month. The social banter was fun, inspiring and a great learning experience. A focus on commonalities and sharing of successful life guidelines further improved the functioning level of members. However, some members were so disenchanted with society they went to the opposite extreme, tuning filters to forbid identifying with any values and refusing to trust and belong to any group.

OCIP type groups could play a role in helping society recalibrate its' filters. Concepts such as competition must be downplayed and replaced by cooperation and partnership. Sharing must replace acquisitiveness, communality can replace individualism, simplicity is more desirable than complexity.

Reframing filter criterion can be accomplished at any age and with most types of personality. Broad-minded, open personalities are usually the fastest at reframing. This means engineers and accountants are in the slow lane, while power personalities like politicians and lawyers can be exceedingly difficult to initiate changes. As we age, time itself can clear away some impurities.

Eventually better calibration of brain filters and balanced maximal PELGAMs will become ingrained in the on-going life of the community, as it is necessary for survival of our species here on earth and in space. This may take several generations. Whether it will happen in the near future, or only after an apocalypse, is unknown.

Chapter 5   Sensory Deprivation

Survival - anywhere, anytime - demands accurate sensory awareness. The range of awareness differs from species to species. Dogs hear a higher pitch than humans, and elephants hear a lower pitch. In some cases, a human's range can be expanded with training. Some people have awareness beyond what we traditionally call the 5 senses; often referred to as 'extrasensory perception' (ESP), or psychic phenomena. ESP is detailed in the upcoming 'wave sense' section.

If you plug up your ears, nose, and mouth; wear a blindfold and gloves, the 5 senses will receive little input. 24-hour darkness and nearby high voltage power lines can cripple the body's bio-clock and the ability to receive electromagnetic waves from the surroundings. A severe lack of sensory input makes it impossible to successfully cope with the environment. Psychosis may ensue.

You are being monitored by corporations, governments… keen to control you. If you wish to control yourself, you must be alert to sensory input, and make optimal use of the brain filters.

Long duration space flight involves sensory deprivation, which manifests itself in negative ways. The first sensory element to go is the pull of gravity and its physical comfort of rootedness. An astronaut's sense of time could also be affected; in the ISS, sunrise and sunset alternate every 45 minutes, the sleep-and-wake cycle seems arbitrary.

Brain filters receive and work simultaneously with data from internal sources and from the seven senses. Both sources of information play a vital role in the maximization of the PELGAMs. Subsequently, a rudimentary understanding of human senses is helpful.

Senses are similar to muscles, extensive training combined with experience produces strong, precise senses. This helps the filters accurately accept or dismiss stimuli. A person never knows when the censor might accept a novel sensory experience that could reignite a turned off gene or suppress a problematic gene. In a natural setting, superbly tuned filters working with the full range of acute senses may prompt a person to wake up and become aware of their connectedness with all.

* * *

I shift the lifesaving cushion that protects my butt from the hard-cold seat of the aluminium row boat, and watch Rich make another cast. Out of the low overcast sky, lazy snowflakes drift down, and meld into the flat lake surface. I toss my spinner lure towards shore 30 metres away. Up in the shallows near shore, hundreds of the long dark shapes of brown trout hover over the sandy bottom of this little bay on Shoshone Lake in Yellowstone National Park. Nearby, a bull moose, knee deep in water lilies, lifts his head from grazing and nonchalantly looks at us. From beneath his two metre antlers his dark eyes briefly meet mine, then he returns to feeding.

Morning mists shroud the surrounding snow-covered peaks, and lingers in and above the pine trees. Down from the heights, the searching whistle-bellows of stag elk waft over a half dozen cow elk in the adjacent meadow; they perk their heads and listen. Over the water comes the honks of a thousand Canadian and Snow geese, plus the clamour from a variety of ducks.

My senses afford me a rapturous awareness. I'm snug and warm in my down parka, as Rich hands me a steaming mug of Earl Grey, its fragrance mingles with the scent of pine and the fishy smell of our catch. The hot mellow taste soothes my cold lips. I sit back, and soak up the waves emanating from the creatures, the land, and the water. On this magic October day, time stands still, I am home in nature's cathedral.

INTERNAL AWARENESS

Physical Body States – advise the person all is well or something needs attention. Pain says an injury is about to happen or has happened. Fatigue is similar, suggesting a suspension of effort. Thirst and hunger require sustenance. If filters block these messages, self-preservation is in jeopardy.

Mental States – may provide information requiring action. Confusion suggests clarification is needed prior to action. When a person receives information from learning experiences, dreams, or the unconscious, they may have the 'aha!' experience, of gaining insight and understanding.

Blockage of mental cues may stifle the ability to interact with the environment.

Emotional States – Being emotionally overwhelmed, severely frightened, or in a rage, is apt to initiate panic. This can lead to inappropriate responses, or it may induce paralysis. The filters may temper the incoming data, leaving the mediation of it to the brain's emotional control centre in the limbic system. If too much data is screened out, the individual's coping mechanisms are marginalized. When the filters fail to acknowledge such states as satisfaction, relief, joy…, the person may continue actions that are no longer necessary.

EXTERNAL AWARENESS

Vision - is the dominant sense of humans; its' goal is to produce an appropriate motor or cognitive response. Vision is more than light from an object casting an image on the retina. Brainline.org stipulates it as one of the sets of brain functions entailing numerous abilities. Vision integrates with auditory stimuli and muscle movements; it registers visual stimuli in the memory and makes possible the recognition of objects or settings. Modern physics suggest perception (all types) is a matter of tuning into the correct frequency of the 'zero-point field' (ZPF).

Visual recognition helped the ancients survive - *is that tan spot in the distance a rock, part of a sand dune, or a lion?* In contemporary life, the ability to visually read facial and body language assists interpersonal relations. Some visual recognition is inherited. A new born gorilla infant is able to distinguish the difference between a poisonous snake and a non-poisonous one. Culture also affects our perception; what a French man perceives as a pretty dress can be vastly different from an English man's perception. Cultural factors are detailed in *Visual Sense,* a 2010 book by Berg publishers.

The visual skill of movement tracking is vital in sports. I have good visual tracking, enabling successful participation in activities like basketball, football, tennis, and skeet shooting. However; my poor long-distance vision makes it difficult to pass the driver's license vision test. The more life experiences a person has, the better their vision will be. Thus, more accurate visual data is presented to the brain filters.

Once I had a young lad aboard ship for his first venture onto the ocean. As we skimmed across the swells, all of a sudden, he hollered 'there's a floating log off to the right.' I looked, and in spite of my poor eyesight, immediately recognized the back of a whale sunning itself.

What visual experiences have affected you? Have you been present to view the birthing process, or the coming of death?

Hearing - is a 'mechano-sensation' process, wherein some action (e.g. a falling tree) sets in motion the surrounding air molecules (vibration). The ear receives these vibrations on incoming air waves, and converts them to nerve impulses. Neuronal encoding lodges the data in both halves of the brain, with some areas specifically devoted to certain types of sound. Wernicke's area, deciphers the sounds of spoken words. The Broca area employs the sounds of spoken words to produce speech. When specific sites of functioning are injured, the brain may transfer the chore to nearby areas.

Auditory discrimination permits the ears to locate the source of a sound, quantify its intensity, and determine whether it has any relevance. Survival of the ancient ones, in part relied on their ability to hear danger approaching. Some of their auditory memory became ingrained in their genes, and this is reflected today in our innate fear/recognition of specific things, and our startle responses. The startle reflex is present in newborns. It is an immediate physical reaction of the body to a possible threat, and can be triggered by loud noise, a flash of light, a nearby sudden movement...

The contemporary human also uses hearing for survival and direction of activity, such as a soldier in a war zone. A pedestrian walking down the street responds differently to the sound of a mosquito, roar of a jet plane, or the rumble of an approaching vehicle. He swats at the first, ignores the second, and checks to see if he needs to move out of the vehicle's way.

My mother, wife, and daughter were classically trained pianists; as a result, I became accustomed to the daily sound of piano music.

Now when I hear piano music it often brings back memories and feelings, sometimes exciting, other times sad or soothing. 'Moonlight Sonata,' sends me to the nearest sofa to relax and occasionally drift off to sleep.

Sound has played a major role in various religions: the Muslim call to prayer, chants of monks, the Buddhist tinkling of bells, the vocal repetition of a mantra…

In quiet settings, such as forests and lakes, the ears can detect and identify a multitude of barely audible sounds. In loud settings, such as factories and cities, the ears ability to differentiate sounds is impaired. Seeking out and attending to novel sounds, or sounds you usually ignore, such as a wolf howl, crashing waterfall, singing chant…, could possibly turn on a dormant gene.

Touch – I am a member of the primate group of animals and share with them a crucial need for touch. Watching the great apes, chimpanzees, and monkeys in zoos and the wilds, has given me valuable clues about my need for touch. Young non-human primates remain physically close to their mother, siblings, or other nurturers for a large part of their childhood. They cling, ride and sleep with this close contact. Moving into adulthood they continue to sleep together, and during the day spend a lot of time sitting close together. They pat, nuzzle and lay a reassuring hand on the back. Grooming each other is the tie that binds them all together.

This information helps me understand why hand-shakes, hand stroking, cuddling, the caress, being hugged and the massive tactile stimulation of sexual intercourse are so vital for the well-being of Homo sapiens. We have a lot in common with our primate cousins.

The human infant spends the first nine months of life cradled in the womb, in constant physical contact. Birth separates him from this contact, throwing him into an alien world of extreme sensory input, except for touch. The new human infant has the same tactile need as a new born chimp, or ape. It needs to be held, to be touched. This is a crucial personality building block for all primates.

During the first year of life children should sleep and have extensive physical contact with others. In Ashley Montagu's book *Touching – The Human Significance of the Skin,* he is adamant the infant should not be placed in a nursery, crib, or baby carriage. During the day the infant should be carried by the adult in something like the Chinese *madai or Eskimo parka.* As an infant I was toted around in an American Indian type papoose board. I have a picture of myself at the age of eleven months, snuggled in a papoose rig and tied to the trunk of a streamside tree while my mother fished for trout.

Montagu says fondling cannot be overdone; the child will soak up as much as it can get. Feeling the soft pressure of human life, its warmth and heartbeat, imbues the infant with comfort. This will slowly build an internal sense of security, an integral element in the building of a successful intrapersonal relationship PELGAM. Likewise, a sense of belonging is established.

Dr. Stanislav Grof, in his book *When the Impossible Happens,* suggests the failure to meet a child's anaclitic cravings to be held, cared for, caressed and played with, impairs the child's future. Provision of ample loving human tactile experience for a child requires the communal family (Hub). It cannot be accomplished by the nuclear family, or non-invested day care providers.

Satisfaction of the need for touch eventually leads to exploratory behaviour: when the child will have the courage to break physical contact and investigate other attributes of the environment. Deprived of physical contact satisfaction, a sense of insecurity permeates the child's existence. This hinders their move into adulthood, and ability to pursue a mature life style.

The sense of touch has always been important to me. I have preferred clothing with soft and smooth textures such as felt, corduroy, and satin. I do not like the feel of fuzzy peach skin or stringy sweet potatoes in my mouth. I love the feel of water, wind, and sunlight on my skin. When I receive a hug, it instils within me a sense of comfort, and gives a clear message that I am cared for. There are many types of touch, and each may provoke a variety of responses.

131

The touch nerve endings in the skin are able to differentiate the sensations of wetness, heat, cold, pressure, pain, hard-soft, smooth-rough and many, many more. The receptors are not spread evenly over the skin; some areas are more receptive to pain, and others to heat or pressure. The areas of greatest sensitivity can vary from person to person and culture to culture.

Regardless of the person or setting, human touch can communicate: emotions, comfort, support, or non-support. Touch can boost the immune system and it also activates the production of the hormone (oxytocin) enabling more effective coping with stress. Touch expedites and strengthens inter-personal relationships. Despite all its benefits, touch has not fared well in contemporary culture.

Human touch has been impaired via the aforementioned turning off of genes and stalled maturational development. A few religions exacerbated the situation when they posited 'sins of the flesh' and demanded monogamy. Current society's preference for digital media contact versus in vivo contact, and legal restrictions on physical contact at work and school, has made matters worse. These factors may have turned off more genes, and reduced human physical, emotional, mental and social capacities. These issues are pursued in the following articles. *March 2015 Psychology Today article by Ray Williams. August 2015 CNBC.com article by Chris Morris.*

Western culture must facilitate greater physical contact amongst the population. They can start by altering those laws and practices currently interfering with human contact, and learn from cultures that practise high physical contact. On the personal level, greetings could include a hug, a common practise in Italy. Daily massages and plentiful sexual intercourse are easy simple means of bolstering the sense of touch. We could learn much from the observation of animals such as puppies and kittens who sleep in a tumble of bodies. Consider also how livestock often draw close together and lean on each other. What happens to you when you stroke the fur of an animal, or dig your hands into soil?

Taste - receptor cells exist in the duodenum and throat, but mainly on the tongue, and roof of the mouth. When you put something in the mouth, the receptor cells determine the chemical makeup of the substance, and transmit the data to the brain, where neurons receive the sensation of taste. For this to happen, the brain must include data from the sense of smell, and the sense of touch (texture and temperature).

Traditionally five tastes have been recognized: salty, sour, sweet, bitter and umami/savoury. Recent studies postulate a taste for fat. The German Institute for Quality and Efficiency in Health Care (IQWiG), state 100,000 flavours are possible when the five tastes with their ten levels of intensity are considered. When the sense of smell and touch are included, the total number of possible flavour sensations is enormous.

Taste played a key role in the survival of the ancients by training their brain filters to detect poisonous (bitter or sour) plants or water, and nutrient rich foods (sweet or salty). Some people are able to taste allergy producing ingredients (from a recent PubMed Health article). It remains to be smelled, if these human capabilities will work in other planetary settings. The palate has been a casualty for current space travellers, astronauts describe their inflight meals as tasting like cardboard.

Taste can produce strong emotional responses: I get the warm glow feelings of Christmas from eating Christmas cookies. I feel February's cold isolation and loneliness, when I drink hot chocolate. Memories of special occasions may produce tastes associated with those times. Research has shown pleasant emotions may arise from savory broth dishes. When I eat couscous, it brings back feelings and memories of good times in Morocco. I have emotional responses to the taste of: BBQ meat, nachos, blood, bile, vaginal secretions, lipstick, perfume, chocolate, burnt toast...According to nihseniorhealth.gov, people over 60 experience a small decline in taste ability, but so small most people don't notice it. If there is a noticeable reduction, it more often than not is the result of impairment to the sense of smell.

Smell - Who knows what the nose knows? The nose can detect: blood relatives, possible sexual partners, spouses (each person has their own distinct odour), fear, disgust, poisonous substances, fire… The nose can distinguish about one trillion unique odors, far more stimuli than the other senses can detect. The smell sense is more powerful in women than men, particularly during ovulation. According to a 2001 report in the *Annual Review of Psychology*, smell is the only sense that connects directly to the forebrain. Hence, pairing smell with brain filter training is a wise idea.

When the nose detects a smell, the data is sent along the olfactory nerve to the olfactory bulb in the brain. From there the information is shared with various brain areas. Smell plays a role in memory, behavior, and emotion, as reported in *fifthsense.org.uk*. Remember the movie theatres that had scent piped to each seat?

The air re-circulating machinery aboard the International Space Station cleans the air, but is limited in its ability to remove odours. Inhabitants describe the ISS as a strongly odoriferous habitat.

Travel is not just about seeing it involves all the senses, including smell. Walking the alleyways of Morocco's medinas, one encounters a stream of aromas from the multitude of spices being sold, camels and donkeys and the overpowering vats of dye. Cultures vary vastly in their approach to body odour. In his book *Lame Deer, Seeker of Visions,* the Lakota medicine man cites the white man's use of deodorants and perfumes as an example of their alienation, not just from nature, but from themselves. They are disgusted by the natural smells of their own body.

The fragrance industry takes advantage of the relationship between smell and human functions, by marketing perfumes and colognes designed to evoke a vast array of emotions. The scent of 'Here's My Heart,' 'Red Door,' 'Shalimar'… always makes me hungry.

While odor receptor genes makeup the largest gene family in a human, they are far fewer than the thousand active odor receptor genes found in other mammals. The Grizzly bear can detect the scent of food from thirty kilometers. I spent many years backpacking in Grizzly areas such as Glacier and Yellowstone National Park, and never carried chocolate or bacon. Both are known to draw in the Grizzlies.

An Idaho road construction worker parked his travel trailer on the remote edge of a forest glade in Island Park, an eight-thousand-foot forest plateau adjacent to Yellowstone National Park. He had been living there a month or so, each morning driving the twenty kilometers out to the new section of highway being built. He eventually cast caution to the wind, and bought some bacon which he enjoyed the next morning with his eggs. That evening he returned to find the side of his caravan ripped off and the frying pan licked clean.

In general, a dog's sense of smell is a million times more acute than a human's. Theo, my present canine companion is amazing. If you take one of her sticks she has been retrieving, and hide it anywhere on the property, she will find it within minutes. Mel, the basset hound I had years ago, was similar. Bassets are the second-best scent dogs after blood hounds. Mel had a problem of self-identity; he preferred being a social butterfly to being a hunter. I'll talk more about him in the animal relationship section.

A massive part of the fish brain is devoted to the olfactory sense. Fishermen will often douse their fishing lures in a variety of odiferous solutions. This, plus the caught fish, and the grubby fisherman, makes a fishing trip a smelly outing.

A rancher relaxes on the tailgate of his pickup in a paddock; a half kilometre away on the other side of the hill, something lies crumpled and bloated next to the swollen river. The rancher cannot see it, but his nose tells him what it is.

Let us probe the sense of waves and time which are ignored in mainstream culture.

Waves – All life and all objects vibrate, giving off electromagnetic waves; waves are energy systems, each having its own distinct frequency. A person emits waves and senses those of humans, animals, plants... Remember when you felt you were being watched, or something was nearby? Studies have shown this awareness to be accurate on most occasions. *The Sense of Being Stared at* by Rupert Sheldrake reviews an array of waves impacting life and extending from the human mind.

Ancient schools of meditation claim to draw upon the surrounding positive waves. This brain based sensory ability has been referred to by many names: intuition, extrasensory perception, enlightenment, genius... It may be responsible for the success of the great scientists, mathematicians..., many of whom, cite intuition as the source of their inspiration.

The senses so far listed are specific forms of wave systems, such as sight and sound. Our vision is a result of receiving waves of light particles; our hearing comes from vibratory waves passing through air space. I place the vast array of other wave systems into this section and refer to them as oceanic.

For twenty years, the intelligence collecting branches of the United States government financed Stanford Research Institute studies of the remote viewing of distant objects. Individuals with remote viewing ability were exceptionally accurate in describing distant objects, such as items in a box, features in outer space, structures at secret Russian sites, and so on. Study findings are available at www.rviewers.com; the *Journal of Scientific Exploration Vol 10, 1996,* contains an interesting article by Russel Targ on the research findings.

The use of brain waves to heal the body has been used in various practises: meditation, self-hypnosis, bio-medicine, massage... A multitude of studies have shown these practises to have significant beneficial results. On the other hand, popular media has been awash with the claims about the tremendous impact of prayers offered for the healing of others. Numerous studies have failed to support distant prayer as a viable healing modality, as reported by Marilyn Schlitz in her article *'Can Science Study Prayer?'* (Published in Shift, September 2006).

I successfully reduced dermatological patient suffering by pairing hypnosis with wave washing. This process involves slowly moving the hands in wave like motions about two inches above the distressed area, drawing, pulling and washing out the unhealthy elements. Eventually, I would change my mental focus, sending my healthy waves into the problem area. This, like a lot of psychotherapy, is a process of empowering the patient to heal themselves.

I incorporate extrasensory perception (ESP), and psychic phenomena (psi) into the oceanic category of waves. These areas are often referred to as the 6th sense and includes mental telepathy, clairvoyance, precognition, distant viewing... In 1973 the 'Institute of Noetic Sciences' (www.NOETIC.ORG) was founded by Apollo 14 astronaut Edger Mitchell to investigate the extraordinary human capacities inherent in the interconnected unified wave fields of energy.

The existence of ESP is no longer in doubt, but how it operates remains a mystery. Ervin Laszlo (*Quantum Shift in the Global Brain*) suggests the old traditional societies probably had people who possessed the sensitivity to tune into: mental telepathy, past life impressions, communication with the spirits of ancestors and so on. Modern society's reductionist and materialistic mindset has led to the demise of these wave sensitivities.

Each person's waves intersect with the waves of others; ZPF physicists theorise these interference patterns are natural holograms. Each person leaves their holographic trace pattern in the ZPF field, and these unite with the patterns of others, to provide a hologram of: a family, group, community... When we heed our AM, we may possibly tap into this group hologram; it is simply a manner of tuning into the correct frequency according to Ervin Laszlo.

If you set aside time to relax from the daily whirlwind, practise tuning into and identifying incoming waves, it could provide many benefits: creative thinking, problem resolution, detecting danger, finding lost people or objects, understanding a person or a group...

Investigate how your waves may affect your surroundings. When you are angry, sad, or happy, can you perceive its effect on the people, animals and plants around you? In the presence of highly performing people, their waves may coax you to get your act together, to move towards optimal functioning.

Extensive research on learning while asleep failed to achieve positive results. I suspect it failed because it used tape recorders which did not contain the waves of the person reading the material. There is an electrical/magnetic component involved in the brains transmission, and reception of data. I theorize the presence of recording equipment with its electrical/magnetic field, may interfere with the brain. It may be possible for a foetus or sleeping person to learn from verbal material presented by a live reader.

Eventually, we will collect, store and harness the waves from: people, plants, the planet and the stars - in a similar manner to our harnessing of solar waves, wind, and wave energy. Sensing the wave forces of growth and decay, we may be able to slow the aging process. Give the oceanic wave sense some thought - you may devise new methods of using it for your benefit.

Time – The solar system primes the human internal clock, which sets standards for physical functioning and monitors activity. Female ovulation is one example; it occurs on a lunar time cycle, and ceases in mid-life. Psychological and educational research has determined peak brain performance occurs from ten am to noon. Heavy work or gym workouts are best left for the afternoon. Humans can sense when an hour has passed, and it is time for the beauty shop appointment. This area of science is known as Chrono astrobiology, and has been studied extensively by Franz Halberg at the University of Minnesota.

Workers employed within buildings do not receive the full dosage of solar light to balance the long night of darkness. This balance is crucial to physical, emotional and mental well-being. The situation is worsened by the cultural habit of staying up late soaking up the blue light of televisions and computers, which interferes with the light balance system.

Night shift workers and students who study for long hours violate the body's clock. Most third shift workers adjust their body clock within two weeks, some take twice as long, and 10% never adapt. Too much study time (specialization), prevents students from obtaining vital experiential learning and social skills. The western mind focuses on the present appearing to have lost grasp of the time line, unable to lay the foundation for a secure future time for their descendants.

Improve your sense of time by paying more attention to natural phenomena- the sun's movements, plant foliage, air temperature. Try to rely less on a watch or your phone. Body states such as hunger, thirst, and stamina level can be accurate tellers of time. It is important to set short and long-term time schedules as part of life's plan.

CONCLUSION

A stellar person has accurate near-far visual acuity and is able to hear across a wide range of the frequency span and at great distance. Likewise, they possess a highly sensitive touch that can detect the smallest imperfections and minute temperature changes. Their reception of wave energies enables them to find: animals, water, mineral deposits, and energy. They may accurately forecast short-term local weather, earthquakes, and volcanic activity. Some may create synaesthesia ability such as the ability to witness colour with the ears.

Society's emphasis on progress and reason leads humans away from the use of their natural sensorial abilities, hence away from nature and each other. Enhancement of sensory awareness can bring about a sense of pleasure, of belonging, and a feeling of broader comprehension of all.

Homo-sapiens survival on earth and in space requires maximal development of the human sensory system so they can be aware of their interconnectedness with people, animals, plants and the biosphere. This will facilitate a higher level of individual consciousness which will aid human interactions with alien life.

Chapter 6 PELGAMs

Doomed Craft

Cold rain beats down from the pitch-black sky; the wind roars, and rampaging waves toss the dinghy about. The oars are flailing as two scrawny hairless apes aim for the feeble speck of oscillating light in the distance. They draw closer and closer till the surf hurls them upon the rocks with a resounding whack. Timbers shatter as the critters are thrown into the maelstrom of water. The undertow's numbing voracious jaws suck at their bruised bodies. Gasping for air, arms thrashing, feet pushing against stones and gravel, they struggle towards the shore. Raw bleeding hands grasp rock, sod and dirt. They pull themselves up the slope, escaping Neptune's tenacious fingers. On their bellies, they squirm like snakes towards the feeble greenish blue light. Aeolus's heinous shrieking gusts attempt to tear them from earth and fling them into the vapour. A forehead bumps a splintery door.

Quivering hands climb upwards to a shaky knob and twist; the winds fury hurls them through the portal. They strain, and push the door shut. Around them, the dull pinkish walls of a cavernous room glow eerily, and pulse with the beat of life. A tall slender hourglass reaches upward into the dark; a thin trickle of sand streams down. Bright flashes of light, sloshing sounds, and chemical odours emanate from behind a multitude of encircling doors. On a shelf, an ancient ever-burning candle casts worrying doubts. They take it down, walk to the nearest door and slip inside.

Rivulets of sticky fluid flow around their bare abraded feet. Naked electrical wires are everywhere. Flying sparks, miniature bolts of lightning, and throbbing tubes and hoses give an air of impending disaster. Amidst vats of steaming goo sit bins of firecrackers. Innumerable colourful bulging tanks appear ready to burst. The walls are festooned with dials, gauges, panels of buttons, levers and tiny hissing atomizers. An infinite array of unrecognizable items clutters the room. A bare white table sits in the centre of the room. Hanging above it an exquisitely fluted crystal bell reverberates a soft pure tone. Fluttering about the bell, a dainty red bird sings a haunting melody. Our apes have stumbled into a PELGAMs quarters.

This story is to raise awareness of the awesome grey matter between the ears. Now, let's take a closer look at the PELGAM concept.

PELGAM – is a combination of environmental learning (EL) experiences, genetic (G) potential, and ancient memories (AM). Chapter 3 introduced this concept and listed PELGAMs of import to daily life. These will be discussed in the upcoming chapters. This chapter is a brief review of PELGAMs as a group.

Unbalanced - An unbalanced set of PELGAMs is the norm in society, partially due to day-to-day demands not requiring development of every PELGAM.

Another factor is the culture's emphasis on specialisation, which results in the development of one or two PELGAMs, while giving little attention to the remainder. When a brain circuit is not utilized, it is apt to fade away. The brain's tendency to become fixated on previously formed neural circuits, rather than creating new patterns, is also to blame.

Balanced - is not a new idea; as I previously mentioned, it was an aspect of the 'renaissance', and a key component of the last century's 'self-actualisation' movement. Genetic intelligence/potential, ancient memories and the ZPF may provide answers and directions for life situations we confront. However, the ever-evolving complexity of modern life demands more. When the environmental learning component interacts with all PELGAMs, understanding and finding solutions to new and unfamiliar situations becomes possible.

Stellar souls have a multitude of skills. Consequently, they live a balanced life style. Such a person is not perfect, nor can they do everything. Yet watching them in action can be daunting, as they flexibly adapt to most situations and achieve success in most endeavours. How do they get that way?

Each time one embarks on learning activities the brain sprouts new circuitry, a potential comes to life (neural Darwinism). PELGAM growth requires action; life experiences (EL) must be organized. Children enrolled in music classes (EL), will over time draw upon their genetic music potential (G) and their (AM), to become musicians. This amalgamation creates a more fully functioning brain. Musicians have 25% more of the auditory cortex involved in musical processing than non-musicians.

A PELGAM has many stages of development, we can quantify its level of progress. For example, the physical PELGAM contains numerous sub-categories (strength, agility, reflex speed...). A person scoring low in most categories would be classified as having an underdeveloped physical PELGAM. A high scorer in most categories would be classed as having a highly developed physical PELGAM.

Achieving Balance - Our ancestors learned from all aspects of the flora, fauna, and humans in their surroundings. Over millennia the genetic encoding of their learning, combined with ancient memory traces, has imbued humans with a fluid intelligence containing a host of potentials. When a potential is subjected to social, mental, emotional and behavioural learning experiences, it will be set into motion, and act on the environment. At this point I label it a PELGAM. Experience is a good teacher. Sufficient experiential time for each PELGAM will lead the way to balance. Each PELGAM chapter contains suggestions for experiential learning.

You can realize how much your PELGAMs have grown in the past by taking a moment to reflect on the environmental learning experiences you have had. Your years as an exploring toddler, time in school, the different countries and cultures you have visited.

You've met thousands of people, and dozens of animal species. You have explored forests, deserts, mountains…, the list goes on and on. Each learning experience strengthened your PELGAMs, providing more tools for you to work successfully with life. Did you collect all the tools possible? Have you used them wisely?

PELGAM potential directs you toward certain preferences: sitting around a fire, living near water, physical activity… An example of AM working within the relationship PELGAM is the ubiquitous preference for hairiness in a partner. Our ancestors were more hirsute than present day humans. When we see people with short or little hair, our AM warns us this may not be a healthy mate, or worse yet, it may not be our species. I'm sure the latter was the case with a couple of those shorthaired so called 'girls' I dated as a teenager.

Utilizing PELGAM potential enriches daily life and makes for a bright future. Therefore, it is wise to delve into the experiences life has on offer. Learn to sit enjoyably atop a mountain, in a cave, on a rolling boat at sea… If you like to ride your bike, try something similar but different, take up the unicycle, roller blading, or horse riding. Study unfamiliar topics. Expand your musical repertoire. If your kitchen is stocked with sumptuous food, why be content with a stale crust? Variety is not only the 'spice-of-life', it is essential for PELGAM growth.

Consulting for corporations and the military, I witnessed the importance of balanced development in group dynamics. When you assemble a group and assign them tasks, the lowest functioning member of the group drags overall performance down. Investing energy in top functioning members will only slightly improve group performance. What works best is to draw upon assistance from the high functioning members, to raise the skills of all the members to a mutual level. Then overall performance of the group will surge ahead.

Balanced PELGAMs is a natural law. The body requires a specific balanced intake of nutrients and expelling of waste, otherwise physical incapacity results. Similarly, the brain needs a balanced inflow of stimulation, and outflow of expressive action. Otherwise, physical, mental, and emotional life will be stunted.

* * *

West of New Caledonia, a twenty-five knot breeze flows over the deck; we are doing five knots. The wind vane auto pilot struggles to stay on course because the sails are not in balance. This morning's winds were only ten knots, so I put up the spinnaker and full main. In the low wind strength this full sail plan had given us five knots. But now the greater wind strength is pulling us off to starboard, and there is a chance it might split one of the sails.

I haul the spinnaker into its sock, and drop it on the deck. Then I furl in 40% of the Genoa. This eliminates careening off to starboard, but lowers speed to four knots. The hull begins rolling from side to side, making it difficult to maintain a foothold. The rolling is a result of the main sail being too high; it is reaching up where the winds are gusting. This repeatedly tilts the hull over till some wind spills out of the main sail and we roll more upright, then the process repeats. I crank the roller furling main down several meters, and we quit rolling.

The Genoa and main are in balance now, but speed is only four and a half knots, not acceptable. If I unfurl more Genoa, I'm sure it will produce more speed, but it may pull us off to starboard again. It's time to raise the mizzen sail.

I winch the mizzen out of its bag between the lazy jacks, and sheet it in till the streamers are fluttering evenly. Speed is up to nearly six knots. Hallelujah! But the wind vane is working furiously; the ship wants to go to port. Too much mizzen. I let off the mizzen halyard, lowering it two meters, and the wind vane quiets down. The sail plan is in balance; the ship smoothly glides ahead at full speed.

* * *

When strong PELGAMs are developed and implemented in a balanced fashion, life can sail on at a suitable clip. Let us inspect each PELGAM

Chapter 7   Physical PELGAM

In Holland, if you do not own a bicycle you are not considered Dutch. Does it follow that you are not human if you cannot swim, lope, and climb trees?

The physical PELGAM governs internal physical functioning (heartbeat, breathing, blood pressure…), external physical interaction with the environment (gross and fine motor skills, use of senses…), and the energy that drives the system. It intermeshes with cognitive and social activity. Therefore, the 'World Health Organizations' (WHO) definition of good health includes mental and social well-being, plus the ability to function well in adverse circumstances.

We will examine some joys of the physical body, like my learning to masturbate; and some of the sorrows, such as aging and my lifetime fear of going blind. I will review some of the strange personalities resulting from poor physical maintenance, as well as, physical break down brought on by career and living environment. Locating and maintaining energy for the body will be covered. I will encourage you to consider what body part you would like to have surgically removed and replaced with a better part. Perhaps you would prefer to ingest a substance to alter your physical morphology?

INTERNAL

The internal need awareness system monitors the bodies' inner workings advising us that all is well, or we should attend to something. Some need awareness is genetically based and automatically sets in motion drives to fulfil the need. Hunger, body temperature, fatigue, pain, constipation, urinary urgency and so forth - these are messages demanding one to eat, get out of the sun, rest and so on. When winter approaches, I retrieve my warm clothes out of storage. When I see a rain cloud, I duck for cover or don a raincoat. Both are examples of how we have learned to use external cues to prepare ourselves for an internal physical need.

EXTERNAL

The external needs monitor detects how much strength, agility, speed and so forth are needed to cope with an environmental demand on the body. We consciously or unconsciously make the decision to jump higher, run faster and so on. Demands exceeding our physical capabilities require our withdrawal from the situation. This may not be possible in a world crisis or a space setting which place high demands on the physical body.

Here on Earth I weigh 84kg, on Mars I would only be 30kg and on Neptune 90kg. The low gravity of space flight and the Martian environment place less strain on the body; however, it leads to bone structure and muscle fibre deterioration. Planets with more gravity than earth will sorely test man's physical agility and mobility. Astronauts need superb physical dexterity as they routinely use about a hundred tools and pieces of equipment. When outside the space craft on high gravity planets, they have the additional burden of lugging around a 110kg cumbersome space suit in life threatening temperatures. On Mars they may have to climb peaks 2000 metres higher than Mount Everest or walk in snow shoes over extensive dust bowls. They will need energy.

The bodies' energy system is similar to the one on my yacht; the diesel engine and solar panels generate electricity which is stored in five deep cycle batteries. Energy for the body is derived from the consumption of food and stored within the body. I envision a storage battery for each PELGAM. Aboard ship the electricity provides energy for starting the engine, running pumps, lights and appliances. Human body energy is used for physical and mental activity. A super athlete draws heavily upon their physical PELGAM battery, whereas the non-athlete uses little energy from their physical battery.

When a person's interpersonal relationship PELGAM involves them with a physically active group of friends, bike riding, tennis, ab sailing… The individual must physically shape up and have highly charged physical batteries. Likewise, a strong philosophy PELGAM will have a highly charged philosophy battery. This would be necessary for performing in high mental energy burn professions such as mathematics.

WEAK PHYSICAL PELGAM

Genetics – may predispose a person to have deficient bone structure, muscles, organs, chemistry, neurological wiring, intelligence… Low intelligence often interferes with the individual's ability to maintain appropriate eating and exercise regimens. Or it could result in negativity, low self-esteem and difficulty handling stress, which can impede physical functioning. The aging process entails progressive degeneration of the physical body in response to genetic guidelines.

Genetics gave me strong muscles and bones, tall stature, and agility, but weak eyes. During the aging process I have undergone a reduction in physical well-being: less energy, stamina, breathing capacity, flexibility and muscle strength… Thus, I run out of steam earlier in the day, have excessive oxygen burn during scuba diving, and have more difficulty stretching or bending to get something. At first these changes were frustrating; I've adjusted to them now, but worry about further deterioration.

Throughout life I have improved my physical PELGAM via a variety of endeavours: weight lifting, basketball, football, baseball, track… I have tried every eye exercise and enhancement program known to man, to no avail.

Internal Cues - Inappropriate responses to internal cues are a common problem. Anorexics respond to their negative image of self-worth by ignoring the need to eat. Workaholics toil on in spite of fatigue. The professional athlete plays on in spite of severe pain. A spouse unhappy with the meagre amount of affection from their partner may ignore the issue and console themselves with excessive eating, sexual promiscuity or abusing their spouse. Those people who sleep a lot and have little exercise are apt to accumulate negative chemical substances in their muscle tissue and excessive carbon dioxide in their blood. These conditions reduce the level of physical functioning and the availability of energy.

External Cues - cultural, career and family circumstances may damage the physical body. Bullied boys may lift weights in an attempt to build muscular bodies as a means of coping with threats. Those boys with light bone structure are likely to incur bone fractures, further negating their self-concept. Striving for the tanned body can produce skin cancer. Loud music damages hearing. Working with asbestos building materials has impaired and killed carpenters. The knee joints are shot by middle age in most tilers and roofers.

Diet plays a key role in the energy system. Failure to eat adequately lowers body and brain effectiveness as witnessed by low levels of strength and stamina, poor dexterity, slow physical and mental responses, mood disorders, inaccurate problem solving and a general lack of energy. If the inadequate intake persists, death will follow.

Too much food destroys balanced body chemistry and can lead to a host of internal ailments. It also negatively impacts the individual's self-concept. An obese person will struggle to have faith in themselves. Obesity strains the entire system and usually interferes with career, interpersonal relations, and the pursuit of a happy life style. I used the term 'usually' as I have known exceptions.

* * *

'You have written here on the counselling application that you both are happy with your marriage aside from an issue of body weight? Please explain.'

Dagnia – I have always kept fit, except when pregnant. During both my pregnancies I put on fifteen or more pounds, which all went into my butt. Buz loved it.'

Buz – 'Well, some went into your boobs. I like big boobs and a big ass.'

Dagnia – 'Our second child was born ten years ago, after which, I lost the excess weight in spite of his beleaguering me to keep it. Now over the past year he has been on my back to put on weight. He brings home endless boxes of candy, pies, cakes and ice cream.'

I asked Buz: 'Most men like their wives to stay thin and shapely - is that not the case with you?'

Buz – Well! I see a big ass as more-shapely than a flat ass.

'Yeah! I can understand that.' I said.

Buz – 'In sex, Dagnia's preferred position is to be on top where she is able to orgasm more quickly and more often, which is fine by me. But I like to get it off from behind, doggy style. Thumping up against a big ass is great, better than a bony ass.

* * *

Some men, out of a sense of insecurity, prefer their wives to be portly, hoping no other man would be attracted to such a female, that wasn't the case with Buz. I spent a half dozen therapy sessions with the couple over a four-month period. They experimented with some unique and interesting solutions till both were happy.

Other folks use their obesity as a tool of power and authority to dominate others. Clinical practices regularly see sexually insecure women who use obesity to keep prospective suitors or husbands at arms-length. Law enforcement (a power wielding profession) has the highest (40%) rate of obesity amongst all careers, as reported in the United States *2010 Health Interview Survey*. Studies printed in the UK mirror (mirror.co.uk) report similar statistics for English law enforcement. Both of these reports found a 32% rate of obesity amongst health care workers. I have always been aghast at the number of overweight nurses.

The power personality focuses controlling others and thwarting control directed at them; however, they often have poor self-control and some become obese. Their obese image in the mirror tells them to eat less; they respond with 'I'll eat as I damn well please.' Some initiate excessive bowel movements in an attempt to stave off getting fat. Un-natural or excessive evacuation procedures can lead to long-term de-stabilization of the general intestinal tract.

A Strong Physical PELGAM - is evidenced by: a high level of body fitness, ample energy and good utilization of the fitness and energy. Such an individual will have a broad range of physical and mental activity, balanced with peaceful, relaxed times and adequate sleep. When the brain consciously engages in tasks, the physical body tends to relax.

Building the Physical PELGAM – Food and drink provide the building blocks for tissue, bone, blood..., and serve as the fuel for energy generation. Hence, selecting the type and quantity of nutrients is important. Consider consulting a dietician. They can provide the best guidance when they have your family history, results of a medical exam, genetic predisposition, activity level, and so on.

Web/library research will give you the food requirements for a human your size and activity level, as well as, your racial genetic data. Talk with your relatives and learn your family's dietary history. When an elf eats like an elephant, you get a fat elf. If you work at strenuous physical labour and attempt to eat the same diet as your partner who has a clerical job, your batteries will go flat, you will collapse.

Consumption of genetically modified food (GMO) can produce allergy and other health problems; you may want to avoid its use till such time research suggests otherwise. Current cultural emphasis on organic food is compatible with our concept of keeping life natural. The goal of non-organic commercial fruit and vegie farmers is to produce food that looks good and will not spoil during shipment and lengthy time in the supermarket. Flavour and nutrient level are usually below that of home-grown products. The freshest, most nutritional, and tasty food comes from your home garden, and contains the micro – organisms inhabiting your specific environment which are more beneficial to your immune system. Home grown food is free of additives and pest sprays.

The use of packaged or canned food should be minimized as they usually have too much sugar, salt and preservatives. Pure water and lots of raw food are important. Good eating habits help ensure you have an adequate uninterrupted power supply.

What goes in must come out. There must be a healthy pattern of expelling waste exhaling, urinating, defecating and skin emissions are the major means of eliminating waste.

In addition to the intake of nutrients, our primate genetic code demands physical activity to build and maintain the body and its energy. Chasing dinner and hoofing it from one place to another was a daily feature in the lives of our hunter gatherer forbears. They extensively used their hands to create articles they needed, solve problems and creatively express themselves. There is some truth to the old adage 'busy hands are happy hands.' Regular use of the hands assists the brain's intellectual and neural processing. Some at home activities can help with this - computers, gaming consoles, love making, musical instruments, wood working, gardening…

Hub children should receive extensive physical training. By age 5 the child could be an adept swimmer, skin diver, a dextrous tree climber, and capable of loping a fair distance. As the individual moves through the stages of adulthood, continuation of physical activities will help them maintain a strong physical PELGAM.

Consider a return to the healthy nomadic life style in which Hub members may rotate between several home sites (beach, mountains, forest...). Natural landscapes are conducive to meditation, yoga, self-hypnosis and other techniques which may help a person learn control of various internal physical functions - their metabolism, body temperature, heart rate, blood flow and possibly the healing of the body.

Thirty minutes of daily vigorous exercise improves physical fitness; it also invigorates mental processing and emotional stability which relieves negative mental states such as depression and anxiety. Physical workouts should not be conducted when one is sick or injured.

Apes love moving about, investigating mysteries and having fun; they are not built to sit or stand all day at a job, or to spend the evening sitting at the dinner table and TV. Some people try to compensate for the days inactivity by having gym workouts in the evening. You only have so much time in life. If you spend your evenings getting the exercise that you should have gotten during the day, what is going to get left out? Research suggests most of us do not make enough time for sleep, sex, social contact and alone reflective time.

I like to follow the example of my ancestors and obtain some of my exercise roaming about the wilds in search of my food. At other times I prefer exercise that fulfils multiple needs. Tennis, dance parties, and group hiking provide opportunity for social time, fun time, time in nature and endless opportunities to learn. As a 'boatie' I enjoy water activity. Water has therapeutic effects on the nervous system and the mind. If the water is cool, the body will burn more calories to maintain body temperature. This makes it a definite aid to weight loss programs.

While scuba diving, snorkelling and body surfing recharge my mind and body, doing laps in a pool is a different story. One bitter Michigan winter I was unable to play basketball due to a back injury. Instead I swam laps at the athletic club indoor Olympic pool. The physical workout was great, but it did not relax my mind. I found it mentally boring and could not keep from thinking about work. Then a solution bubbled up.

***

I drop into a lane next to a lane occupied by a skimpy bikini. I don my snorkel mask and swim contentedly gazing out of my mask. My fantasies are entertaining, and it increases blood circulation in certain body parts. Unfortunately, it dampens my immediate interest in gym exercise. Eventually it gets boring, some people you can't please.

***

Consider participation in sports that utilize a large percentage of the body's muscles (swimming). Table tennis improves eye-hand coordination, agile foot work, and timing. As I have gotten older, I have shifted from weight lifting to stretching exercises and cycling. These things, as well as the work I do around my property keep me recharged and fit.

In recent times the old standard of endurance training has been somewhat supplanted by 'high intensity training' (HIT). The individual quickly pushes the muscle group to its point of failure. *'Fitness First Australia'* and other websites extoll HIT benefits. An article at www.shape.com/fitness by Charlotte Anderson lists some of the benefits: increase in body metabolism, boost in the body repair system, improving cardiovascular health, and slowing the aging process.

HIT expects a person to have already achieved a fair degree of fitness and be on the young side. I suspect a blend of endurance and HIT might bestow the best outcomes. Given the complexity of physical functioning and the plethora of information about it, it is wise to maintain a close liaison with a medical practitioner and perhaps your own personal trainer.

Additional Methods – I favour natural means such as social interaction and pet ownership. Social interaction has been shown in a multitude of studies to provide great mental and physical benefits. I have seen the physical health of clients improve when they form a network of close friends. Such a network produces more stable pleasing emotional states. Hence, people are not as likely to eat out of frustration, overwork due to boredom, or avoid appropriate exercise due to a lack of interest.

Pet ownership is equally important. Lisa Fields in a 'webMD' feature discusses how pets can improve health. Pet owners have fewer stress reactions, lower blood pressure, are happier, more trusting, more socially involved and less lonely. Family pets strengthen a baby's immune system, such infants have less allergies, asthma, colds and ear infections than children in homes lacking pets.

Chemistry - There are chemical substances which may improve the physical PELGAM without negative effects. One would need to review the literature and draw upon the wisdom of substance experts. I have focused on limiting my intake of substances that might be physically harmful such as alcohol, nicotine, anti-biotics, prescription drugs, salt and sugar. I expect the future will bring forth new substances offering enticing possibilities for physical improvement.

Surgery - procedures are available to alter physical morphology. I have known several sinus sufferers who have had their nasal passages drilled out - sounds gruesome to me! Malaysia, Singapore and Thailand have billion-dollar plastic surgery industries. Breast implants and removal of the epicanthi eye fold, are popular with Asian women. Penis and testicle enlargement are popular with Asian men.

Manufacture - of physical prosthesis, such as hands, arms and legs has been around a long time. The recent break-throughs of manufactured body parts via 3D printers, suggests a future where weak or damaged body parts will be routinely replaced.

Neurological – Physical and mental ageing is in part a result of the reduction of mitochondria in brain cells. The November 2011 issue of *Life Extension Magazine* has an article by Michelle Flagg titled '*Reversing Brain Cell Death by Growing New Mitochondria.*' Creating new mitochondria is also hinted at in some of the HIT research. Genetic engineering and cell therapy are in their infancy and will no doubt over time have much to offer. Neurological implants and brain stimulation are also on the horizon.

Energy - The generation and maintenance of a constant, even flow of energy is a prerequisite for stable physical functioning. Some of us are born with large batteries and some with smaller batteries. During certain times of the day or year, some people may experience energy brown outs or energy spikes. This is of no concern if it is a short time period. Extended periods of low energy can be seen in slothful people (couch potatoes and bookworms). This of course, results in poor physical health.

Long-lasting high energy spikes can lead to hyperactivity and a frenetic life.

Human batteries are similar to the standard car battery - they require fresh non-polluted air and an even temperature. I'm sure you remember how sluggish you become when you are too hot or too cold. Partially depleted batteries impair overall functioning. If the level of charge is taken below 25%, a nervous breakdown may occur.

Energy channelled into only a few areas may produce narrow minded high achievers who often end up mentally and physically burnt out and unable to cope with the vicissitudes of life. Low energy and wasteful fluctuations are generally not a result of small batteries, but rather a lack of appropriate action and not understanding how to regulate the power. One must avoid the endless number of battery drainers such as fear, stress, anger, illogical thinking, senseless behaviour, loneliness, the presence of certain people, unpleasant surroundings and so on.

Re-charging Human Batteries - Physical dormancy (relaxation, sleep, trance) burns a tiny bit of energy while at the same time giving an energy boost. There are many energy restoring activities- listening to gentle music, being in natural settings (beach, mountains), viewing a comedy, socializing, reading and so on. If the birds in the trees are fighting, your book is a thriller, or your mind is agonizing over something, then your recharge may be minimal. When we got a tropical fish aquarium, I thought it would be a tranquil addition to the house, till I witnessed the ongoing fights for dominance and territory.

Sleep recharges the batteries, improving brain receptivity, cognition and physical abilities. Genetics seems to be the culprit in determining how much sleep is needed. The range required by the general population runs from two to ten hours. If you are not sure how much sleep you need, experiment. Stick to the same hours of sleep every night for a month, perhaps 7. Sleep 8 hours per night the following month. Confine sleep to 6 hours a night on the third month. When you pin down your optimum sleep time, adhere to it. Deviations of one hour has little effect, but your recharge may fail when you miss your required sleep by more than two hours.

Occasional sleep difficulty is common and nothing to be concerned about. You can facilitate sleep by avoiding the intake of stimulants, strenuous physical activity and highly emotional TV shows several hours prior to bedtime. On the other hand, a day of mental challenges and physical activity, followed by a hot shower, a sumptuous meal and passionate intercourse, can bring a deep sensual sleep in the arms of a beloved.

Hypnosis, yoga and meditation are battery chargers. They may in fact be the same process. Mindfulness Meditation (no religious affiliation) is currently all the rage. Many kinds of meditation are portrayed as a physically and mentally relaxed state in which the conscious mind is emptied. Its benefits have been widely documented and plentiful training exists to help one learn these techniques.

I have reservations that some meditators may slip into daydreaming fantasy and wishful thinking to escape from our acidic society. This may be relaxing, but leaves unresolved the needed changes in society. The world needs those who challenge the status quo.

Trance is commonly used by athletes, mathematicians, musicians, actors and so on. I have observed numerous meditation practitioners and experimented with a few. Most of them show the signs commonly associated with being in a hypnotic trance state.

Trance is basically self-induced. When first learning to enter trance, being relaxed can help. In the long run it may not be necessary as trance can occur spontaneously. Some people may enter a meditative state or trance as they walk a forest path. It is common to enter trance when driving your car on a familiar route or when watching TV. Afterwards you may not remember the details of the journey or the TV program because your mind and body were semi-dormant and automatically executing necessary actions, while the rest of your mind resolved some issue or rested. Workers on boring repetitive jobs spend most of the time with their minds elsewhere and this is comparable to the trance state. If you sit relaxed with your cup of tea, and stare into space, you are probably in a trance.

As strange as it may seem, there are physical activities that burn a huge amount of energy while at the same time generating lots of energy. Sexual intercourse, learning a piece of music and then playing it, running a marathon..., are examples of high burn and high recharge.

Sexual intercourse is genetically programmed; its positive energy charge has a whopping impact on personality, physical health and relationships. Having a solid sense of one's sexual identity is important in mammalian species and all human cultures. Like species identity, it forms a crucial element of personality development.

Regular sex reduces the risk of prostate cancer in men and gives women shinier hair and softer, healthier skin. It strengthens muscles, bones, heart and the immune system in both sexes. It reduces cholesterol level, combats asthma, calms the nervous system, relieves pain and boosts olfactory abilities. Intercourse promotes sound, restful sleep, and results in a longer life span. The physical togetherness and orgasmic response strengthen the bond between partners. Sounds like a snake medicine advertisement, doesn't it?

The bonding resulting from orgasm may have led to sexual monogamy. In the early communal Hub, having sex with all the opposite sex members would have been the norm. Thus, the group would have had a robust sense of bonding and mutual support that was resilient to outside forces. Power wielders would not have been able to have much impact on such a group; hence, to break down this stout solidarity, sexual monogamy was initiated.

Given the benefits of sexual intercourse, it is appalling how distorted the issue has become in western culture. Such as the practice of monogamy, prohibition of sex outside marriage, ban on public nudity, ignoring child sexuality, celibacy… There have been numerous intensive studies of over one thousand societies. Monogamous beliefs exist in less than two hundred of them; however, adherence to sexual monogamy is almost non-existent.

During my Doctoral training and on-going education, I reviewed reams of sex research program results and received sex therapy training from some of the best experts in the world. Studies have generally found twice weekly or more intercourse to be the norm up to the age of thirty and once a week or more up to age forty-five. Nonetheless, the majority of people report they do not have as much sex as they desire, nor is it as satisfying as they would wish, boredom being a major complaint.

Generally, the '*sexless marriage*' label is applied when intercourse occurs ten or less times a year. The *1994 U.S. National Health and Social Life Interview Survey* found only 2% of couples reported no sex in the past year. In my review of other research, my practice statistics and discussions with colleagues, I surmise the absence of sex for two or more years probably occurs in less than 1% of couples. It damages the mental, emotional and physical health of the couple. Furthermore, it often turns families into a toxic environment, poisoning children and all those in close proximity.

In families where intercourse is occurring, but at an insufficient level, depression, anxiety, frustration and aggression are usually in evidence. This may lead to long term gastro intestinal and muscle-joint problems in males; whereas, women often have re-occurring dermatological and respiratory complaints. These problems are summarized in a number of softpedia.com articles.

Most cultural restriction of sexual expression and celibacy are simply insane behaviours; they defy the laws of nature and are essentially inhumane and immoral. When you prevent the old, infirm, handicapped or single people from having sex, you might as well limit their sleep and reduce their food intake. You are in essence torturing them, which has many negative outcomes. It lowers the individual's psychic and physical energy, it forces them to accept rejection, accept something is wrong with them, think less of themselves, expect less from life. It prevents the development of a self-confident personality.

Society's that ban nudity and put an emphasis on clothing contributes to the problem. The wearing of clothing in a tropical climate is only necessary when one is in direct sunlight or celebrating a festive occasion; otherwise, it is an irrational behaviour, particularly during strenuous physical labour. Plentiful studies have shown a higher degree of personal identity and self-satisfaction in societies where limited clothing is worn.

The acceptance of nudity and females going about topless, is an integral part of French culture.

During the early seventies, I spent part of a summer enrolled in Carl Roger's '*Institute for the Study of the Person*' in La Jolla California. There were one hundred and thirty therapists from around the world. We spent twelve to fourteen hours a day, seven days a week, exploring and learning from alternative ideas, concepts and actions. At one point I was in a group of twelve who began to consider experimenting with nudity. Most of us had read about nude therapy groups run by California psychologist Paul Bindrim.

The group spent several hours discussing the pros and cons of spending part of a day nude together, deciding they would only do it if there was unanimous agreement to do so. As they talk about it, I relax, knowing I am a very liberal person and game to try just about anything. Besides, I know they will never do it, too many of them are conservative types. There is the thirtyish wife of a Lutheran minister who is trained in religious counselling. Plus, a nun in her forties, and a Catholic priest, aged 60, from New York City. As we converse, I keep an eye on a shy female psychiatric nurse, who I expect to get up and walk out at any moment.

I listen attentively as they deliberate each person's issues. Several men mention the sensitive topic of not having a large penis or possibly having an erection. But, one by one people are giving their approvals. Then they come to the Lutheran minister's wife.

* * *

'Look, I want to do this, but, I'm on my period and wearing a tampon. I would prefer being able to leave my underpants on.'

A discussion ensued, and everyone was ok with that. The group continued working through each group member, getting assents, including the shy nurse, then unbelievably it was my turn.

'How about you Roberto?

I thought this can't be happening. The only other person left was a hip female psychologist from San Francisco, who was likely to go along with the idea.

'Oh! I've enjoyed the discussion, it has been amusing and a learning experience, but I'm shocked that everyone has approved it. I haven't really thought about doing it.'

'Do you have feelings you want to talk about?' 'No, the only thought that comes to mind has already been brought up; the common male fear of not having a big enough penis. I'm excited to have the opportunity to do something so unique.'

* * *

Squeals of laughter and joking came forth as we disrobed. One of the females I thought was flat chested, wasn't. One guy looked like a skinny ape; he had lots of hair over his body. We spent hours talking about our feelings.

In the afternoon, we sat on the floor with our legs wide apart; a line of females, facing a line of males. Not allowed to talk, we had to stare at each other's genitals for a half hour then move on to another partner for a half hour. We did this desensitization exercise with four partners. A fantastic learning experience, but genital gawking does get boring.

I highly recommend learning to be comfortable in the nude amongst family, friends and better yet, in public. It engenders a new sense of respect and wonder of one's physical being. I often encouraged this for weight loss patients. When one sees their real body in the glass door or mirror as they walk by, they are more apt to become motivated to take better care of their body.

French schools have explicit sexual education classes. It strikes me as ironical, that USA society places a heavy emphasis on education, but tends to ignore sexual education. This has brought about untold harm to children, adults and the culture as a whole. Today, some sexual education is available on the internet, and a few schools have formalized classes. But, for the most part children and adults have scant knowledge of sexuality. As a child, my culture only provided sexual education on the playground.

***

As a young lad it was my job to wash the dinner dishes. One chilly fall evening as I laboured at my chore, my mind was contemplating a new activity I had learned from guys on the playground. I wanted to try it again. After finishing the washing up, I snuck a piece of lard out of the fridge and wrapped it in a piece of brown paper bag. Then I watched the new-fangled invention TV till I was told to go to bed.

I took a leak in the bathroom and grabbed a handful of toilet paper. I could still hear the TV. In bed I pushed the sheet out of the way and used the blanket to form a tent over my mid-section, it gave me room to move my hands. I slowly began fondling myself, while in my mind I visualized Annette, the bumpy chested girl on the school playground who insisted I kiss her. In no time Pete stood at attention, straight and hard, it was amazing. Then I took the lard out of the paper and rubbed it on Pete. It began to melt and felt warm and slick. In strong fast yanks I began to beat my meat. It was exciting. I went faster and faster. I could feel it coming and then like an explosion, Pete spit all over me. Wow!

In the morning I awoke and reached down to check out Pete. He was ok, but my abdomen was swollen. How could this be? The guys never warned me this might happen. I was horrified. I even had the morning sickness, felt like I wanted to throw up. I was distraught. I must be a really weird kid. I had no one to go to for help. Frequent vomiting throughout the day suggested I had the flu. It was the only time in my life I was glad to have the flu.

* * *

Given our societies inadequate sexual education, the past two decades of child sexual abuse revelations comes as no surprise. However, untold numbers of clergy (some supposedly celibate) are involved in fairly normal sexual behaviour. In discussions with other therapists, many revealed they were aware of priests regularly having intercourse with the females of the Parish. I too have had patients, usually married women, who in passing reveal satisfying intimate relationships with their Priest or minister.

The justice system hands down punishment to the individual perpetrator of sexual abuse, the truth is that everyone is to blame. The citizen has a responsibility to force governments and schools to provide thorough sexual education to everyone and remove barriers that interfere with citizens having a satisfactory sexual life. Otherwise we all suffer the dire consequences.

When a Hub creates a golden ambience learning environment, members may want to consider a radical alteration in sexual education. Children could be extensively trained to masturbate and eventually participate in sex. By the mid-teens sexual intercourse might be a common facet of life, like eating and sleeping. Sure, such a change will have problems. Will the problems be as severe as the harm brought about by society's insecurity and paranoia of all things sexual? What do you think?

One sunny afternoon the Rogers workshop held a session on the university lawn beneath the palm trees. A half dozen Catholic nuns and priests discussed the ins and outs of their marriage with each other. For a young fellow like me brought up in the conservative Bible belt

Midwest, this was mind blowing stuff. It would be interesting to know what percentage of priests and nuns are actually celibate.

Development and maintenance of the physical PELGAM, and subsequent growth of a robust self-concept, can be severely hampered by inappropriate cultural attitudes towards sex. One should routinely review what family or societal themes might be interfering with personal development. Keeping in mind that each culture has its' own slant on what is appropriate. Learning sexual guidelines on how to speak, act and dress sexually is a necessary ingredient in creating the personality. Some cultures (Spanish and others) have formalized teaching of this. Make sure you learn how to present yourself in such a manner that others readily perceive you as feminine/masculine, enticing, and you feel it yourself. This also applies to homosexuals and bisexuals.

* * *

It is a calm turquoise anchorage in the French islands d' Hyeres, but too many boats for my liking. I'm not long from the states and still trying to adjust to European crowding. Less than thirty feet separate each of the sixty boats. If a storm comes up there is going to be hell to pay.

I spot an inflatable dingy, carrying a large ice chest, slowly buzzing through the anchored fleet, like a puppy rushing about to make friends. Soft tresses blowing in the breeze, two scrumptious sixteen-year old girls in string bikinis (minus tops) are at the helm. Fantasy is a wonderful thing. When they finally come alongside, I can barely control my drooling in anticipation of the ice cream bar I buy. Funny thing, the ice cream does not cool me down.

A couple months later I am more attuned to Med. life, a little more blasé. We are just a normal middle-aged couple from the states lounging naked in the cockpit on a hot Mediterranean afternoon. The water is crystal clear in this pristine Corsican bay south of Ajaccio. I'm flying an Italian flag, it nullifies the prevalent anti-Americanism. A sleek sloop is coming into the bay with stars and stripes fluttering, headed straight for our anchorage. Nude inhabitants on the surrounding European boats stand up go to their rails and give friendly waves to the approaching vessel. Bingo! She swerves off and heads to an unoccupied area of water. It works every time. Europeans know how to get rid of the sexually uptight Americans.

* * *

Let us get back to the energy issue. A delightful and sensible lifestyle may only burn 25% of the daily energy allotment. This means you have 50% available for emergencies or to invest in new ventures. Whereas those living at the survival level may burn all their energy on basics, with none left for emergencies or PELGAM development.

'Nobody realizes that some people expend tremendous energy merely to be normal.' Albert Camus.

Staying in sync with nature, your biological clock, and keeping life in balance, will help you maintain a steady flow of energy.

Store bought batteries have a specific limited amount of power, this is not true of your PELGAMs batteries. They have a reserve generator similar to the body's use of oxygen. Research clearly specifies blood oxygen levels required for survival. A recent trip up Mt. Everest by medical researchers, found stable physical functioning on blood oxygen levels normally associated with death. In oxygen deprived environments the brain turns on reserve mechanisms allowing life to continue. I am suggesting a similar reserve power exists for each PELGAM.

When all PELGAMs are firing in the upper range of their capability, this reserve booster may kick in when needed and provide two or more times the usual power. When all the boosters have kicked in, higher optimal functioning becomes a reality. Consequently, current world sporting records will be surpassed.

In physical appearance the stellar person is apt to be smiling, bright eyed with copious hair, clear in complexion, with a trim, well-muscled body. Their immune system is at its' genetic full strength; thus, they are relatively free of physical illness and may have a life span of 150 years.

They would be like the ancient ones, having the physical where with all to grow their own fruits and vegetables, hunt for protein, procure building materials and construct housing. With ease they can run, jump, climb, swim, and have strong and revitalizing orgasms. They would possess a tremendous sense of physical confidence.

Why don't you go climb a tree where you can relax and contemplate these ideas, then go for a half-hour run, followed by a half-hour swim. Last of all enjoy an hour or so of spirited activity in bed.

Chapter 8   Spatial PELGAM

I feel like hell: my muscles ache, joints are stiff, my head aches and my stomach is rumbling; the usual results of spending a day on a bus. I stash my gear in an eight-bed dorm room, and set out to find a restaurant. I rush through the twilight lit alleyways and streets of Valdivia, anxious to find an eatery before closing time. A sign beckons from atop a German style cottage near the river. The Germans and Swiss settled southern Chile; the local architecture and cuisine reflect this, and German is the second language.

They seat me at a corner table, and inform me they have just opened. I forgot Chilean restaurants do not open till 8:30pm. A stein of ice cold Kunstmann lager begins to relax me, it is a highly regarded local beer. I sip my beer and soak up the mixture of Bavarian and Chilean ambience. A stream of patrons enter. by their looks, dress and mannerisms, they are Chileans, not a foreigner in sight. I linger over my dinner plate size burger; relaxing and people watching. Slightly apprehensive about returning to my hostel; it will be my first time in a hostel dorm room.

Back on the street, I watch colourfully lit boats ply the river. I'm tempted to walk about and investigate the town. It is dark and I'm whipped, better head for my lodging, a five-minute walk away. I cross the street, and go up one city block to a lane I remembered. At the bottom of the lane, I turn right and go two blocks, then left. There is a six-story apartment block that has replaced my two-story hostel.

Maybe it is another block up. No luck. I retrace my steps back to the street one block from the lane. I follow this for two blocks and turn left. It is a nightclub, not a hostel. After thirty minutes of searching, I am definitely lost; Valdivia's layout has defeated my spatial ability. Not an easy thing to admit, for a sailor. The night club manager graciously leads me on a three-minute walk to my hostel.

Definition - Brain specialists tag spatial perception as a primary thought process, an intellectual function consisting of numerous interrelated sub-skills that reside in various brain areas. The bulk of the spatial function is to the rear of the right hemisphere. It has the capability to distinguish depth, and to comprehend and remember the relative size and juxtaposition among objects. Western culture has suggested men have more spatial ability than women. A John Hopkins university article *(www. jhu.edu/cty)* claims there are no gender differences.

In the everyday world spatial ability fosters the appropriate physical response for navigating through the physical environment. This becomes problematic in space due to low gravity. Walking, running, tossing an object or catching something mid-air requires less musculature response in low gravity and more effort in higher gravity. There is no up and down, left and right in the International Space Station; this makes it difficult for the brains' spatial function to construct a mental map. New crew often wreak havoc: running into people, dislodging equipment …, until they adjust their physical response to the spatial cues in low gravity. It will be interesting when we place people on high gravity planets.

Spatial function assists in the comprehension of a plan or blue print, and allows manipulation of objects, such as constructing a bird house or a mansion. It also comes in to play when we view a visual artistic expression or participate in sports. It supports our need to explore and sense what is about us, helps our memory, boosts our creativity, gives pleasure; the list goes on endlessly.

Weak Spatial Ability - The inability to: catch a ball or hit it with a bat, aesthetically arrange the living room furniture, find your way around town or the mall, comprehend left from right… Spatial disorientation has commonly been labelled *'Directional dyslexia;'* I prefer the term 'dysorienta.'

One of my relatives when given the task of digging a straight trench or raking a straight row in the vegie garden; will always wander off the straight line and make an arc. When they leave a movie theatre, concert hall…, they always turn left.

I was born with extremely small eyes, overtime they failed to grow as much as would be expected. This resulted in bi-lateral amblyopia. No structural abnormality exists; the brain simply fails to fully accept and integrate what the eye is viewing, commonly referred to as 'lazy eye'. My right eye is the one most severely affected. My functioning is primarily guided by my left eye. This impairs my spatial ability; depth perception is challenging with only one eye.

During my teen years I enjoyed playing tennis and became quite skilled. Occasionally I would play one of the guys on the high school team. I could not beat them, but I came damn close. It is tough to win when you don't see the returning ball till it crosses the net. It was similar to when I went clay bird shooting with my brothers and friends. When the projectile was fresh out of the thrower, I was fairly deadly. If it got out-a-ways - then my success rate plummeted. As an adult dirt bike rider, I could twist on the throttle with the best of them, but in the turns my eyes slowed me down.

Spatial ability is required for success in: mathematics, engineering and the natural sciences. It comes into play in a vast array of life situation, yet it has received scant attention. A 2010 Duke University article (duke.edu), labelled it a neglected area.

Building Spatial Ability - Training and practice improves the spatial PELGAM and slows down its' decline with age. Wear a blindfold when you do chores or walk about the house. Enrol in a 'how to' course: paint, draw, sculpt, read blueprints, build, cartography, photography, play a sport, dance… Computer games and the study of geometry can help.

Dysorienta may involve short term memory problems, such as remembering the sequence of turns one took to arrive at the post office.

Hence, memory improvement efforts may be beneficial. Keeping notes as you travel can be helpful. You might think a GPS would solve the problem: guess again.

***

My camper van is third in our camping club's convoy of eight motorhomes as we approach Proserpine, a little town in northern Queensland. The voice of my GPS lady directs me to bear to the right up ahead, but our leader and the rig in front of me go off to the left. I follow as the group behind me goes to the right. Maybe our leader knows a shortcut? We proceed through the village and out into the country, where the lead man turns down a dirt lane in a sugar cane field. He abruptly comes to a halt, hops out of his rig, comes back, and tells me we should have gone right back at the entrance to town.

***

Recent technological advances in imaging, computers, graphics, data visualization and so on, are heavily imbued with spatial ability factors, thus requiring more spatial skill to use these modern innovations. An article by Gwen Dewar in *parentingscience.com* discusses the importance of providing spatial training for children. The Hub could provide orienteering courses.

Acute Spatial Ability - Architects, visual artists, athletes, engineers and others, typically have outstanding spatial ability. For most people vision plays a major role, yet a blind person can have good spatial ability. They utilize their ears to establish an accurate knowledge of the surrounding spatial characteristics. It works like electronic sonar, the individual makes sounds (tapping cane or voice), and the sound echoes off the surrounding objects, giving the details of their size and location. The visually impaired have a highly developed sense of touch, which facilitates spatial recognition, and is particularly useful in hands-on construction activities. The olfactory sense may assist in the identification of objects and the space about us. I don't need eyes to know I'm in the chicken coop; my nose and ears tell me.

How much development is enough? Who knows? I reckon one ought to be able to: read maps well enough to go anywhere (GPS is cheating), join friends in a ball game, arrange a meaningful and aesthetically pleasing personal living space, design better work environments, help foster communities harmoniously blending into the natural environment and just maybe, assemble that thingummyjig made in China?

* * *

It is 2.00 am, I need to take a leak. I cannot turn on a light; it might disturb the seven sleepers. Gingerly, I crawl out of my bunk; in the dark my spatial orientation relies on my sense of touch. Fingers skim along the bed frame to the wall, and then to the door. In the hall I flick on my LED and proceed to el bano.

The second night is more problematic. I awake in the middle of the night. The 45ish bicyclist from the bunk above me is on his hands and knees, in the middle of the floor, rummaging thru his saddle bags. He is constantly flicking his LED head lamp on and off. I swing my legs off my bunk and collide with him. He flicks on his light, scoots aside as I make my way to the door, and out into the hall. During the past two days I have had contact with him at breakfast and during evening leisure time; he seems to be an unusual character.

I make my way back to the room, turn off my LED and enter. He is still on the floor, fussing about. He makes room for me to crouch down and get into my bunk. He continues messing about, I reckon he is an obsessive compulsive. I can't get back to sleep; I want to get up and strangle him. After a half hour, he climbs back in his bunk, and within minutes is snoring. The guy across the way rips off a fart and the teeny bopper girls in the end bunks giggle.

Chapter 9   Emotional PELGAM

The Question is What!

Moves you to the core of your being?

Love warms your heart?

Is so disgusting you feel sick?

Makes you see red?

Brings utter despair?

Emotion/affect eludes precise definition; a consensus on the classification of the various emotions does not exist. Likewise, acceptable emotions and their appropriate level of intensity, varies from family to family and culture to culture. I suggest emotions include a range of subjective mental states, each accompanied by a physical state (crying, rapid heartbeat, sweating…). I favour a two-part breakdown; primary emotions are genetic and ancient memory based. They may serve as survival mechanisms, helping to determine what action is needed at a given time. Secondary emotions may have these two components, but are to a great extent based on learning.

J. Panksepp, suggests that there are seven 'primal based emotional states' (I refer to them as 'primary'). 'Seeking,' is the urge to get up and do something. 'Anticipatory joy,' is generated by the brains seeking mode, it is one of the first primitive emotions. Humans share it with animals. 'Rage,' is an aggressive defensive state; I include in it the venting of tension from fear. He labels 'Fear' a cautionary protective state. An unfamiliar setting or person may provoke a 'fear' emotion. 'Lust' is the desire to procreate. Looking after the well-being of others he calls 'Care,' and 'Play' is listed last. I group 'Care' and 'Play' together, as part of the genetic necessity for social contact; together these 2 states can be understood as the need to love and be loved, to have fun and seek connection with others.

I class empathy, love, and altruism, as secondary emotions, encompassing a blend of thoughts, body states, and actions. Thinking processes play a crucial role; an emotional response will fluctuate depending on how a person assesses the situation. Does this person care about me? Is this a poisonous snake? Is bungee jumping safe? Is this holiday going to be fun or a hassle? Emotions have a polarity and may seek balance over time: hope and despair, joy and sorrow. Secondary emotions are so puzzling to pin down that entire books have been written on each one.

Emotions may be initiated by stimuli in the surrounding world, or stimuli in the person's body or mind. Basic emotions are quick, short lived, intense responses. If the emotion builds slowly, is milder and tends to last a longer time; I refer to it as a 'feeling or mood' state. Emotions are an attempt to decipher what action is needed. If the assessment is incorrect, it may result in erratic, chaotic, disorganised behaviour; if valid then appropriate resolution seeking activities are initiated.

A Weak Emotional PELGAM – may be suggested by the lack of emotional response, inappropriate intensity, a response when one is not needed, having the wrong response for the situation, and unstable emotional responses.

Lack of Emotional Response - The failure to respond emotionally may result from genetic factors, defects in brain chemistry and/or neural processing, family upbringing, or cultural influences. The individual may be unable to show love, care, anger, sadness, empathy, joy, awe… The psychopathic personality has little or no emotional response. They commonly have no qualms about causing grievous harm to others and can be shockingly violent. Genetics is thought to be the causal factor.

Familial or cultural pressures may forbid or limit the expression of emotional states. Emotional repression usually leads to high levels of mental frustration and a host of physical maladies. Intestinal disorders are high on the list. Insufficient emotional responses can wreak havoc in a family.

* * *

After fifteen years of marriage, George, towing wife behind, initiated counselling. He described his wife, Robin, as a 'cold, hard person.' Throughout several counselling sessions her stone face, icy demeanour and verbalized apathy supported his complaint. If she did not change, he and the two daughters planned to move out.

189

At one point I was attempting to build some form of physical contact between the couple. I assumed she, like any mother, was physically supportive of her children. I asked her when she last hugged a daughter.

'Never.' She replied.
'Surely at some point in the past you have cuddled or hugged the girls?'
'No, why would I do that?'
I was dumbfounded.

* * *

Robin refused to return for further therapy, I gave her the names of other therapists, she did not contact any of them. George and his daughters moved out. I helped the three of them make the transition. A year later I heard Robin was working in the county dump re-cycling facility and living alone. I often wondered what she did with the rest of her life.

Low Intensity - There are few Robins and even fewer psychopaths in the population; however, there are numerous people with weak emotional responses. I refer to such people as having flat emotional batteries; the diagnostic term of schizoid personality disorder might be used. These people typically avoid contact with others, tending to be loners. It could be their emotional modulating centre in the brains limbic system is malfunctioning. Or, inappropriate tuning of the brain filters could be at fault.

When a parent is a low emotional responder, their child's emotional responses may be ignored, punished or labelled as not important or bad.

For example, some parents teach their children that 'only girls cry', 'only boys get angry and violent', 'it is a sign of weakness to show you are upset.' Some children respond with belligerent, acting out behaviour: fighting, stealing and refusing to obey. Others may feel rejected, and become shy, withdrawn, depressed or suicidal. Psychotherapists in Western countries are inundated with tearful depressed patients who complain of being unloved, unimportant or controlled and demeaned. This is a massive societal problem resulting in mental distress for individuals, broken families, and exorbitant national health costs.

You may meet a low emotional responder and not realize it, as they typically do not stand out in any way. Fear of hunger or homelessness drives most to hold down a job. At work they may partake in organized activities; otherwise, they generally have little involvement in social interactions or hobbies. While they may discuss any subject you bring up, their talk is apt to be superficial and boring. They have difficulty making decisions or taking action. You usually cannot involve them in an argument.

Some philosophies teach a path of minimal emotion; excessive sadness, hatred, joy... are to be avoided. The focus is on a loving awareness of the universes unity of one. This may be viable when we have achieved balanced development. At our current stage of understanding, low emotional response is more indicative of problematic personalities. Despite the widespread negative impact of these personalities, they receive little attention from the community at large. Perhaps it is an example of the 'squeaking wheel' getting the grease; our daily media overflows with examples of excessive emotional expression.

High Intensity –Intense feelings of fear, anger, hate, and jealousy can fuel actions that bring sweet revenge, but tragic repercussions. A Dunedin New Zealand study followed children into adulthood. Children low in self-control became unstable adults unable to achieve success in career, marriage or the community. Other studies have suggested high intensity emotions debilitate the immune system and cognitive thinking ability. Captaining your life - or a vessel - demands emotionally stable responses and clear concise thinking.

* * *

It is a moonless, pitch black night; the thirty knot winds are on the nose, and two metre seas are breaking over the deck. I point the bow towards Middle Percy Islands' south bay. I'm physically and mentally exhausted from twenty hours of rough seas. I feel alone, and there is fear in the pit of my stomach; I cannot see the rocky outcrops on either side of the bays' entrance. The air is pungent with the eucalypt.

The chart plotter is erratic; the rhumb line flits about on the screen. There are no lights on the uninhabited shore, and it is too dark to see if there are boats at anchor. I watch the depth sounder, and listen to the roaring wind. Water is crashing on the deck, and there is a continual thudding, as the hull rises and falls in the waves. Then there is a rumbling sound off to starboard, rollers breaking on the entrance rocks. I sense their angle from the ship, and compare chart depths to the depth finder reading. I turn the wheel ten degrees to port, ease the throttle back, and creep forward. The thunder of waves on the rocks gets louder. Then I hear the roar of waves breaking on the portside rocks, and turn another ten degrees to port. Depth remains good. Little by little, we come abreast of the unseen rocks and slip into the calmer bay. I flick on the spot light just in time to avoid smashing into an anchored yacht. Cautiously, my ship weaves its way between four anchored yachts, and drops the hook in four meters. Reversing, the chain snubs and the anchor holds. Stumbling below, I fall into the bunk - physically, emotionally, and mentally spent.

* * *

I like life too much to purposely seek out thrilling emotional experiences. Virtually every day in the news there are reports about fatalities caused by sky diving accidents, cliff jumping, running rapids, mountain climbing, and once in a while boating.

If you wish to avoid the high intensity emotional person, be wary of the mouse. Quiet mild-mannered people may have intense emotional feelings raging beneath their calm demeanour, often they are complete emotional wrecks. Not knowing how to lower their internal stress levels, their bodies may vent the distress via various illnesses. Others take out their frustrations on those about them via a passive-aggressive manner; with subtle elusiveness, they smile as they sabotage the plans and goals of all nearby. Then there are the bombs that explode and lash out.

Western society glorifies the expression of anger and hatred; the portrayal of violence is the second largest category within media entertainment. Some sports teams encourage the development of violent feelings towards the opponent. Cultures often emotionally over react to other cultures, depicting them as immoral, inhumane, or evil. Ubiquitous emotional trauma is a part of modern western culture.

The histrionic personality is a label given to those with high intensity emotional behaviour. In English speaking cultures it is most often associated with females, while more common in men in some eastern and Asian cultures. Histrionics tend to be 'over the top,' dramatic, attention seeking, and sexually provocative. It is a prominent feature in Italian culture. Histrionic personality traits make for a successful career in acting, media and marketing.

Unnecessary Emotional Responses – Our ancestors developed fear and other emotional responses to survive and cope with their threatening environment. Some of these learned emotional responses remain in today's emotional PELGAM: the fear of heights, snakes, and loud noises are a few examples. Modern life does not require some of these ancient fear responses; yet they remain active and generalized in many people.

Fear of loss (job, spouse, assets) is wide spread. Interpersonal relationships are often weighed down with paranoid suspicion, jealousy, contempt, hate, anger and indifference. Some people are emotionally distressed (anxiety) by the array of goods in the hyper market, by the overwhelming stimulation in the city, by the pace of life.

Excessive or unneeded emotions can stifle awareness and cognitive functioning. This can disrupt families, schools, workplaces and the community. Most of us have witnessed someone becoming emotionally upset or wildly excited over virtually nothing. A few of these people are simply overly sensitive. In a social interaction they may overreact to the faintest hint of a slight or affront. One type is the agro, the forever angry person, who responds with fury. Another type will break into tears or run away. Some people are overly effusive in giving thanks.

Wrong Response– When you are too anxious to take a test or perform your sport ('emotional blockage'), you are allowing emotions to limit your life. If the gift you receive is not what you wanted, and you become angry; the giver is apt to become upset. Do you remember the time you were so enthralled with feelings of love, that you were unable to think clearly, and said or did something that did not turn out well?

Emotional Instability – How do you cope with the person who is happy and enthusiastic at breakfast, sad and depressed at lunch, angry throughout the afternoon and blasé by evening? These people are difficult to live with, as you never know what to expect. In its severe form it is clinically classed as an 'affective disorder.' A common form is the cyclic expression of inappropriate elation and depression, termed bipolar disorder.

If a parent has this, the children will be unable to successfully tune their brain filters. United States eastern seaboard longitudinal studies begun in the early 1900's, found these children had a high incidence of psychological problems when they moved into adolescence and adulthood.

Once in a while, you may come across someone who relates to you in an open, friendly, and emotionally expressive manner. But when you check out their private life you find they are just the opposite. Usually it's a fear of emotional investment in others.

Conclusion of a Weak Emotional PELGAM –The home environment is often the culprit in creating this problem. Vast numbers of youngsters spend five days a week in emotionally chaotic day care centres or schools; then come home to spend their evenings with a nuclear family of exhausted working parents, who do not have the stamina or ability to teach or meet emotional needs.

When these children move into adolescence, they may be unable to find emotionally sound role models or mentors. As they move about the community on subways and buses, they are aware that their fellow adult travellers ignore each other. They see that most pub patrons are emotionally about sixteen years old. On TV they watch bickering ten-year old parliamentarians.

Adulthood in over populated Western society presents an unnatural, surreal scenario entailing excessive emotional states of fear and anger, which results in emotional out bursts of violence. The nuclear family's inability to meet genetic needs produces emotionally distraught humans feeling unloved and unwanted. Mankind's separation from nature leaves the human animal in an identity crisis; they don't know who they are (animal), nor where they belong (in nature).

Many of societies emotional problems are the result of too much emphasis on the so-called 'hard sciences'; with its focus on human tangible needs, such as, food, water, housing, clothing and so on. While ignoring the soft or intangible qualities of existence (emotionality, creativity, social cohesion...) that nurture good mental and emotional health. Our planet is past its' carrying capacity in terms of meeting these delicate needs.

Humans are genetically geared to cope with the emotional thrill of hunting a large beast or being hunted. They are not emotionally equipped to cope with subtle threats in pleasant surroundings or threats that last months or years. A problematic spouse, manipulative boss, political abuse, legal injustice, and bureaucratic fumbling are major causes of emotional distress.

If the daily genetic need for love, caring and touch is not met then the emotional bond with others atrophies and the self-concept withers. This often leads to excessive egocentric behaviour, the constant seeking of food, sex, achievement... If a person is not loved, it does not matter how successful they are, how much money they make, or how much power they have - they will not experience satisfaction or lasting happiness. If societal practices continue to turn off the emotional genes for love, caring, empathy..., and strengthen the hate, anger, distrust and violence genes, what will happen to the human species?

Building - a viable emotional life entails awareness of existing assets, attributes that need to be deleted and those that need to be added.

Current Assets - In traditional human communal families of up to fifty people, children and adults learned comprehensive emotional expression from each other, resulting in strong emotional bonds within their living group. This history plus innate factors has given the contemporary human a dynamic genetic requirement for regular intense emotional and physical involvement with others. Enduring relationships in the family and with friends are based on emotional attachments.

What Needs Deleted? – The emotional system may be likened to the physical system of waste removal; if the bowel and bladder are not emptied regularly, toxins build up and poison the body. One must rid themselves of the tendency to bury or ignore emotions. Emotional angst needs to be emptied daily (catharsis). Otherwise, the venoms of fear, jealousy, and anger can poison the mind, eat away the physical body, and defile the soul.

The Hub group in a survival or space setting cannot afford explosive emotional outbursts. This is a real concern in the space programs employing large numbers of engineers and scientists who tend to be introverts and personality types that are inclined to suppress their emotions. When groups are composed in this way, there can be communication breakdown in the face of pressure.

Life is full of emotional perils and hardships; seeking the easy way out is common. Startle a deer on a hillside and it will run downhill. Hook a fish in the river and it will swim downstream. Stress humans and they may run to Religion or go on a war rampage. Some people keep fear in check by hiding in known routines, becoming slaves of habit, and avoiding change. When life becomes a rut, it stunts the human. They are unable to flow with the universe's ever evolving changes.

Excessive activity is a common feature in contemporary western life. An adult or child may spend all day on the job or in school, and every evening involved in a sport, music lessons, scouting… Such a schedule reduces the individuals' ability to emotionally bond with other family members, thus creating an emotionally stunted home life.

In Japan (and other countries) the excessive emphasis on academic and workplace achievement has placed excessive emotional stress on students and workers; resulting in a high youth and worker suicide rate. The workaholic ethic has emotionally scarred many, disabling their ability to form emotional bonds. Marriage is on the wane, and the birth rate is falling.

What Needs to be Added? - Emotional satisfaction and interpersonal emotional harmony are hallmarks of well-functioning. This requires learning to feel and express a variety of emotions which are acceptable in the context of the situation; bearing in mind that each family and culture has its own emotional expression guidelines.

Jumping, screaming and throwing things is ok at England's sporting events; but not at a bar mitzvah. Singing a jazz song in joy as you walk behind the horse drawn hearse of a New Orleans funeral procession is fine - but this would be frowned upon in a New England funeral. The Spanish and Italian cultures are emotionally effusive, the English quiet and reserved. If you need to become more expressive, spend time with the former; if you need to learn how to calm down, spend time with the latter.

In several chapters I have stressed the importance of sharing life with animals. Extensive research shows the presence of animals in the home helps strengthen the emotional system by reducing stress, fear, and loneliness. My little blond God adds to my happiness with her affection, tricks and antics.

A few philosophers claim emotions are solely a human characteristic. Animal owners know better. I heard a cattleman describe the emotional makeup of his livestock. 'They can be happy, angry and I have seen them cry.' Theo exudes emotion; when I prepare the truck to set off without her, there is a plaintive whine, a drooping of the tail and sad eyes. When I take her with me, she jumps for joy, tail madly wagging, and yips excitedly for the first few minutes of driving.

Ignorance of animal emotions created a tragic scenario in Africa a few years ago. During an elephant culling, adults were killed and butchered as the baby elephants looked on. This resulted in post-traumatic stress disorder for the juveniles. Traumatized, and lacking adult role models, the youngsters acted out aggressively and killed other animals and humans.

Building stronger emotional ties in family relationships is a common counselling task. Often it requires teaching men to be more verbally and physically affectionate with their families and friends. The process can be comical.

Having boated all my life, I at one point was fed up with all the boat maintenance work, and sold my cabin cruiser. At the suggestion of friends, I filled the void by joining a prestigious country club. The social life was good, and the food excellent. However, playing golf was a demeaning joke. I did not like the game and frequently could not see where the ball went - when I managed to hit it.

One of the club members was my client. He was a successful businessman, and he had formerly been a well-respected football player in his university days. Learning to be physically affectionate was one of his marriage counselling tasks. If I saw him while I was having lunch or dinner at the club, I would walk up, ignore his outstretched hand and give him a big long hug. Turning every shade of red he would return the hug and whisper "SOB" in my ear.

He finally mastered it. I got a kick out of watching him distress his male friends at the club by giving them a big hug. Don't underestimate the impact physical contact has on emotional wellbeing. You may wish to review the research literature on touching. *Touching, The Human Significance of the Skin*, by Ashley Montagu is a classic book on the topic.

A man who expresses a wide range of emotions can be a role model for children, and a soul mate for his partners and friends. When a pregnant mother experiences and expresses an extensive range of positive emotions and minimizes problematic states such as fear and anger; she too is a good role model, and strengthens a positive emotional PELGAM in her unborn child.

In his book *Lifting Depression,* the neuroscientist Kelly Lambort posits his "effort-driven-rewards" theory. He believes physical movement aimed at achieving a desired goal can foster an emotional sense of well-being and help deter the onset of emotional disorders. My experience as a clinician, family member and friend, supports physical activity as a powerful tool in building a strong emotional PELGAM. I wonder if emotional maturity requires a self-determining, nomadic, free-range human?

Being in the presence of dominant, self-absorbed people will emotionally drain you; you deserve better. You need those who demonstrate love and caring behaviour; this includes you. Showing care and love for one-self is a prerequisite to showing care and love for others. Caring and loving of others, is an emotional investment in something or someone that goes beyond your self-interest. Milton Mayeroff in his book *On Caring,* suggests caring is a process of giving fully of oneself to help another person to be all that they can be. This process also helps bring order and meaning to the carer's life.

The giving of unconditional love is touted by numerous schools of thought and may well be something to strive for. I have only been able to achieve this up to a limit. When a person's behaviour seriously damages others, I opt out and refuse to support them. In the wild, a group of animals will drive out a member whose actions threaten the security of the group.

The giving of warm, effusive love has the power to transform individuals, groups, and entire societies. Intense emotions can enrich life, such as giving or receiving plentiful amorous attention. Lovers may overcome huge difficulties just to be together.

203

Groups often set aside personal interests to strive for the well-being of the community. Sometimes a hard-assed resolute person will leap across the chasm separating their inner being and their outer life. They bypass their mundane everyday personality, to bestow authentic love and caring on another. Actions inspired by the heart bring a deeper sense of satisfaction than actions directed by the logical brain.

The burden rests on each of us to help one another, our children, and community to grow a strong and flexible emotional life. Mortar, brick and timber are needed to construct a house; love is required to make it a home. Contemporary families have goals to obtain better appliances, clothing and so on; it is more important to strive for positive emotional states like love, happiness and security. A simple action that has dramatic results is grooming. Do you remember film clips of primates grooming each other? When you brush the hair, massage the body or bathe a loved one, it instils a sense of pleasure and contentment in both of you. To flourish, one needs the love and respect of others.

We need more media depicting healthy images of affection and intercourse, and less portrayal of hatred, anger and killing. Educational institutions need to include emotional training in their curriculum. It must include first-hand experience of emotions and sensations, which is far more enlightening than reading about it.

Some suggest our purpose in life is to learn. If true, I suggest learning how to feel and express emotion, and to have empathic awareness of others is one of the most vital learning experiences.

Robust Emotionality – Stellar humans capably handle a wide range of emotions, neither hiding nor overly expressing them. If they are angry, jubilant, upset, or sad, you will know it. Their emotions fit the context of the situation, and are of the appropriate intensity. While tending to remain quiet and lead by example, their socially outgoing cheerful aura of happiness, vitality and contentment provides comfort and motivation for those about them. Love and empathic emotional stability are readily observable.

Depression, anger, fear… are often pigeonholed as negative emotions; however, they may reflect the existence of a significant issue. If someone has experienced a series of devastating life experiences, some long lasting depression or anger is to be expected. In a similar way, it is natural to experience fear and panic if an uninvited masked person entered your house.

Emotion may serve to impel a person into action or cautiously restrict their behaviour. Stellar souls know not to make major decisions when emotionally upset. Appropriate emotions involve a sense of timing, an accurate appraisal of one's assets, liabilities, and values. Such a person perceives and understands other's emotions as well as their own (proprioception). They grasp the ins and outs of the cultural milieu and adapt accordingly.

Check out Daniel Goleman's research articles and his excellent text 'Emotional Intelligence.' All-in-all, the accuracy of the emotional response and its' appropriate physical action is a key factor in a successful life.

When people fluently express a full range of emotions and perceive them in others, social conflict will diminish. Then love, respect, empathy, caring, and a sense of community will expand to help create a society embracing differences, providing a more meaningful and secure existence for everyone.

Chapter 10 Creativity PELGAM

Plant a seed: a cabbage sprouts, a baby pops out, a thought germinates, a resolution is found, distrust is born, a revolution explodes. We join together in love creating tender relationships and new life. Empathy creates charitable behaviour. We invent, form, produce new items, and breathe life into broken things and refuse. Random thoughts, unusual actions and strange experiences create innovative values, ideas and concepts. Whether it is engineering, painting, writing, music, building houses or polishing stones, your brain does best when it is creating.

Creativity is a cognitive thinking processes derived from genetic and ancient memory components and often incorporates new learning experiences. Thought is energy and the first level of creation; it incorporates polarity as the very basis of creation. The expression of creativity is a human need - it is a factor in all of life.

Weak Creativity - may be associated with certain types of environments, cultures and personalities. Sitting on the 12th floor balcony of my holiday apartment in Santiago Chile, I'm overcome by the visual, audio and air pollution. The six million inhabitants, dwell in a setting common to people all over the planet. The metropolitan profusion of sensory data overwhelms the brain filters, dulls the senses and bogs the brain down in a foggy state of semi-awareness.

Large cities replace the natural environment with manmade structures and swarms of people. The inhabitants spend most of their waking hours striving to meet food, shelter and clothing needs, a difficult task in an unnatural setting. The abundance of unemployed and under-employed people threatens personal, family and job security. Daily metropolitan life has too much anxiety, and too little free time to cogitate or playfully entertain wild, creative ideas. Nevertheless, there are bound to be a handful of specialists and aberrant types, who thrive on the excess of stimulus and use it to inform their creative endeavours.

Life in a small village can be claustrophobic and just as inhibiting as a metropolis. Villages usually have a narrow range of personality types, less mental stimulation and a paucity of new learning experiences. Village and rural folk do not witness the almost daily changes, to which city dwellers are accustomed; hence, rural people may be suspicious and inflexible, regardless of their creative, positive characteristics.

A mid-forties couple came for counselling to map out the next segment of their lives. He was a corporate executive and she owned a business. They initiated many lifestyle changes, one of which was to move to a small village. They loved their new modest home on two acres of land, in spite of the forty-five-minute drive to work. They expended tremendous effort to become part of the community, but it failed. The locals did not like them, and avoided them if at all possible. After five years the couple sold out, and after much research moved to another village they felt would be more welcoming. Two years later I ran into them, and they reported they were doing great in their new community.

One can expect to witness less creativity in a conservative or rigid cultural milieu; particularly if there is a pressure to conform to the established provincial way. As a graduate student I was involved in a psychometric testing program administered to high school students belonging to a highly structured and conservative religion. The test results were similar to results from other high school groups, except for the creativity measures. Their creativity scores fell significantly below the other group averages.

The world has numerous religious cultures, many demand obedience to narrowly defined modes of thinking and acting. This places groups at odds with each other, and disables humankind's ability to creatively work together towards a progressive evolution of life. Similarly, there are a multitude of despotic and dogmatic political regimes, wherein creative thinking can cost you your life. Western culture's emphasis on the work ethic and economics further inhibits creativity in the community.

Personalities unable to experiment with different ideas, thoughts and actions are likely to be uncreative. Such as the shy and withdrawn, the fearful/anxious, and the narrow-minded or inflexible thinkers. Never attempting to create (a poem, structure, idea...) is an error in living, which creates a person who never fully appreciates the talents they possess.

Harmful Creativity - Some schools of thought reserve the term creative for those productions deemed good and useful. 'Useful' may not be pertinent, as some things may not be useful at the time, but will be at a later date. When I go to those two-dollar shops it makes me wonder - I can almost always find something to buy. It is creativity gone mad. To me, a lot of the items are junk, and are a waste of effort and resources (junk and waste are both subjective terms), which do not add quality to our lives. As apes we are fascinated with trinkets. And as humans we have been trained to buy.

Creativity, like emotional expression, must meet the criteria of timeliness and appropriateness. Have you ever met someone so busy being creative they failed to deal with the basic issues of life? The unkempt, unfit, sickly artist is a part of our cultural lore. As we wandered about Vienna gazing at the multitude of awesome art works, sculptures, fountains and palaces, I wondered if all the Viennese had adequate housing, clothing and food; when these masterpieces were crafted?

Humanity creates more and more humans, who create new ways to destroy each other and the environment. Politicians create programs and structures of questionable value, reams of paperwork, and a plethora of laws, while ignoring fundamental community needs. Societies create elaborate self-portrayals, ignore the negatives, avoid the truth and disparage beauty. Many of our belief systems are creative fairy tale fabrications.

Boosting Creativity - requires combining the genetic potential and ancient memories with learning experiences. When a person selects a topic to be creative with, investing ample hours of study and hands-on practice will bring forth their creative potential. Ample research has shown creativity in the art forms is not a gift of birth, but rather a result of learning. Likewise, learning is the key to develop creativity in other realms, such as cognitive processes, the emotional system and physical body.

Increasing cognitive ingenuity requires free time to let your mind wander. Daydreams often provide new ideas and insights. When you kick censors off the brain filters and attend to new types of stimuli, it can result in a different world perception. You may think, talk, and act differently. Clinical psychologist Deidre Barret of Harvard Medical School suggests reducing the inhibition of the filters as a vital constituent of creative thought. This occurs naturally in senior citizens. Brain filter controls weaken with age, allowing seniors a revival in their creativity.

Could the game of chess be modified to portray our contemporary life? Kings become industry moguls, pawns blue-collar workers, and knights are the police. The slippery hard-to- pin down characteristics of politicians are well represented by the queen's ability to move just about anywhere. Rook is a good name for a lawyer. Bishops could become scholars, except scholars have little impact on society; where-as, religion continues to be influential world-wide. I guess we should leave the bishop as a bishop. Should there be a taxman? Chess piece moves could be changed, and the board altered to reflect things like off-shore tax havens, media propaganda and third-world slavery.

Consider expanding your repertoire of skills, range of reading material, and breadth of physical activity. Visit an alternative life style commune or social organisation. A diversity of new acquaintances may add, subtract, expand or simplify your concepts and actions. This in turn could help you to re-evaluate and revise your notions.

Learning new skills in an unfamiliar physical activity came to play for me when I built the pilot house on my yacht. I had no experience working with alloy. Every day, almost every hour, I learned techniques for cutting, drilling and shaping the aluminium. During free time, inventive construction methods would pop into my mind and I would immediately enter them in my notebook.

In daily life I carry a notebook or tape recorder, enabling me to save ideas and thoughts as they come to me. Author, professor, and long-time psychology researcher Robert Epstein labels this recording process 'capturing.'

Comprehensive knowledge increases the likelihood of creating original ideas and products. When you decide to save more money to finance longer annual holidays, having a complete listing of all current and future income and expenses will help you creatively tailor the budget to accomplish your goal. Likewise, the design and building of your picnic table will be facilitated by a thorough working knowledge of all the tools and building materials. Knowledge and imagination are keys to creativity.

An emotional boost to creativity can occur when fear is thrust aside and the boundaries of our comfort zones are pushed. Happiness and a positive passionate outlook can help. When you become frustrated attempting to solve a problem, take a break, perhaps a nap, brain filters relax during sleep. Solutions may arise in a dream. I have used hypnosis to help clients improve their creative output. The hypnotic state is similar to daydreaming and meditation and is easy to learn.

A life of wide-ranging experiences enhances creativity: climb a tree, walk in the river, paint a picture, write a poem, sing a song, build a trellis, alter the organization of your file cabinet/workbench/kitchen cupboard, change the sequence within your work tasks. Variations in your approach to daily chores can significantly increase your creative processes. Have a read of *'Your Creative Brain'* by Chrysikou, E.G., in the August 2012 issue of *Scientific America Mind.*

Robust Creativity - The ancients resided in natural resource rich surroundings that provided diversity and a fairly predictable ebb and flow of conditions. Under these conditions, needs were well met; they had a full belly, ample social support, no immediate threats and heaps of free time to wonder, to experiment and be creative. Creativity bloomed in every type of geographical terrain and climate; they devised new tools, art, protective clothing, housing, astronomy. Every discovery laid the foundation for contemporary life. Human inventiveness continues today at an accelerated pace, but is confined to a narrow range of endeavours: engineering, chemistry, biology…

Much of this creativity has resulted in a scenario that posits a threat to human existence: pollution, destruction of planetary biology, over population, exploitive systems and warfare. Chaos survivors will need a great deal of creativity to regenerate human existence on earth's barren, lifeless terrain or the topography of inhospitable planets. The future demands more creativity in the social sciences. Humans must learn how to live cooperative, caring and respectful lives.

The creation of a slow simple communal life style in tune with the natural environment could provide the security, time and space for humans to reinvent themselves. When I relax on the veranda, seashore, mountain …, unique ideas, questions and solutions burst into my mind.

* * *

I'm pulling our travel trailer along the winding back roads through the picturesque villages of southern France, after having spent the winter on the 'Costa del Sol' of Spain. We are on our way to England to find a boat to cruise the Mediterranean; we failed to find a suitable one on the Spanish and French coasts. Entering Toulouse mid-morning, the Opel engine running erratically, we leave the caravan in a treed caravan park and locate an Opel dealer for repairs. During the repair time we plan to have a look about town.

A short bus ride delivers us to the central business district, where we seat ourselves at a sunny sidewalk café and patisserie. The selection of a French pastry is a religious experience; should I have an éclair or pain aux chocolat? No! I'll have a religieuse with my tea.

I enjoy the morning's ambience, and observing the people passing by. A nicely shaped lady of about thirty years sports a wide-brimmed hat and long beads straight out of the 1930's, while her skirt and blouse are contemporary fashion. A gruff-looking guy in farmer's overalls walks by in the shiniest pair of patent leather shoes I have ever seen.

In French society, topless swimwear, nudity and having a lover are all acceptable. The variety of expressed emotion, while not as flamboyant as the Italians, is much more colourful than that of the dull grey tight-

215

lipped English. I wonder if this personal freedom and diversity has contributed to the well-known creativity of the French.

The setting has a strange impact on me. I feel alive, free, as if I can be myself and nobody will object. I do not speak French, yet I have a strange feeling that I have come home. In spite of speaking Spanish and being captivated by the people, I did not feel at home in Spain. I suppose it is because Spanish culture and social customs are more narrowly defined than in France. I wonder if I should set up permanent residence in France?

* * *

When the French political theorist Alexis De Tocqueville visited the United States two hundred years ago, he described the U. S. people as similar to a herd of cattle, all looking and thinking the same. If that were true, the United States culture would have been low in creativity, which hasn't been the case. It seems likely he was responding to surface characteristics and not cognizant of the population's underlying makeup. The North American culture at that time contained immigrants from cultures around the world. Such a diversity of cultural beliefs placed in a political structure based on individual freedom was bound to bring forth richness in creativity.

The creative personality has cognitive flexibility, an open mind, and a sense of adventure. The creative PELGAM exists in everyone, its expression a matter of degree. It comes back to the necessity for balanced development. The backward, socially reticent engineer may contribute creative inventions and solutions. His colleague who has achieved a balanced set of highly functioning PELGAMs will create more and of a greater quality.

Contemporary creativity can be seen through-out society; governments, industry, agriculture, science, education… During the past several decades creativity has been most evident in various branches of technology. I am sitting in front of a computer, and of course, have access to the internet. My mobile phone sits an arms-length away. These are useful tools, but otherwise not of interest to me. Let us look at literature, music and the visual arts, where new creations are a daily event.

Linguistic Creativity – Linguistic ability begins in the genetic language/communication process functions of the brain, draws upon ancient memory material, and possible input from the ZPF. This involves the physical elements employed in speaking/writing, and the senses of hearing, vision, time and waves.

Linguistic patterns differ from culture to culture, yet their goal remains the same, to communicate and to comprehend the verbal and written output of others. Modern technology provides instant means of doing this; however, there is a glut of information, finding what you want can take extensive time. Likewise, if you wish your linguistic output to be consumed by others, it will have to be of excellent quality.

I have from an early age read and written profusely, nevertheless I struggled in high school English classes. Diagrams to set off prepositions, verbs and so on left me in a stupor; I failed to grasp the structural dynamics of the language. Years later, studying Spanish and books on how to write, my linguistic skills improved. Although, I still feel inadequate with English grammar.

Two hundred years ago reading and writing was the domain of the university educated upper class. With the advent of public education, fundamental reading and writing skills were provided to the populace. In the recent past, most people only attended school through the eighth grade, currently in Western culture, the twelfth grade is the standard.

The 2008 'Social Trends' (4102.0) review published by the Australian Bureau of Statistics, lists some current life issues that require significant literacy skills (filling out forms, finding information on the internet...). This study used a five-point scale (1=low, 5=high) to rank reading ability. Level 3 is considered the minimum level required to meet the increasingly complex demands of a knowledge society. Almost half of all Australians aged 15-74 years had literacy skills below level 3. 83% of low scorers either had not completed grade 12 or English was their second language.

The consequences of these deplorable findings are obvious. A huge percentage of people do not understand their insurance contracts or loan agreements. How many people can have a productive exchange with their auto mechanic or electrician? Pity those with timid personalities and poor linguistic ability; they cannot confront someone who has short-changed them.

As a result of low literacy skills many newspapers, magazines and books are written at a fifth-to-seventh grade reading level, far below the linguistic quality of published materials two hundred years ago. Today, high verbosity and extensive reading do not necessarily indicate good linguistic ability.

Traditionally, women have been seen as more verbal (linguistic) than men. This may be the result of millions of years during which the female primates spent time screaming from the treetops, warning the troupe a predator was nearby. This distracted the predator so the males could take defensive or offensive positions. Today, if I am confronted with an overly verbal female, I look around for a tree to hoist her into.

Education has traditionally relied upon linguistic teaching methods favourable to the female brain. This left males and some female students in the lurch. One day a short grizzled forty-year-old plumber showed up in my office.

***

'Doc, I got a problem with readin and writin dat frustrates da hell outta me'

'As a plumber, I wouldn't think you would have to do much reading and writing?'

'I got tree employees now, da paper work and supervision is driving me nuts. At home the
kids ask for help with der homework and I'm hopeless.'

'Have you tried the reading and writing classes offered by the community's adult education programs?'

'I called em, it's for foreigners.'

**

A test battery revealed he was low in linguistic potential, but high in spatial, musical and kinaesthetic ability. It was music, pictures and 'hands on' tasks he needed. I referred him to an educational specialist and six months of effort produced amazing improvements.

In our society of specialization, there are people well-read and linguistically adept in a few areas, but linguistically poor in general. This can also result from poor emotional development; a lawyer or politician may create a beautifully crafted law or policy, yet be unable to grasp the essence of a love sonnet.

Boost Linguistic Creativity – This begins in the womb as the unborn learns some of the mother's vocabulary. Daily reading (various voices and languages) to the foetus will set in motion the development of a strong linguistic PELGAM. After birth this can be continued via daily reading to the child, plus discussions and eventually teaching them to read. Neither infants, nor the unborn should be subjected to complete silence or overly loud raucous noise.

At birth the visual system is genetically geared to recognize various forms. Auditory training assists the infant to recognize and identify these forms. Using all its' senses, the infant begins to learn word and thought patterns from observing and interacting with the environment. Extensive reading or listening to various genres, such as biographies, science fiction and mysteries, quickly expands the linguistic ability.

Adulthood participation in: theatre, music, world travel, social activities, sports and hobbies can be helpful. A playful personality will be more creative than a stern, regimented personality. Creativity is enhanced when you tell and write stories or poetry. When you write, play around with the word order and substitute words. Question everything. Long ago some cave woman gnawing on a raw hunk of meat wondered what it would taste like if she stuck it in the fire. This anecdote is from *'Every Idea is a Good Idea: Be Creative Anytime, Anywhere.'* By Sturges, T. Tarcher Books, Penguin Group USA.

Educational institutions offer formal training in linguistic skills. Community groups such as debating societies, speech and writing clubs, and drama groups provide further help. There are a plethora of books, CD's and DVD's available. Each new language you learn increases your linguistic ability. Linguistic creativity, like all creativity, is enhanced by diversity in thinking, action, experience, social contacts and environments.

How much linguistic material is enough? This varies depending on a person's present level of development. An older person, having accomplished much of their development, has time to invest in whatever they wish. A young student must spend more time in the 'book learning' phase of life. A mid-life adult might read/write an hour or two a day, five days a week. More time may interfere with maintaining a balanced life style.

A stellar individual might possess outstanding linguistic and communication skills, including mental telepathy and the ability to dialogue with animals. They would be fluent in the international language plus several others and they would be able to learn a new language in a matter of months.

Musical Creativity - Is not all sound musical, the rhythm of machinery, the symphony of nature, the sing-song of conversation? Music can evoke a vast range of emotions and it helps us relate to those around us. The foetus can recognize differences in music and sound patterns. (*'Origins of Music'* Cosmos issue 38, April 2011). Music transcends foreign languages; Longfellow called music 'the universal language of mankind.'

Problems - Musical creative is problematic for the hearing impaired and tone deaf. Australian government publications estimate 16% of the general population, and 70% of older people, have some hearing impairment. Research statistics at *Musicianbrain.com* claim 17% of people have some degree of tone deafness (congenital amusia*),* an inability to distinguish between musical notes.

Solutions - More solutions to help the hearing impaired are becoming available: better hearing aids, surgical procedures, implants, drugs and special training programs. The individual can do their part by being careful not to injure their heads or allow the ears to become infected. Avoidance of prolonged loud noise and keeping ears clean is important. Given that musical sound waves are a vibration, improving one's kinaesthetic sense of feel and touch could be helpful.

Musical creativity draws upon the genetic musical potential, ancient memories, and the broad-based learning of musical technique (explore be-bop, jazz, classical). This genetic potential allows an infant to hear tones and interpret them into vocalizations, while their body moves to the beat. With a little creative effort, we learn to sing. Vocal music pulls the sometimes-ambiguous lyrics from the linguistic brain and blends them into the fluidity of musical notes. Include some fine motor and breathing skills from the physical PELGAM and you learn to play an instrument. Writing music becomes possible. A child can become a talented musician by their teens. An adult can become a musician, it just takes them a little more time and effort.

***

A mid-forties member of my Thursday evening group therapy had always wanted to play an instrument; the group encouraged him to pursue his desire. He found a music shop that offered group lessons to older adults and with some trepidation signed up. One evening three months later, grinning broadly, he announced to the group that he would be playing in a concert on the weekend and we were all invited to attend. We were shocked. This is not possible. You cannot learn enough in twelve weeks to play in a concert. He assured us he and the others, who were also oldies new to music, had the skills to perform. The repertoire would be eclectic; the most complex piece being the 'Mickey Mouse' theme song. A roar of supportive laughter ensued.

***

I recommend weekly singing and dancing as the minimum involvement in music. If you do not learn to sing or play an instrument, then be sure to attend symphonies, concerts and other musical venues. A daily half hour of listening to music could be uplifting and enriching.

The midbrain emotional control centre gives emotional feeling to a musical piece. A performance can be expert in all the technical aspects, but if it lacks emotional impact, the performance will be poor. Playing emotionally imbued music requires memorization of the musical notation; this allows the performer to focus on an emotional delivery. If there is emotional depth in the music, a technical error or two will not matter. There are world famous singers whose vocal abilities are mediocre or even poor. Their fame derives from their emotional charisma and their ability to emotionally captivate you with lyrics that pluck the strings of your heart.

* * *

I hike the sun-dappled paths of the forest listening to the bird song, the humming insects and a whispering breeze through the trees. As evening approaches I pause beside a gurgling brook and listen to its' plaintive ballad. Enticed, I pitch the tent in this sylvan setting. A fox yips in the background as I collect fire wood. The snapping, crackling flames blend in with natures evening symphony. It has been a day, like every other day, full of music.

I bed down beneath the canopy of a primeval gnarled oak tree and listen to a distant owl and the syncopated rhythm of frogs and crickets. The eerily haunting laments of loons assure me I am in my northern forest home. The night time orchestra and chorus of thousands slowly builds its' forte, a soothing rhapsody slowly carrying me off to blissful sleep.

<u>Rhythm of Life.</u>

It may begin softly and gently
The purring of the strings

Then there comes a melody
All kinds of emotion it brings

Your body swings into motion
you begin to hum
Feel the driving base beat
staccato of the drum

A trilling harp's refrain
A mournful saxophone
They take away your pain
Give you courage to roam

The clashing of the castanets
Strumming of guitar
Flashing of a golden thigh
Take your thoughts afar

A soprano softly quavers
To the background of a chant
These are moments to savour
No further need to rant

In the keyboards run
You can dissipate your fear
Learn to have fun
It is ok to shed a tear

The regal golden horns come alive
Giving you a new-found strength
A new way to survive
Through life's eternal trials

Somehow the organ has found
The very depths of your soul
You find that inner calm

Peace with the world is your goal

The final crashing crescendo
Gives promise to your hopes and dreams
For the universe that is full of wonder
It is all within your means

Visual Creativity – involves the eye, the optic nerve and the visual receptive area of the brain. The brain forms an image of what the eye perceives or what the mind dreams up. This latter ability is in fact creativity at work. Conscious thoughts and memories can form realistic or unique visual images in the mind.

I was given a Kodak box camera for my tenth birthday. My friend Ron (he had several cameras) and I set up a dark room and experimented with photography - microscopic, 3D, portrait, landscape and so on. Our photographic creativity was fun and I learned to achieve quality picture composition. Ron was a genius photographer, actually he was just a genius. He went on to get his Ph.D. in physics at Yale and later worked in various famous laboratories. Photography was his life-long hobby.

As an adult I expanded my visual artistic expression via watercolours and acrylics to paint people and landscapes. My visual handicap led to products of questionable artistic value. I still have a boat painting in spite of it looking as if it were about to sink. My best portrait was of a pretty lady, but I got the neck wrong, she looked like a giraffe. Don't know what happened to that painting, it seems to have disappeared.

* * *

Dodging peniches (barges) and other vessels, a thousand years of French history slides by as our motor yacht makes its way up the river Seine. Waterways were the highways of yesteryear and upon their banks lay the human story. I am not fond of large cities; however, cruising into Paris we pass the heaven pointing Eiffel tower, small statue of liberty, Notre Dame and the Louvre. It is a peak experience.

I coax our craft alongside a floating pontoon adjacent to a canal that runs off the Seine. The crew leaps off and fastens the lines to bollards. Pushing a voice box button, we advise the port authorities of our wish to enter the canal's marina. Within the hour the lock gates open allowing us to move into quieter waters. Using old auto tires as fenders we dock alongside a pre-Napoleonic stone quay.

Here we are in the heart of Paris within sight of the metro and a short walk to the landmarks mentioned, all for fifteen dollars a night. This includes electrical hook up, a spotless toilet block, hot water showers, modern washing machines and dryers. The cheapest B & B rooms in the area are US $150 per night. For over a week we walk our legs off. The only other time I have seen this much visual art was during our stay in Vienna. The cruising lifestyle is hard to beat. After a full Paris day of gardens, galleries, sculptures and exquisite cuisine, we come home to our own snug beds.

* * *

My brother Phil was the most creative and intelligent member of our family. He had phenomenal eyesight, he used it to become an exceptionally talented sculptor. He has a fantastic bronze bear statue he sculpted and other wildlife statues. His visual creativity of animal art was in part due to his lifetime immersion in nature with animals. Yet another example of how creativity demands thorough familiarity with the topic.

At present my visual artistic endeavours involve creating a vibrant botanical landscape around our Bavarian cottage, a blend of plants that produce fruit, shade, perfume, colour, and homes for wildlife. The cottage walls are adorned with photographs, tapestries and paintings, that add to the natural beauty of the pine cladding and wood furniture. There are a few sculpted pieces collected during my travels.

A quality photograph or painting requires repeated accurate visual observation of the subject from all angles, and under all lighting conditions. The artist's efforts have been abetted by recent technological advances in photographic equipment and computer software. These factors combined with formal training give the average person the opportunity to create spectacular visual artwork. This could change the way you view the world.

CREATIVITY WRAP UP

I liken creativity to the sour dough bread starter that I mix up. Into the bowl you throw novel experiences, new acquaintances, passion and crazy ideas. Mix it up, then let it ferment. In time it gives off gases, swells up and grows a porous skin. Then I dip a bit out and bake a book, invent a gizmo, paint a picture, foster a relationship...

Western culture is too ensconced in the hard sciences, technological creativity and economics, it tends to overlook the importance of beauty. If we could instil an appreciation of beauty in scientists, politicians and business men; it might stem the annihilation of the planet. Beauty can instil peace, love, awe and a host of other qualities which give meaning to every-day existence. Hence it is important to implant within children (via filter training) an appreciation of beauty and an interest in fostering beauty.

Beautiful creations often contain genetic underpinnings. An article in "Developmental Science" January 2008 details how infants world-wide are pleased by specific facial features we commonly call beautiful. Some human physical characteristics are considered beautiful by all cultures. On the other hand, learning accounts for many concepts of beauty. Thus, conventional beauty differs between cultures and individuals.

Beautiful, beauteous, something very good, pleasing to the eye, pleasant, a skilful action, an emotionally moving experience or event, a logically sound idea, a naturally flowing complex thought process. Beauty is all of this and more.

On the downside we have been warned not to judge a book by its' cover. Beauty can seem magnificent, but it can also be destructive, wasteful or frivolous. For example, beauty contests, physical disfigurement, overly ornate décor, grandiose structures, clothing and accessories that demean the natural beauty of the human body. When we are ignorant of individual and cultural differences, it is easy to quickly label something ugly.

Listen to music on a rock, classical or country western station and individual differences are obvious. Driving through our nearby suburbs it is easy to spot Italian homes with their columns, statues and fountains. In one of Jared Diamond's books there is a hilarious conversation amongst New Guinea natives about a visiting attractive (by western standards) blond female. They cannot imagine why any man would want such an emaciated, sickly pale woman with a small narrow hatchet shaped nose.

Time can be a relevant factor; the birth of a child may not be a beautiful event if you are currently stricken with malnutrition and poverty. Last year's beautiful fashions may be seen this year as gaudy, non-descript or ugly. When life is stressful beauty may disappear. Are flight controllers and soldiers less able to perceive beauty? When I was twenty-five I could differentiate a beautiful car from an ugly one. Today they all look the same to me, neither beautiful nor ugly. All is not lost - I am still awed to silence by the presence of a beautiful woman.

Location and knowledge can make a difference in perceiving beauty. Hand digging a trench is hard work; sitting atop a trenching machine, the work is easy and the machine seems beautiful. A six-foot high termite mound appears as a featureless pile of dirt. When you study the intricacy of its tunnels, the engineering of the structure, and its' air conditioning efficiency; you may then marvel at its beauty.

Beauty became comprehensive for me on the several occasions when death at sea seemed imminent; during those times, I saw land and things on land as beautiful. Arriving safely in port I felt the universe and life were beautiful. Now when I am confronted with obstreperous people or difficult situations; I bring the situation into perspective by reminding myself I am not caught in a dangerous storm at sea - I am not about to die, this is real life and it is beautiful.

Purple, Chopin's piano nocturnes, trees, fresh baked bread, the Sydney Opera House, golden retrievers, the national anthem, soft cashmere sweaters (nicely filled), snow-capped mountains, Khalil Gibran's poetry, are a few of the things I find beautiful.

A person may expand their creative ability by improving their appreciation of beauty. This could occur via a near death experience or creating life, boredom or a full active life, a cross-mix of friends, or a pet. There are formal courses such as art or music appreciation. Consider writing down what constitutes an attractive face and voice, a beautiful piece of music, a stunning idea, a gorgeous personality? Bearing in mind, a work of art may be assessed on its technical skill, imagination, message, degree of abstraction... In the final analysis, we have no way of delineating art from non-art.

Share your ideas and beliefs about beauty with the rest of your group. This could be the catalyst for your Hub to determine the beauty characteristics you wish to impart to the children. List your own personal characteristics you consider beautiful. Modern society contains multitudinous formal methods of improving your creativity (workshops, brainstorming, self-help books, training videos, hypnosis).

The ever-widening planetary chaos and the eventual venture into outer space will inspire an unparalleled surge in creativity, greater than the invention of the wheel, the agricultural revolution, nuclear fission... This progressive evolution will not be carried out by the large nations, they are too inflexible, paralysed by vested interests. It is more likely to be smaller countries that will have the courage to support the creation of Hubs, Circles, and Constellations, which will fashion a living environment and society conducive to the full empowerment of Homo sapiens.

Currently, most employees labour at tasks requiring minimal levels of cognitive ability. This is a huge waste of talent. The intellectually challenged and other disabled people could do this work and do it more effectively. Those freed up can apply themselves to more intellectually demanding work and research. Since we have adequate resources, all people can excel at all facets of existence and do so with only a few hours of work a week.

Creativity in general requires an uncluttered, unrestricted mind to speculate about possibilities and free time to observe, dream, imagine, and experiment. The Hub society provides the venue for this enhanced life style. From this, creative changes in government, education, business… will completely alter society as we know it.

Chapter 11 Intrapersonal Relation Ship PELGAM

Learn to know

understand

and like yourself.

You are the admiral of a fleet of ships; each conducts your affairs in different areas of life. In this chapter we will go aboard your intrapersonal relation-ship, which navigates the sea of interactions within yourself.

A Festive Party

It all starts when the egg and sperm are formed in the respective female and male body and begin a relationship with the host body. A further intra-personal relationship commences as the attributes within each sex cell acclimate to each other. The sex cells also begin to relate to sensory input from the adult (emotions, physical body states…) and from the external world (oceanic waves, sound…).

***

Once upon a time a princess and a prince met in darkness.

Vaginal microbes.

'Where da blip did that flood come from?'

'Beats me! Never seen such huge long tailed whales.'

A wild party ensued as the princess (egg) was visited and admired by a host of princes (sperm). She was eager to dance with one of these squirming guys, but acted coy and demure at first. She was enjoying sitting around looking pretty and being popular. This boy meets girl stuff is groovy.

The poor guy has had a rough time of it - he had to leave his home and travel a long distance. His first relationship was meeting all the critters in the tunnel, hardly seems fair to me. He got into a few fights with rivals before he finally managed to greet the princess. I wonder if he would have backed off had he known what lay ahead.

Not wanting to be a wallflower, she gave in to his pestering and accepted him. Perhaps it was love at first sight and the two of them joined as one. Or maybe there was an initial squabble and bonding was only achieved after a struggle. Either way the union of the two produced you.

You began your existence in the amniotic fluid (did you have your snorkel?). This is very natural given you reside on a water planet and as a human you consist mainly of water. You did some good work on furthering your relationship with mum. Of course, relaxing back in a warm bath is a rather nice place to work from isn't it! How did you feel about your earliest encounters with others? For example, when your dad thumped on your living room wall? How did you like it when the doctor snooped about with his stethoscope and bounced sound waves off you?

Then came the day you left behind your warm, cuddly, safe and sterile home to travel down the tunnel, past all sorts of microscopic and ultramicroscopic critters, out into the cold blinding world. It was a good time to get even with dad and the Doctor; did you plan your arrival for two in the morning?

I remember how it was for me; I popped out to a shower of fluids sprayed upon me; that was ok, but the rest of this relationship thing was a bit much. All of a sudden there were thousands of those microscopic living beings. On the opposite extreme there were giants physically bullying me. It was my first group inter-personal experience - not the best way to start life when everyone treats you like a baby and they are dressed up like spooks. I opened my peepers to a dazzling brightness and broke into song, 'blinded by the light.'

The cacophony of sound was deafening and the commands confusing; open your eyes, smile, it was difficult to think. Then into view popped dad's face, Wow! Talk about ugly. I didn't want to admit I was related to this monkey. The real shock came when they put me on mum's belly and I saw her face: a big white ball with a long pink nose. No! Wait a minute, that's a teat. Yeah!

The number of my relationships increased tremendously; one was awesome and incomprehensible. I can only describe it as spiritual – it felt like it had been there forever. It was like a glowing ring above my head. Who knows! Maybe I'm special?

A spook unnecessarily carried me to mum's room. I could have wiggled my way! I began my fundamental relationship with nature; flowers welcomed me with open petals and bestowed upon me their gifts of fragrance. It was going to be the same for me as for my ancestors - plants would provide me immeasurable joy, sustenance, shelter, clothing and tools. The room itself was a bit drab, no aesthetic appeal.

Those first days were perhaps the most blissful in my life. All I did was eat, sleep, shit and piss; sooner or later all good things have to end, it was time to go home. The journey home took more time than the tunnel trip. My bassinette was strapped into a large covered bed that roared, rocked and jerked and had a loud horn. I was overwhelmed by the multitude of humans along the way; how would I ever get to know and relate to so many? Everywhere I looked I saw box shaped structures with shiny rectangular bits. The ground we moved over was flat rock with coloured stripes. It was as if I were on an alien planet.

Nevertheless, the motion was nice. It was like being back in my womb bath; I took a nap. When the motion stopped I woke up to see what was going on. I heard entrancing music, singing birds, whispering trees and humming insects. Beneath me a shaggy haired creature looked inquisitively at me and wagged its' tail; the beginning of my relationship with the animal kingdom.

Lifted from my hot rod bed, I saw grassy fields, a meandering stream and groves of trees. I instinctively knew my relationship with the botanical world of mother earth was precious. I could not survive in the cold emptiness of space. Yet it was in space that I began, I am a star child; some of my elements came from space a long time ago. My relationship with the universe began before my present totality had come into existence. That glowing bright spot in the sky kindled a spark in my deepest being, 'You light up my life.' I felt the warmth and intuitively knew its' light enabled my existence. Whoa! That's enough of me waffling on.

* * *

Let us take a closer look at the intrapersonal relationships in your life. They govern how you interact with yourself, helping you stay internally consistent in your thoughts and actions, which is necessary to successfully relate to the world about you. We will look at three components: the impact of micro internal elements, ancestral contributions and your conscious relation with yourself.

Micro Elements - (cells, chromosomes, microbes, genes…) within the human body play a major role in every aspect of life. There are a lot of them. The bacterium in our body out -numbers the number of cells. Proper diet, exercise and living environment are required to maintain stable micro relations.

Ancestral Contributions – consist of the genetic DNA elements, which also contain ancient memories (AM). The DNA transmits hereditary characteristics down through the generations. The question of which specific DNA characteristics come from the universe and other unknown sources, such as plants and animals, remains a matter of speculation. The rest are inherited from your long line of ancestors. Which of the available inherited DNA characteristics will be used to form the final product, you? An automatic internal selection process takes over and decides which DNA features to include in your makeup.

The Conscious 'Self' component includes internal thoughts (talk), unconscious revelations, as well as the spontaneous actions a person takes for their own well-being.

Weak - intrapersonal relations are in part a result of our modern frenetic life style: blaring radios, TV, stereo, phones, busses, planes, the glut of visual stimulus in books, emails, text messages, advertising materials…, these things make it difficult for us to hear our inner voice or see the reality of nature about us. If we take the time to heed our internal messages, they help us pinpoint the things we are doing wrong and suggest changes we could make. Both bring us closer to authentic reality. If we know we are acting inappropriately but do nothing about it; we lose self-confidence and feel haunted by our weakness.

If there are too many or too few microelements, intrapersonal problems occur. For example, an unbalanced ratio of red to white blood cells or an aggressive infectious microbe that overwhelms the immune system. Both can lead to poor health and the loss of life. Imbalance may result from aging, toxicity, insufficient nutrients… Hormonal changes can wreak havoc with self-awareness. Women may alter their self-perception during the menstrual cycle.

Life can be sheer drudgery or even hazardous if the individual does not accept and work with the driving forces of genetic input (G) and the intuitions of 'AM'. Take for instance a small, lightly muscled human struggling in a career that involves heavy, strenuous manual labour. Or consider an even simpler illustration – a person who fails to notice and steer clear of a poisonous snake.

To avoid weakness at the 'self' level, self-assessment is required. The narcissist focuses on self-aggrandisement and thinks he can do anything. He leads a stressful life attempting to accomplish feats he is not capable of and leaves a path of foul ups behind him. Some people are lured by the wealth and fame of movie stars and they set out on this career path without realising that they do not have the most basic skills - a sufficient grasp of language, a strong memory capacity, or social skills.

There is of course the opposing tendency: the insecure personality afraid to attempt much may set goals that are far below their talents, resulting in a life that fails to meet needs and lacks meaning.

Slouching in my office recliner, Tom, his voice full of resignation said, 'Looking back now, I should have joined my wife in some of her hobbies, taken some of the management courses at work, learned to play golf with my neighbours. I didn't feel I had the ability to do any of those things; I was afraid I would make a fool of myself.'

241

Tom's wife left him ten years ago, 'She said I was boring.' Tom held the same engineering position in a manufacturing company for twenty years, declining their encouragement to strive for a higher-level position. Lonely, bored and depressed, his impending retirement 'seems like death.'

Workplace statistics reveal large numbers of employees hate their jobs; this dissatisfaction could have been avoided if they had done an accurate assessment of themselves

Poor 'self' relations can be the result of taking on board too much societal nonsense. Western culture often demands sublimation of the personal self for the betterment of the family, community, corporation or other entity; some of these requirements are good and necessary. Others distort a person's sense of personal value, for example the excessive emphasis on being a hard worker.

A diligent worker provides more profits for the business owner and more tax revenues for the government. For these types of employees, excessive time and effort achieving career success often destroys their family. For others it narrows and de-stabilizes their self-concept; they only respect and value themselves as workers. Consequently, being sacked or going into retirement produces high rates of depression and suicide. A significant percentage of male retirees simply give up and die pre-maturely.

Parents with faulty brain filters create a family unit wherein the children have an inaccurate perception of themselves and the world. Good traits may be seen by these children as bad and bad traits as good. Dishonesty is the norm in some families; in others it is ok to exaggerate. Some children are belittled, while others receive praise no matter how odious their behaviour. The destructive influence of friends on children is well recognized; bullying and name calling are rampant in school and the neighbourhood.

When children move into adulthood, the negative impact of family and friends on their self-perception puts them at odds with other people and the general culture. Therefore, success in the career, social and marriage arena is difficult, if not impossible.

Modern culture provides a daily bombardment of concepts that poison intrapersonal relationships, for example narrow conceptions of physical beauty, the pressure to overcommit to careers and the prevailing consumerist atmosphere. Failure to meet these and other cultural prescriptions often demeans the individual's self-perception. There are those who feel so worthless, they cannot expend time or energy on themselves.

Building Strong Intrapersonal Relationships – Our perilous trip across the seas of life demands boldness, knowledge and understanding of the intrapersonal ship's intricate components: the G and AM factors. Taking good care of our well-being fosters faith in our selves. At the micro G level physical health must be maintained; this includes an avoidance of toxins and de-stabilising physical regimens, while ingesting the proper nutrients and being physically active. When confronted with infection or disease, the intake of antibiotics may be necessary to reclaim good health.

Testing of intelligence, memory, cognitive abilities, vocational skills... is an easy first step towards understanding self. Plotting your genetic makeup (genome) is wise. Minimally, make a list of your good and bad traits. Remember your traits are not set in concrete, they are malleable. The details of your assets and liabilities assist you to identify potentials worth investing with training and negative behaviours that need to be eliminated.

For the AM component, reviewing research in the social sciences may help. It is known we are born with a number of fears: loud noise, snakes, height... Whether they are from the 'G' or 'AM' area, or both, is not known. The AM is not just the voice of our human ancestors, but also from the other life forms from which we evolved. This includes our early primate relatives and all the way back to our small multi celled ocean dweller.

Your ability to receive communication from the G and AM is crucial. We currently have a so called technical 'communication revolution'. This term is somewhat misleading. Optic fibre, micro waves, and the

internet are fantastic tools for transmitting numbers, theories, concepts…
but they fail miserably in conveying mental, emotional and other
intangible states of human existence.

Reception of internal information does not require an antenna; it
requires free time to listen to your inner voice, your intuitions and
hunches. Emotional calmness is needed to ask your true self what it
wants or suggests. Physical rest can allow you to decipher the body's
messages. If you spend half as much time on internal listening as you do
on text messages, phone calls, emails and social media, your life could
dramatically change.

Good internal reception helps develop the self-understanding needed
to expand assets, reduce liabilities and obtain a solid well-founded value
of 'self'. This in turn cultivates self-satisfaction, courage, perseverance,
peace and contentment. These dispositions are necessary in forming and
contributing to a loving and nurturing family. From this basis you are
able to set priorities for a meaningful life.

Attending to the inner world is similar to surfing the net; you can
spend endless hours viewing material that has no bearing whatsoever on
your life. Some of it may be ridiculous - only good for a laugh. There is
a tendency for the mind to get stuck on issues having to do with things
we are anxious about, deprived of, or fantasies. Change channels.
Meaningful material may come in the form of a serial drama requiring

attendance at many sessions; each one giving more clues and information until you are able to construct a clear image or idea.

A meditation type practice could prove fruitful. Meditate ensconced in a comfortable position amidst natural terrain, animals and other humans, so their oceanic waves can wash over you. Pay attention to whatever comes up in your mind; it may talk, provide TV like images, or form thoughts and ideas. Heed feeling states, an uncomfortable feeling may be a warning; a pleasant feeling may be an 'all-is-well' signal. Use a note pad or audio recorder to save the important info.

The average person is unaware of the strengths hidden in their G, AM, and ZPF connections. This is understandable given contemporary emphasis on 'sensible cognition' the process of learning via the senses. Deep introspective thought is frowned upon, as is heeding one's intuition. However, ample studies reveal that emotional calm, peace, quiet and solitude, often reveal what is meaningful and what is not. The fulfilment of natural instincts is the ultimate goal of Chinese morality according to the writer Lin Yutang.

Partial determination of 'self' worth can be attained by comparing yourself with other people, but it also opens you to the possibility of nonsense. You may attempt to bolster your self-worth by noting how much better you are at something than someone else. What if that person has a disability in that area or perhaps they outshine you in every other respect? Maybe your issue is of little importance? Conversely, you may deride yourself for not being able to succeed in ways others do, when the reality is you have a disability - or you may be envious of something lacking value altogether.

Altruistic behaviour and looking out for the welfare of other people can increase one's personal sense of value and contentment with 'self.' This may be as simple as wishing someone happy birthday or doing volunteer work. When you contribute to society, you gain the respect of others, and this helps meet your need for belonging and increases your self-respect and self-value.

In the term 'self-confidence', the word *self* is crucial; confidence in ones' self must first come from the self. When the person (self) is functioning well, they possess confidence. If the core self is weak, containing extensive neurotic behaviour (phobias, obsessive compulsive disorder, control freak…), or poor self-control (obesity, consumerism, addictions…), then attaining self-confidence becomes almost impossible.

A stellar personality is not free of self-doubt; they simply do not let doubts interfere with necessary action. They study and draw upon humanity's accumulated knowledge to enhance the vitality of their genuinely robust centre. They grasp the subtleties of their innate desires, values, motivations, goals… and heed their messages. Their internal voice of wisdom is strong, providing valuable assistance.

Those with a weak core must address and eradicate the relevant problems. This requires accurate self-assessment, followed by behavioural remediation. For most of us this means enlisting professional support.

Role playing is one psychotherapeutic technique for altering one's self. Through your life experiences you have collected hundreds of characters and stored them in your conscious closet of people. In the front rows of each shelf, are the characters you use regularly, such as when you are happy, studious, selfish, angry, pompous, hardworking, a liar, a show-off or whatever.

Try this little trick. Pick a character that represents the personality and type of person you wish to be, or choose a character from history, a movie, book or an acquaintance. Then study how this person reacts to the ins and outs of daily life, till you have a thorough understanding of the new role. Print up a document detailing how the new you will act in any given situation.

When you tuck yourself in at night, place this character or characters you are going to use the next day, to the front of the shelf. Think about them and your document as you drift off to sleep. Your eyes will pop open in the morning and you will be off and running, playing the role of the grouch, irresponsible clod, loving friend or brilliant musician. Review the prompt document in your pocket every hour.

A mid-twenties carpenter came to my office with multiple complaints; he wasn't sure what kind of person he was. He did not like himself, was bored, tired of being single with no direction in life. It took several counselling sessions to pin down what kind of learning he wanted and what type of roles he might play to acquire the new knowledge and skills. The role he chose to practice flabbergasted me. He chose a catholic priest as the role most likely to provide him with the desired learning experiences.

He spent hours researching the role and filling pads of paper with descriptions of how he would act in every conceivable situation. Hiring priest garb was the easy part. Where he might go to play his role was more difficult. Trying on new roles is difficult amongst people that know you. Through some of my contacts we came up with the perfect location.

On the far side of town, university students in a large rooming house were throwing an open house party for the entire neighbourhood. It was a mixed socio-economic area of students, professors, tradesmen, factory workers and clerks. This was the perfect opportunity to interact with all kinds of people who did not know him.

We met for a final briefing a few hours prior to the party; he was trembling in his collar but eager for the challenge. I was almost as nervous as him. I knew he would learn heaps that would bring about great changes if only he could stay at the party rather than running home. I fretted he might have bitten off more than he could chew.

Late Sunday afternoon I got a call - he was over the moon. He had been at the party till daybreak, completely ensconced in the interactions. As a priest he had no fear of relating to the women, thus he relaxed and learned about females. He related to males without the usual male competition and met the openness of others with sincere interest and care, no longer needing to focus on his own worries.

He is an excellent example of how role playing can have a dramatic impact on your life. A good time to try this is when you move to a new neighbourhood or take on a new job. Halloween and New Year Eve's masquerade parties are a chance to practise other roles.

Learning new roles raises the question of what roles we act out on a daily basis. We may be cognizant of our role as a student, parent, employee... But what roles are we not aware of, the ones we unconsciously perform? In psychotherapy we help a client uncover hidden roles; awareness of hidden positive traits bolsters a person's self-esteem. Likewise, finding a hidden shameful role can pave the way for its eradication.

A good relationship with one's 'self' smooths the way for building meaning and harmony in natural, interpersonal and spiritual relationships. It requires action - make sure you always celebrate your birthday; it is the one day in the year you have every right to claim as your day. While it helps enhance your self-worth when others show they value you by acknowledging your birthday, it is even more important that you honour your 'self.' Consider taking the day off work and schedule things to please yourself: special activities, food and drink. Include at least one unique gift to yourself. After all, if you do not take good care of yourself, why should anyone else?

Strong Intrapersonal Relationships – The stellar soul deletes negative traits and replaces them with positive ones. They nurture their uniqueness but have no need to flaunt it. They socially adapt in any setting or happily spend time alone.

They detect and symbolize their complex and highly differentiated sets of emotions. This skill in part is the ability to recognize the difference between when they feel happy and pleasant versus unhappy and troubled, and how to obtain the former and avoid the later. Numerous people actually have happiness and unhappiness intertwined and confused - this is reflected in the person who excessively moans and complains about their problems. They may be happy because it is a way of obtaining attention. It could be a cultural attribute. Australians label people from England 'whingeing Poms,' as they are viewed as constantly complaining. I probably would be disagreeable too, if I started the day with grilled tomatoes. I'm not sure cardboard tasting powdered eggs would be any better.

Long term confinement in the ISS or a rocket headed for deep space necessitates a strong belief in self. This is an individual who maintains a lifetime of internal inspection and dialogue; they know their shortcomings and their assets, their life purpose and the steps they need to take to achieve their purpose. They feel good about themselves and the world, inherently having worth, dignity and beauty.

Intrapersonal strength produces physical strength, good health. and a meaningful life. They follow their passions, have a positive self-concept and treat themselves with love, care and respect. They maintain close contact with the natural realm and pursue loving inter-personal relationships.

Self-Acceptance.

Once I lived the life of a poor man

Now I have found true wealth

I have friends that love me

And I love my 'self'

Chapter 12 Nature Relation Ship PELGAM

You cannot see the wind,

yet it can devastate the landscape

or softly cool you on a hot day

FLUIDS, FLORA, PLANETARY.

Mankind's relationship with nature is unavoidable and necessary; he requires nature's oxygen, water, animals and plants to survive, and these earthly elements require the sun's energy. These factors create our planetary ambience which allows us to live and progress.

Fluids - Millions of years ago our forbearers thrived in salty oceans and eventually crawled out of the sea to live on land, although still dependent on water. The fluid that the human egg and sperm inhabit has remained unchanged since the beginning of time. Humans live submersed in fluid the first nine months of life, so it is no surprise that water is the major ingredient of the human body. Water envelops three quarters of the planet's surface and is a survival necessity for life forms. Humans do not relinquish their relationship with water till long after death when the body returns to dust. Rumi suggests the most precious of all fluids are the lovers tear drops.

Since we evolved from water, consider re-establishing your ties with water; living next to water and regular swimming may fulfil unknown needs. It can be particularly enlightening for those interested in stellar travel. Don mask and fins; experience weightlessness, drift amidst a spooky outlandish world and you will encounter awesome alien creatures.

***

The warm clear water of the Australian Barrier reef holds me as I zip up my Lycra diving suit. My marine geologist buddy and I hold our respective BCD (breathing control device) relief valve hoses in the air and press the valve button. The hiss of escaping air quickly becomes bubbles as we sink below the surface. I slowly rotate, my eyes scanning the bottom fifteen metres down and the surrounding coral. No sign of white or tiger sharks, only three of the harmless metre long white tipped reef sharks.

Descending five metres, I kick my way to a three-metre diameter coral bommie. On its top, bright blue and green trumpeter fish nibble the coral. I move to the far side and drop down alongside the bommie, marvelling at the coral's vast array of vibrant colours. A metre-wide school of minute fluorescent blue fish hover in front of my mask. Slow intermittent releases of air take me deeper amidst the plethora of multi-coloured fish living in the nooks and crannies. I maintain a two-metre distance from the coral face; it is sharp and can give nasty cuts susceptible to infection. Some corals are poisonous to the touch.

A half dozen bright yellow and black angel fish come up close, checking me out; one places his nose on my mask, peering in at me. I turn slowly to view the waters of my twenty-five-metre range of sight, still no man-eaters in sight. A pair of black Queen Angelfish with shimmering gold trimmed scales; dart out from a crevasse and confront me. They are protecting their territory.

Nearing the bottom, we are careful not to kick up sand and reduce the visibility. Brad is two arm lengths off to my side and a metre below me, floating horizontal a metre above the sandy bottom. He motions to me, pointing to a recessed dark area at the base of the bommie; two thirty-centimetre lion fish hover, their toxic spines and feathery fins quivering. We give them a wide birth. Brad turned his face up towards me and gave me the pointing finger and thumb round sign, asking if I was ok. As he peered at me out of his diving mask his eyes suddenly enlarged and he pointed above me.

I turned my head to look and gasped at the huge dark form suspended a half metre above my shoulder. A two and a half metre manta ray lay suspended looking at us. I regained my composure and was tempted to reach out and touch him but didn't. For a half minute all of us observed each other and then the big fellow lifted up like a live space ship and slowly flew off into the blue haze.

***

My childhood and teen years were spent amongst the streams, lakes, great lakes and temperate forests of Michigan and Ontario; which is in contrast to my present hot sub-tropical life in rural Australia, where

255

water is scarce or non-existent. The water and forest wonderland of my youth no doubt played a role in my becoming an avid boater. I consider lakes and forests the best of all habitats, my preferred living environment. I know it's not true, but I tend to view deserts as dead places.

A Hub dwelling site must have ample clean water for cooking, bathing, drinking, crops and livestock. Members may need to learn water rationing, purification and how to use a water testing kit. Presently our house water comes from a tank, which is the run off from the roof. This still seems strange to me, I grew up with well water. Here well water is often too saline or full of minerals to be useable.

When it comes to water extreme caution is warranted when selecting a Hub site. World-wide, some communities have been dismayed when they discovered, that although the nearby streams and lakes were clean, the ground water table was contaminated.

The rejuvenating power of water has been documented throughout history; Roman baths, Turkish steam baths, mud baths and other cultural iterations of this. Fascination with water continues as contemporary humans participate in all manner of water sports; they seek out water's ambience at the beach, at a spring, a bubbling stream or waterfall. Waterfront properties sell for a premium.

I enjoy walking in the rain, sitting next to a fountain, swimming, snorkelling, scuba diving, water skiing and sailing. Fishing is just an excuse to be near the water. I get a kick out of sprinkling the lawn. What would I do without my shower? It always perks me up. It is even better when a love joins in and she bathes me.

I asked Theo how she felt about water. She looked at me intently, wagged her tail and woofed. She is obsessed with retrieving things and being in the water, jumping in our dam several times a day. Sooner or later I think she will quack.

Flora - During our previous existence in the oceans, survival was dependent on the undersea botanical world; migration to land continued our reliance on plants. Today plants provide clothing, cotton and silk... (with a little help from the leaf munching silk worms). Trees provide materials for home construction. A host of medicines and other consumer products, contain vegetal ingredients. Society is dependent on the energy from previous plant life; peat, coal, gas and oil. The stellar soul raises all manner of plants around and within their dwelling.

Being curious about the history of plant usage, I asked a knowledgeable chimp friend how it all got started. He tells me that life in the old days was pretty easy going. Fruit and nut trees were everywhere; since housing and clothing were not needed, the troupe spent most of their days eating, drinking, playing tennis, making love and farting around. For social life the different troupes would congregate in trailside cafes eating tapas and sipping daiquiris.

They learned how to make fire so every evening they partied with a barbeque, this created problems. Too many fermented banana and lime daiquiris left a few chimps unable to haul their futons up into the trees. Onlookers had a good laugh as the climbers repeatedly tumbled back to earth. Before the troupe retired into the trees for the night, they quickly wove fronds and branches over their comatose friends to protect them from the rain and chilly night air. This is how drunkenness begat housing.

Several million years of life in the natural milieu instilled within primates a genetic need for such settings (Biophilia hypothesis). Then and now it provides a sense of security and contentment. I surmise at some point in history a bully (power) ape and his hench-apes took control of the banana supplies, requiring the rest of the troupe to earn their bananas by building him a castle with tall towers so he could look down upon them. This bully ape demanded they give up the forest and live around his castle, so he could keep them under control and make sure they came to work every day. This is how the first towns were created by egomaniacs.

Many of today's city dwellers run helter-skelter through the alleys and streets, like confused and frantic rats, searching for they know-not-what. Estranged from mother-nature, they tremble at the very thought of stepping into a forest, shudder at the sight of humble creatures.

The urban dweller may create a lovely home ambience by cultivating indoor and outdoor plants, which also provide shelter for critters. Building water features like ponds and fountains also adds to the atmosphere.

Our property has a variety of flowering shrubs and trees that show off a dazzling array of shapes, colours and fragrances. Alamanders display yellow, wine and mauve. Mock-orange bushes give off a sweet fragrance. Fragrant port wine Magnolias and night blossoming Jasmine encircle the sleeping area. Since purple is my favourite colour, I am fond of the Lilac, Geisha girl, Tibouchinas, and Jacaranda trees. This bouquet provides fresh oxygen and a beautiful ambience.

Before going to bed, I like to sit quietly gazing over our reservoir and listen to the murmurs of the abundant plant life. They have tales to tell of ancient times when their brethren covered all lands. It's nice to drift off and dream of how it will be that way again.

I was 11 months old when taken on my first camping trip to experience the natural environment of earth. Mom tied my papoose pouch securely to a tree trunk so she was free to cast for bass and trout. Throughout my early years I spent extensive periods of time within natural settings; this combined with my genetic predisposition for nature, has created a strong internal need. I must live amidst forest and meadows, lakes and rivers. To smell the freshness of the breeze, feel the patter of rain, hear the birds and insects, see the clouds and sun above, taste a wild berry and sense the animals about me. What the town folk regard as dark, foreboding and sinister, I view as a haven, my home, a sacred place.

Planetary - Mother Earth is a wondrous woman with curves galore. She is clothed in rich browns, soft tans, cool blues and vibrant greens; a welcome symbol of life amidst the black void of our solar system. Deep within her being a heart of intense heat generates magnetic rainbows protecting terrestrial life from solar radiation. The planet's animals inhale her breath, drink her tears, eat her fruit and shelter amidst her flowers.

Our circular shaped solar system contains earths circular globe; a unity of life forms and elements exist within this earthly ball. Humanity originally dwelt within the earthly circle but detrimental forces have cast him out on his own. He no longer is in partnership with the planet's flora, fauna and elements. His survival as a species requires he re-enter the organic wholeness of the united earthly circle. He needs to clear the pollution, so he can heal himself and allow mother earth to once again radiate her beauty to the universe.

I have been in awe of the night sky since childhood. It may have started at age four when my grandmother insisted I be taken to an eye doctor; she thought I could not see well. She was right. The following week I came home wearing thick glasses. The trip home was a blur, startling my brain, stomach, and puzzling my senses. I entered the house and gasped at the huge peanut butter jar sitting on the kitchen table; I wanted to know what store it came from. Everyone was amused; they repeatedly removed my glasses and put them back on to convince me it was the usual peanut butter jar.

I spent the afternoon in the backyard marvelling at nature, little things like bees, flies and ants, the huge houses and trees in the neighbourhood, flitting birds, butterflies and leaves drifting on the breeze. I was enthralled with the immense sun and the vast expanse of scalloped clouds. As evening approached I was in for more shocks.

The family sat down for dinner as usual. Being a bit clumsy, I worried about handling the large spoon and fork. As mom sliced hard-boiled egg on top of my spinach, I commented it must have been a really big chicken. My slices of ox tongue looked like enough for three people. I would never be able to drink all my glass bucket of milk.

After dinner I fingered through large magazines, noticing details in the pictures I had never seen before. For long periods I sat admiring my big strong hands and feet. When the women finished the kitchen work, grandma said:

***

'Come Roberto, we go into the yard.'
'Where are we going?'
'Only into the yard'

As the family traipsed into the back yard, the gigantic steps got the best of me and I fell off the last one. I was not hurt. Mom helped me to my feet. As I looked up I was amazed.

'Oh my-gosh, the moon has grown!'
'No Robby, it's the same moon; look at it with your glasses off.'
'Wow, what are all those tiny white dots?'
Grandma smiled, 'I told you so, he has never seen the stars!'

I sat on the ground for a long time, staring at the stars and talking to the moon. I have often remembered that night when I have been out on my yacht on a night cruise, or when camping up in the mountains. At night, the moon, planets and twinkling stars still instil a sense of awe in me. Besides providing fascination, the universe has numerous influences upon us.

Solar flares leap thousands of miles into space affecting the earth's weather, our temperaments and bio-rhythms and even our electrical energy systems. Solar light is the source of life for flora and fauna that provides our food. The moon's phases control the ebb and flow of our oceans and the timing of the female menstrual cycle. Every year astronomy and astrophysics discover more effects on our planet and its life systems, arising from distant heavenly bodies.

Weak Natural Relations – Nature has always been the home of animals, including humans - until last week. Suddenly, humans in a fit of confusion, gave up the grasslands, forests and mountains, to live in the city. The 'Qatsi Trilogy' films by Godfrey Reggio, depicts human alienation from nature's harmonious, balanced existence. Matters have been made worse by the loss of the communal lifestyle. Today's individual truly has no home no genuine connection with family.

My dad had a low opinion of cities; he referred to apartment buildings as rabbit hutches. Of course, no self-respecting bunny would be caught dead in a hutch system; only those too dumb to figure out how to get back to their country burrow. If you attempt to raise goldfish in a sandbox, parakeets in an aquarium, or cows on a tree limb, then your family is going to have you committed. We accept other animals are best in their specific environments; why people think they can live removed from their natural habitat is beyond me.

***

"The most destructive aspect of cities is the profound schism created between human beings and nature. In a human made environment, surrounded by animals and plants of our choice, we feel ourselves to have escaped the limits of nature. Weather and climate impinge on our lives with far less immediacy. Food is often highly processed and comes in packages, revealing little of its origins in the soil or tell-tale signs of blemishes, blood, feathers or scales. We forget

the source of our water and energy, the destination of our garbage and sewage. We forget that as biological beings we are as dependent on clean air and water, uncontaminated soil and biodiversity as any other creature. Cut off from the sources of our food and water and the consequences of our way of life, we imagine a world under our control and will risk or sacrifice almost anything to make sure our way of life continues."

Excerpt from 'The Sacred Balance' by David Suzuki reprinted with permission from Greystone Books Ltd.

* * *

People have a one-sided relationship with our planet; nature provides and humans take. In the process, we pollute (air, acid rain, subterranean water tables, rivers, lakes and oceans). We abuse the botanical realm, drive fauna into extinction and litter the vacuum of space with technological garbage. A break from genetic endowment is evident in those who do not know how to swim and others who are afraid of being in the water or the forest.

Our divorce from the natural world is evident in urban populations striving for achievement and progress; while ignoring maintenance functions. Vast numbers of humans are physically unfit, emotionally insecure and mentally confused, unable to decide their fate or to run their lives successfully.

History warns us. Populations who ignore their place in the natural scheme are eventually over-come with diseases, famines, wars and human chaos. If this continues then our planet may be taken back to the insufferable heat, toxic atmosphere and barren landscape of her violent youth.

Building - ties with nature requires removing obstructions. There is no 'G' or 'AM' genetic priming for city living; humans are geared to live in forests, mountains and on the plains. The message is clear, get out of town. The human sensory system requires stimulation from the relationships available in nature. These needs are as crucial as the need for social interaction and a night's sleep. Fulfilling them helps one to behave naturally in a relaxed manner without deceit or exaggeration. Addressing these needs leads to a more productive and sane way of living. This may alter career choice and reduce financial income but the benefits of living in nature far outweigh financial concerns. Money cannot buy love, health or happiness.

There is a myth that cities increase communication between people, leading to greater creativity and advancement of society. This runs counter to sociological studies and my experience showing more contact and communication amongst rural folks than urban people. If the communal group had prevailed down through history, today's cities would be collections of Circles and Constellations. Wherein, interpersonal communication would be at a stupendously high level, producing far greater innovation. Cities are a boon only for the power elite.

Moving out of the city to nature may entail long term planning. In the meantime, weekends and holidays can be devoted to visiting diverse topographical wilderness settings. This will help adjust the kids' brain filters and teach them multiple skills. By age twelve children could be able to camp with small groups of their friends, some distance from the adults' campsite. By age fifteen they can spend a week alone in the wild setting, minus the smart phone, tablet and electronic games. They will develop an appreciation of the flora and fauna, plus a confident sense of where they fit into nature. Back at home, children should be living, playing and sleeping amidst plants, water and animals

As you prepare to move back into nature, scrutinize other cultures. Vanuatu tribes mark off a garden site and plant a coconut tree when a child is born. As the child grows there are additions to her garden and she obtains domestic livestock (chickens-pigs…). She begins working her garden at an early age. By age ten she can identify and understand the life cycle of the local flora and fauna. She can prepare basic meals. By adulthood she has a reliable source of food and building materials, plus a wealth of survival skills. This approach nurtures a close bond between humans, flora and fauna. It also enhances personal identification and security.

Migrating to another area of the planet may be necessary. Having large financial resources will usually gain admittance anywhere. When wealth is lacking and the usual immigration channels are problematic, there often are other circuitous routes. Visit the local and research possible avenues. Learning another language and new occupational skills could be a prerequisite.

There could be several ideal places for your group; in which case, rotating amongst them during the year or lifetime is an option. This way of living is in our very genes, our ancestors were nomadic.

It might help to scan your collective unconscious (AM) to discern what lifestyle characteristics you have inherited. Is a person predisposed to flourish in an explicit geographical setting? Would a Native American infant growing up in the Kalahari adapt as well as a bushman's infant?

Let's review priorities when selecting a Hub site.

Animals - A suitable Hub building site must meld into a natural environment that includes the presence of local fauna. Wild and domesticated animals are part of the human heritage and a vital element in the ongoing welfare of the homo sapiens species. Regardless of where you reside, whether it be a modern contemporary society, a survivalist group, a Stellar age Hub or a Martian colony, involvement with animals is inescapable and desirable.

The family must avoid dangerous animal territories. Decades ago conservation efforts increased grizzly bear numbers in the Rocky Mountains; with resulting threats to the local humans. Crocodile protection in Australia has had similar results.

I watched with sadness a TV interview of a mid-aged couple holidaying in Australia's Northern Territory. Their teenage daughter had been sitting on a pontoon jutting into the local river when a croc leapt up and took her. Modern humans tend to view wilderness areas as being un-owned. Debating this issue with a Grizzly, elephant or crocodile is a no-no.

Little critters can be just as problematic; Australia claims to have the world's largest range of poisonous spiders and snakes. This is of concern to me because of my poor eyesight and I do not want to lose my dog. Walking between trees and shrubs on the property I run into cobwebs and end up with bites that swell up and itch for a week. So far, I have avoided the deadly spiders.

Our property has the red bellied black snake and the occasional deadly brown snake, generally neither is a problem. Keeping the lawns mowed short helps. Snakes are highly visible in short grass and subject to attack from the meat-eating Kookaburras and butcherbirds.

Australia has eight hundred species of birds and I reckon the butcherbirds are one of the most aggressive. Their hooked beak tip tears apart the flesh of its victims. They get their name from the habit of hanging/ their victims on a tree branch or thorn (as your butcher hangs a carcass) to be consumed at their leisure. They prey on small lizards, snakes, insects and will catch small birds in flight. They love Theo's dog food and will eat it out of my hand or catch it mid-air.

Several summers ago, I stepped over the ditch leading into the dam and mid-air saw a metre-long brown snake beneath me. I nearly did the splits, with my foot coming down a half-meter from the snake. He struck, but was a couple inches short of my leg. He quickly slithered into the ditch and disappeared.

Last summer I was on my knees weeding around a mango tree when Theo yipped her 'pay attention to me' message. I looked up; she was ten meters away staring at me. Then she began furiously digging in a hole in the old petunia bed. I ignored her and went back to weeding. She yipped again. I looked up as she reached into the hole, trying to pick up something. I got up and went over. I could see a lizard's tail in the hole. I told her to leave it alone. I had my leather work gloves on, so reached down to get the lizard so it could run away. I hesitated, looked closely and thought 'could be a snake tail'. I got the shovel, and sure enough scooped out a red bellied black snake. It attempted to slide off into the tall grass, but its' rear section was a bit chewed up. I put it out of its' misery. It is amazing Theo didn't get bitten; it certainly would have killed her.

Neighbours claim the battery powered electronic snake repelling devices are effective. A friend suggested I buy a sacrificial Jack Russel or other small terrier, as they are well known snake killers. As the dog ages and its reflexes are slower, a snake will eventually nail the dog, which would definitely make me feel guilty of murder. Authorities claim most snake bites occur in city suburbs. Let us examine other safety issues.

Safety – Survival requires a location out of harm's way, free of threats from the geography, geology, weather and people.

The geographical home site should not be near air, water or sound pollution. Urban air pollution claims life every year. A Mexican study of urbanites found a large percentage had impaired air ways and blood vessel damage. Brain inflammation was common across all age groups. Most alarming were the persistent brain lesions in children that impaired their memory, problem solving and judgment.

Other studies have found pollution damages the bodies' telomeres; leading to early aging. It makes you wonder if the world will evolve into two populations, a mentally and physically fit rural group and a group of halfwit physically disabled city dwellers?

* * *

A clear October morning, wind behind me, the 140% genoa unfurled, I glide south along the broad estuary doing four knots. My eyes scan the banks and every floating log; it would be nice to see a crocodile in the wild, but I only spot a few cormorants and herons. The bow swings up Graham's creek and the sail luffs. I pay out the head sheet, haul in the furling line and scramble to the foredeck as the ship slows to a stop. I release the anchor winch and the hook plunges to the bottom. Reckon I'll spend a few days in this pristine setting, one of my favourite anchorages along the Australian east coast, now for some crabbing and fishing before dark.

This morning I'm feeling pretty content, with a cup of Earl Grey and glass of fresh orange juice. A little plump from last night's meal of jasmine rice and butter drenched mud crab. The boat is covered with black soot; the morning dew washes it into grey pools along the deck, I probably ought to wear a breathing mask, like Asians in big cities. I am seven miles from Gladstone, the coal shipping port; obviously I'm not far enough away.

* * *

Generally, I find the auditory output of the sea and forest to be musical and pleasing; however, some natural sounds can be annoying. Once I lived in a house where my bedroom was 3 meters from a pond. During frog mating season the croaking would begin at dusk and build to a din that lasted till dawn.

Another time I lived across the street from a family with a mulberry tree in their front yard. When the fruit was ripe, the flying fox fruit bats came at dark and spent the night feasting on the berries, their constant loud squabbling was horrendous. One night I was lying in bed trying to ignore the ruckus, when all of a sudden, the owner of the tree screamed out 'shut up' and slammed his window. For five seconds all was quiet then the racket resumed.

On Saturday mornings my next-door neighbour put his caged pet cockatoo on the vacant lot between our houses, as far away from his house as he could get, which meant the bird was only 3 meters from my house. It would see me and begin squawking, 'Hello, hello, how are you, no worries, no worries.' Waltzing Matilda was sung incessantly. It imitated the other neighbour's barking dog; you could not tell whether it was the dog or the bird barking. The bird's squawking attracted wild cockatoos, soon there would be twenty of them rustling about in the trees and feeding in the grass. The cacophony of noise was unbelievable. If you had been out late the previous night, you were in serious trouble. There was no way you could sleep through the hullabaloo.

Noise pollution creates emotional stress and diminishes mental efficiency. Prior to finalizing on a chosen Hub location, check with governmental agencies to see if they have given permission in the general local for the building of an industrial site, or they plan to construct a freeway or some other noxious installation.

I love the rolling coastal plains, forested mountains and friendly people of Chili; however, the nation sits astride the 'ring of fire,' the juncture of geological plates in the earth's crust. Such areas are prone to frequent earthquakes and volcanic eruptions which destroy property and take lives. Japan, New Zealand, Iceland… have the same liability.

My mid-west United States upbringing gave me a keen awareness of mother-nature's powerful weather systems. Cabin fever is a reality when trapped in the house for 3 months of sub-freezing outdoor temperatures. Then summer comes and you are ever alert for that threatening dark swirling vortex of wind that heralds death and destruction. I remember the sick in the gut feeling and cold chills when I watched a funnel careen across a rural township uprooting huge trees, sucking the water out of ponds and obliterating barns and houses. A neighbour related how his father had been thrown out of his airborne car as a tornado swept it high into the air, his flailing body fell to earth, where it was impaled on a picket fence.

Cyclones regularly clobber the south-sea islands. I asked a young divorced Vanuatu mother of two what hardship would occur if her thatched home was blown away?

'Mum and I build again.'
'How long would that take?'
'Tre maybe four weeks.'

Simplistic home construction from natural products allows south sea islanders to survive most cyclones with minimal hardship. The severe cyclone of February 2015 was an exception, leaving Vanuatu's infrastructure in ruin. In February of 2016 a cyclone devastated the Fijian archipelago.

Australia suffers during the hot summer months when bush fires destroy entire villages, people and all. These are often followed by monsoon floods devastating the environment and also taking lives. In western society buildings are complex constructions assembled from expensive manufactured materials; it can take years and massive amounts of money for a western community to re-cover from a natural disaster.

Choosing to live in an area free of weather hazards is wise, but you will still have to contend with human threats. Half the population of a city will be similar to you and thus easier to understand and get along with, without significant threats to safety. A percentage will have neurotic problems and could pose safety issues, the depressed, silly, shopping addicts, hyper-actives and so on. Approximately 3% of the inhabitants have mental disabilities that might adversely affect you. 10 percent or so are financially disadvantaged and desirous of your possessions. Then of course there are the dangerous drivers, feuding families, organized crime, politicians, cops, druggies and a host of others who could pose a threat. Is the city worth the danger? That is your decision to make. Living in a rural community of three hundred or less will free you from most human threats. Country people tend to stick together and support each other.

Emotional stress is as much a threat to your safety as physical threats. Be wary of land areas (usually border areas or islands) whose ownership is a contentious issue between two nations. Likewise, locales inhabited by a single ethnic or racial group could be problematic. Do your research. In reality, complete safety is un-obtainable.

Life Sustaining Environment – Artic cold and equatorial heat threaten life; a pleasant year around temperature supports life. From birth to mid-life I lived cooped up five months a year trying to keep warm. Huge fuel bills, costly clothing and imported food made for an expensive life style; quite a contrast to my present life in Queensland where heating and clothing are not necessary. Starting in December I get to loaf for three months, you cannot work in 38C/100F plus heat. You just keep the faith that the bush fires don't get you. It cools down a bit when the monsoon rains and floods come.

In North America I used to worry what would happen if heating fuel was not available. The ducks and geese had more sense; they flew south for the winter. I could only afford to do that for a week or two, usually visiting some Caribbean island. On one such trip my inquisitiveness led me to meet some of the residents in a shanty town.

***

Lola, a lowly paid janitress makes her way home up the slope of tin and tar paper shacks, toting a bag of fried chicken. Crouching, she enters the small hovel to the embrace of her nine-year old daughter. They share the shack with Carmen, Lola's sister and her eight-year old daughter. All sit down to their evening meal of chicken and water brought up from the tap at the bottom of the hill. Both daughters have unusually voluptuous breasts for their age, resulting from many fried chicken meals. The baby chicks were given huge doses of hormones to speed growth.

The shack lacks plumbing or electricity. A five-gallon rusty bucket sits on the dirt floor in the corner with a black garbage bag over its top; it's the toilet. At night they sleep on old carpets, mats and rags on the floor as the rats come and go. In spite of the hardships, they are a happy group. This setting is not natural, safe nor sustaining. When cruising in the south pacific I encountered natives living in an excellent setting.

Sailing amidst the Vanuatu archipelago I was impressed with the friendliness of the locals and their self-sufficient life style. First world folks consider these natives poor, as they have few material possessions. I think they are rich in the quality of their life. The twenty-year old in Western society endures great stress trying to obtain a career, food, clothing and transportation. He then faces a lifetime of fulltime work to pay for a thirty years mortgage and maintenance of his way of life; all the time he lives under the threat that he could lose his job at any moment and be plummeted into poverty.

The south pacific child receives a garden plot at birth; as a young person they work a few hours each week in the garden, a few hours tending their free-range chickens, cattle, and pigs, and some time crabbing and fishing. The year around warm climate negates the need for clothes or weather tight housing and insures a ready supply of flora and fauna resources. You can breathe deeply here the ocean breezes are clean.

***

A home site needs to be self-sufficient in food, water, shelter, clothing and energy. Good soil is needed for growing fruit, vegetables, grain, grasses and timber. The local Queensland soil is primarily clay and low in nutrients. I dug a metre of this worthless soil out of the vegetable garden and replaced it with high grade top soil, sand, mushroom compost, cane mulch, cow manure, garbage compost and alfalfa. Our new garden soil is friable, moisture retaining, easy to work with and produces high yielding crops.

Here in the sub-tropics; my love of fruits is satisfied with mangos, bananas, lychees, oranges, tangerines, nectarines, peaches, apples, star fruit, loquat, custard apples... A host of vegetables keep the diet in balance; while kangaroos, wallaby's, wombats, echidnas, parrots and reptiles keep life interesting, and could meet my protein needs in times of crisis.

Housing – At the present time the onsite construction of Hub accommodation must bear in mind the coming civil unrest; the Hubs location should be at least a two day walk from the nearest large town and not adjacent to rail lines, nor major highways. Consider defensible housing similar to historic communal groups. Minimal ground entrances are wise. An elevated site adjacent to a protective barrier (wall, waterway…) has merit. Bear in mind, the invasion of needy hordes has already begun in Europe and the Pacific basin.

Hub members may select an abode style incorporating the elements of the groups' personality and preferred environment. Natural building materials such as stone, mud brick, and concrete are safer than flammable wood structures and are preferred as they lower costs.

The Neolithic in ground dwelling offers significant financial savings and other advantages in a cold or hot climate. The South Sea post and beam structures with roll up mat walls are inexpensive and great in a tropical temperature. Have a look at the book *Home Work* by Lloyd Kahn, a photographic display of hand-built shelters around the world. Many of these are constructed from naturally available materials, blending into the surrounding environment.

I prefer a dwelling with separate rooms where I can cloister myself away. Others fancy the open design where several adjacent rooms meld into each other. You may be rapt with two stories or split level; another personality might select the raised Queensland styles with verandas on four sides. Have fun selecting the best type of abode for you and your family.

When building the cottage, I made frequent trips to the recycle dumps and demolition yards on the fringe of the city; where I found an amazing amount of useful building materials for a pittance of money. Used furniture shops and pawn shops can keep house out fitting costs down. The Brisbane city council sets aside one day a year, when the trash trucks drive about picking up anything placed on the curb. This is the time to rise early in the morning and drive through the wealthy neighbourhoods, where you will find an absolute treasure trove of free goods. Be sure to take your trailer and tie down ropes.

The civil unrest decimation of the population will leave behind plentiful buildings and a wealth of building materials. One might convert empty apartment blocks, warehouses and manufacturing plants into Hub accommodation or Circle service centres. Vacant lots could be used for food/timber production, native animal habitat and recreation areas. In the rural areas a Hub or two might occupy an empty village or farm, which already contains much of the needed infrastructure and cleared fields.

Energy – A dwelling needs energy - sun, wind, water, and thermal are all excellent natural power sources, but only under certain circumstances. Research the pros and cons of alternative energies. It is hard to beat the soul soothing comfort of trees, nature's re-chargeable batteries. They provide - shade in the summer, warmth in the winter, light at night, beauty in the day, fresh air and fruit, fuel to cook your food and heat your dwelling, a windbreak, housing for animals and man, and come with built in bird song.

Our forebears spent many years living in trees; this has imbued the 'G' and 'AM' to prefer abode positions with a view. As a youngster I spent hours climbing and sitting in trees. I still like climbing trees. Consider spending time weekly sitting in a tree; it might surprise you.

Here in the sub-tropics, it took me a while to accept cutting down banana trees. Once the tree produces a bunch of bananas, you have to cut down the tree, so a new tree can grow from the roots of the old tree.

Decision Time - When you find a spot that meets your qualification criteria and gives you a sense of belonging and happiness; arrange to live there for six months. If you have made a mistake, you will know it shortly. This means a bit of upheaval, but you would have learned much and you will be wiser in making your second choice.

Having selected your living environment, learn from the local life forms and inanimate elements. Strive for a sense of harmony and belonging. Once in a while, set aside a time to focus on a small natural segment, a tree, rock, ant..., and advise your vacuum hose censors to filter out any stimuli not associated with the object of your attention. Your awareness will expand to perceive all the nuances of that small world. This is likely to bring forth new realizations, ideas and questions which enrich your life. Your ancestors profited from this type of keen awareness to successfully live in the wilds; 99% of human history has been spent living in the natural environment.

***

Pine needles cushion my footsteps as I tread the game path deeper and deeper into the luxuriant forest; the trees whisper, birds sing, the fragrant breeze fills my nostrils. I come upon a gurgling stream flowing over rocks into a clear pool that reflects the blue sky and clouds above. Knelling, I place a supporting hand on a soft moss-covered rock, my other hand cups the cool water, I drink.

***

Development of PELGAMs is dependent on a natural environment. I prefer a dwelling on a knoll with a hill or stand of trees as a protective backdrop, with a vista of rolling grasslands, forests and water; populated by a wealth of flora and fauna. Being nomadic I prefer a change in local as the seasons or my mood changes. At times I seek out ocean beach to draw upon the sea's rich food resources and entertainment activities like boating and swimming. Other times I enjoy the mountains with the panorama of snow covered peaks and cascading waterfalls feeding into fish filled streams that meander across the valley floor.

CONCLUSION

The Norwegian philosopher Arne Naess was adamant that humanity was an integral part of the environment. Studies have supported his theories and shown our best functioning can only be achieved in a natural

281

environment. Emily Anthes reported on research that revealed students in classrooms overlooking natural settings such as gardens, parks, fields, trees, lakes and mountains scored higher on academic tests than students in classrooms overlooking parking lots and buildings. *'Building around the Mind' Scientific American MIND Vol. 20, #2, April 2009*

Volume XIII of the *'Journal of Therapeutic Horticulture'* contains a research article indicating plants were effective in reducing anxiety level, improving mood and creativity, and restoring stamina after fatigue.

The relationship with nature is a two-way street as shown by researcher Daniel Benor. He has brought together research results showing how human thoughts significantly impact single celled organisms, seeds, plants, insects & animals.

From a very early age I was aware of my affinity for plants, animals and nature's wildness. As time progressed, I took every opportunity to escape the pavement, the calamity, the falseness of the societal display.

In my twenties I vacationed in the Smoky Mountains. Standing atop Clingmans Dome, I acquired an appreciation of our planet's beauty. The downwardly rolling slopes of trees interspersed by tumbling brooks and over flown by various types of birds was captivating. The scenario lies in complete contrast to my recent cruise of New Caledonia with its mile upon mile of denuded mountain ranges. Mining bauxite is their major industry.

During undergraduate days I worked two jobs during the summer break. 7:00am to 3:00pm in a clinical psychology research lab and 3:30pm to midnight as a janitor in a factory that made soft ice cream machines. Friday nights they tested the machines made during the week. I sampled so much soft ice cream, that by the end of the summer I couldn't stomach the stuff and don't like it to this day. We used a bit of the money from the two jobs to finance a small vacation.

Mom offered her Plymouth fury as well as some financial support, given she could come along. My wife, six-year-old daughter, mother and I set out for the Rockies. I did most of the driving, which thoroughly wore me out. The term 'Great Plains' is a gross under-statement; hour after hour for two days, the straight slightly undulating road cuts its swath through unending fields of corn or wheat. I could now believe that the plains once supported one hundred million head of bison.

***

'There they are! There they are!'
I said. 'No that's not them, it's just a bank of clouds.'
'I agree with Mom, that's the Rockies.'
'Well ok.' I said. 'You guys have better eyes than me. But I still think it's clouds.'

***

After another two hours of driving, even I could see the north to south line of the Rockies. We stopped for lunch at a diner in a small town, a couple miles off the highway. There was a buffalo head mounted on one

283

wall and the opposite wall held a jack rabbit head sprouting antelope horns. Apparently, some western critters like sexual diversity.

Lunch finished, we drove for hours and hours and the mountains never seemed to get any closer. As dark closed in we finally arrived at Estes Park Colorado, the gateway to Rocky Mountain National Park. I had done all the driving, only getting four hours sleep in the past two days. I was completely exhausted. I haggled with the owner of a group of cabins and after taking a leak dropped into bed. In the background my family was muttering that I had been rude to the owner. I never claimed to be perfect.

Our time in the Rockies was fantastic; we saw mule deer, antelope, mountain sheep, mountain goats and marmots. The mountain's splendour is on view from many lookouts; on a clear day, for as far as you can see, it is snow-capped mountains. We had snowball fights, made snowmen and slid down snowy slopes on our butt.

During graduate school and after, I backpacked much of the Rockies and always felt as if it were a special place, perhaps a holy place. It is certainly awe inspiring. My brother Phil lived most of his life outside Golden Colorado, a good spot for a hunter and fisherman. I had a laugh once when he told me about a Swiss Alps documentary he saw on TV.

Scowling he said, 'Why would anybody go there? Their mountains are not as high as ours and Colorado alone has seventeen times more mountains than Switzerland!'

I have to say something about the Grand Canyon, it is breath-taking. I have been there several times but was too lazy to walk the cliff face trail down into the canyon and didn't trust the donkeys enough to ride them down. When I finished my Ph.D. at Utah State University, my mother flew out for the graduation. While she visited, we drove her to Las Vegas and the Grand Canyon. At the canyon she got out of the car and wobbled on her phlebitis legs over to the lookout. She looked this way and that, tapped the ashes off her cigarette and simply said 'Well that's not so much.' I was speechless.

Throughout my life I have continued my adventures into many of our planet's awesome features: the cliffs of Dover, Swiss Alps, Rock of Gibraltar, the Atlas and Andes Mountains, Sahara-desert, jungles of Costa Rica, the South Pacific and Asian archipelagos, and many others. These travels have engendered in me a sense of wonder and belonging. This planet is my home; affronts to the natural world of our planet are attacks I take personally.

At this point in life I'm missing the forests and lakes of Michigan and Ontario. Plus, their wild inhabitants – deer, elk, moose, bear, raccoon, the lovely Canadian goose and of course, the silly chipmunk. No longer owning a boat, has made my nostalgia worse. I often dream of getting another vessel and cruising some of the areas I never got to do. Such as the Trent-Severin waterway, Rideau canal and the Thousand Island areas of Canada.

At the societal level every citizen can help our return to nature by not patronizing businesses that are destructive to the natural realm, and pushing the government to reduce the population, de-centralize, eliminate large cities and restore the health of the natural environment. Legislation will need to limit the land occupied by humans. Much of the land and resources stolen from other species needs to be returned.

It would help matters if the media cutback its' negative output and drew more attention instead to examples of positive progress. It would be uplifting to hear about thriving communal groups, reduction in personal debt, greater numbers of happy, multi-skilled and well-rounded citizens. Such media would boost social cohesion, raise community morale and motivate people to strive for their goals.

Books and videos are a good means of learning about the natural world. Familiarize yourself with the plants that provide our food and oxygen, remove carbon dioxide and build our soil. Weekly traipsing into the richness of nature for short solitude periods gives one a chance to hear and feel the voice of the planet and all its natural inhabitants. It may turn on the genes that were shut down as man abandoned his original home. Such experiences drive home the importance of interconnectedness with nature, fellow humans, and all existence. It helps create a sense of contentment; an awareness that one is a shining star amidst a magical universe.

No matter how exquisite and satisfying your home, you are not designed to hide away in its' confines. The fields and streams, mountains and oceans, the starry firmaments beckon; your fulfilment lies in assuming your place as a participant in the natural realm of our planet. A natural setting is your default abode due to your specie's history and the genes you possess. Consider going home.

Chapter 13 Interpersonal Relation Ship PELGAM

My god.
If I could be like my god
Who on any given day
Loves every single person
Who comes her way.

FAUNA, HUMAN

The interpersonal relation-ship PELGAM allows a person to sail out of individual isolation into the communal world, opening a myriad of possibilities to interact with other humans and other species. It can be witnessed in the fullness of intimacy amongst adults, the togetherness of a family, chatting friends, symbiotic communities and the love of a pet. First, we will investigate impoverished relationships and their consequences with fauna, then with people. Finally moving on to rich relationships and how to build them.

RELATIONS WITH FAUNA

Impoverished - fauna relationships are an endemic feature of the un-natural human who gave up nature to reside in a false man-made world. His primary concern with animals is how to use the creature for his own benefit. It is not necessarily an attitude of dislike for animals; they are seen as un-thinking, emotionless objects like rocks or fallen branches. A dead bear provides a carpet, clothing, or a wall hanging. Cows, pigs, chickens, tuna and whales are a rich source of food. Elephant ivory makes nice ornaments.

High rise occupants are only familiar with venues where animals do not exist - the apartment, local shopping strip and entertainment settings. Slum dwellers face a similar lack of contact with animals. Stray dogs and cats are quickly eaten and the residents do not have the money to visit the zoo, parks or the rural scene. City folk are all too familiar with the common rat and often regard all animals as being dirty and problematic. This can produce anxiety, unreasonable fears and abusive attitudes towards animals. Mistreatment of other species is a societal problem. The "Society for the Prevention of Cruelty to Animals" (SPCA) addresses this problem.

Suburban governments demand vacant lots, drainage ditches and parks be kept tidy; thus, they provide no habitat or protection for animals. This leads to an 'extinction of experience' thus named by Robert Pyle in his book *The Thunder Tree*. In this situation local residents have no experience with fauna. Therefore, as Pyle points out, you cannot expect people to have empathy for a creature of which they have no knowledge.

RICH Fauna Relationships – facilitated human evolutionary success, canines, beasts of burden, cats, birds and other species. These associations continue in the present; dogs are hunters and herders, horses, mules, donkeys and llamas are ridden or carry loads, cormorants capture fish and eagles hunt. Cattle, chickens, pigs and sheep often exceed human numbers. A Boston bull terrier pup greeted me at my birth; we were inseparable until she died of illness when I was five. At the age of six we moved from Springfield, Ohio to a large rural house outside Niles, Michigan. One exciting day, dad brought home chickens and bales of straw.

I spread the straw around the coop and in the nesting boxes, repeatedly putting hens in the boxes, hoping to get an egg. Every day after walking home from the little red brick three room school house, I fed the chickens their 'chicken mash' from a burlap bag. It was pretty good stuff, had a unique taste. I continued placing the hens in the nests; they had more patience with me than I did with them. I finally gave up, and weeks later they started laying eggs.

One Easter, each of us kids were given a bunny; I loved holding and stroking those soft cuddly bundles. Their pellet food left a terrible taste in your mouth.

One of my chores in the family was to fetch the butter. Mom gave me the proper coins and I trudged through the snow to farmer Carnes down the road. He took me through the barn where I said hello to his dairy cattle, then into an adjoining shed. Lifting the lid from an old wooden tub, he used a flat wooden paddle to dig out a gob of butter. This was slapped onto some old newspapers and rolled up. On the walk home, fingers would slip into the delicious butter; I'm still fond of butter.

At the end of the day during the summer months I often brought the dairy cattle back to the barn from the pasture. I was a real cowboy, wearing my huge ten-gallon hat that had a habit of falling down over my eyes. I pulled the lead cow up to the wood rail fence, clambered up the fence and onto her back. We ambled towards the barn with the herd following. Mr. Carnes would lift me off, complementing me on a job well done.

I wonder if that had anything to do with me being fond of dairy products. I daily drank two quarts of milk right up to midlife. Oh! How I used to love dunking doughnuts in milk. A quart of milk and a dozen chocolate chip cookies is a great afternoon snack.

Occasionally I visited Kent, a school chum down the road. His family used draft horses on their farm and nursery. I loved the warmth and smell of horses and stables full of fragrant hay and straw. We would lead a couple of these monsters up to a fence, scramble up the fence, throw a blanket on its' back and hop on.. These critters were so broad my legs stuck out straight.

Daisy, my usual steed, would not run, but she steered well. Once I was sitting too far up her neck, when she bent down for a drink from the pond. I tumbled down her neck into the water. Bewildered, I sat in the water; Daisy looked at me as if to say, 'Why did you do that?'

In adolescence my younger brother Phil and I raised pigeons: tumblers, rollers, homing, French mondaines and others. Each bird had its' own personality. A pair of bronze Shetty's hatched a little fellow of great courage; when you stuck your hand on the shelf to check the nest, this three-inch-high bundle of feathers rushed out to protect his home. Wings spread wide, he slapped your hand till you withdrew.

In adulthood, my brothers Phil, Don and myself kept up the hunting and fishing tradition of the family. Like Thoreau, I felt a special sense of excitement in being a predator. As a hunter pursuing game I felt at one with nature - just another carnivore out for the kill to fill my belly. It was especially true when hunting with Gods. I was a member of the pack and we worked together to get our quarry, assuming you had well trained Gods.

Marriage reduced but didn't stop the hunting trips; my wife came from a hunting family. When our daughter was a toddler we purchased Mel, a twelve months old basset hound, from a couple living in an apartment. I figured he would make a good pet for our little girl and a hunting companion for me. One evening a week later, our daughter toddled up behind Mel as he was eating and grabbed a hunk of skin on his back. Being too far away to reach them I hollered at her to get away from the dog. She proceeded to twist Mel's skin; he growled, she twisted, he turned and snapped, coming an inch short of her hand. She twisted more and he went back to eating. We knew then he would never hurt her.

You could hear Mel's howl miles away; this no doubt annoyed the neighbours but no one called the police. He was a lovable house pet and a joy for our daughter. I should have left it at that and never have taken him hunting.

I spent at least a hundred hours training him, laying scent trails of rabbits or pheasants. No problem, he could follow any trail faster than you could keep up with him. It was obvious he was going to be a first-rate hunting dog.

When hunting season opened, Phil came over with Lucky, his oversized German short hair. The goDs were put in the trunk of the car and we drove off to farmer Brown's on a warm autumn afternoon. We started in a field of corn rubble where we knew pheasants often fed. Lucky swung back and forth in front of Phil, but Mel refused to stay in front of me. He kept running over to play with Lucky. Phil got irritated, to say the least, and decided we should split up.

I took Mel off to another field bordering a wooded area. He worked for a while; then I lost sight of him. I called and called, no Mel. I skirted the woods and saw him lying in the shade of a tree. I didn't think it was that warm. I booted him in the butt and told him to get going. He worked ok for fifteen minutes and disappeared again; sure enough, I found him lying beneath a tree. This was one lazy goD.

As the hunting season progressed and the weather got colder, he improved slightly, pointing several pheasants and cottontails. He regularly disappeared and could always be found resting in some comfortable place. His last hunting trip was a corker.

293

Phil and I went different directions so Mel would not distract Lucky; shortly I lost sight of Mel. There were no shade trees around so I knew he would go find Phil and play with Lucky. I just kept on hunting and got two rabbits and a pheasant.

At the agreed upon time I headed back to the car knowing I was going to catch hell from my brother for Mel ruining his hunting. As we converged I noticed the back of my brother's hunting jacket was bulging and he was smiling; he had done well. Lucky was there but, no Mel. The thought crossed my mind – surely, he wouldn't shoot my goD!

'Where's Mel?' I asked.

He looked incredulous. 'How the hell would I know?'

We spent hours driving the countryside searching for my lazy God. Near dark we drove into a remote farm. An old lady was standing in her doorway holding two Chihuahuas.

'Bet you're looking for a hound dog?'

'You bet, I sure am.'

'He's out in the dairy barn, been playing with the cows all afternoon.'

The drive home was a stream of profanities and castigation from my brother about my stupid dog. After assuring my daughter we would get her another dog. I sold him to a young couple who did not hunt, they were happy and so was Mel.

A few weeks later Phil and one of his pals went hunting; Lucky broke into a farmer's chicken coop and killed 14. A week later Lucky mangled a neighbour's cocker spaniel. The police came, took one look at Lucky and jumped back into their patrol car. One more goD sold.

A couple of years later, Phil and I went hunting on a dull-grey miserable morning late in the season. Driving cold sleet stung the face, watered the eyes and numbed the fingers. The weather wasn't fit for man or goDs, so we left our goDs at home. Hunters know it is ok to mistreat yourself and even some people, but you never mistreat your goD.

Tromping through knee high icy wet grass is loads of fun. Thirty feet to my right Phil kicked up a bunny that ran in front of me; stopped and looked back at me. They do not like moving in these conditions as they get soaking wet and that's not good when it is freezing cold. I looked down the sights of my 12 gauge, at the bunny looking back at me, slowly squeezed the trigger and blew his head off.

The furry headless lump lay there, gushing blood over the wet icy grass. I shivered as a cold rivulet of water found its way down the back of my neck. What a hell of a way to die on such a miserable day, when all you wanted was to stay holed up warm and dry. I have not hunted since. I miss having guns and shooting and would have no qualms about shooting game for my survival if need be.

If you want a real adrenalin rush, exchange your role as a predator and become the prey. My wife, daughter, myself and friend Ron were hiking across a narrow cliff face trail headed for gun sight pass in the high peaks of Glacier national park. Rounding a bend, we came upon a grizzly foraging in the rocks below us, only a hundred feet away. My heart started racing as I looked for a tree to climb. But, there was only the narrow path ahead and behind us and the sheer cliff face above and below.

He looked at us, stood up in the attack position, the long hair on his back standing on end. His ten-foot stature wavered back and forth, a normal precursor to dropping on all fours for the attack. He realized he could not scale the fifty-foot cliff we were atop. In a flash he sped down hill through the boulders and out of sight, it was enough to make you soil your pants.

Here in Australia there is an over-abundance of small, hard to see dangerous critters. Occasionally I encounter poisonous brown snakes and red belly blacks on the property. Deadly spiders spin their webs between shrubs and trees. Once I fell off the dirt bike, landing on a nest of black bull ants, their ferocious attack was painful and left swollen welts on my legs and arms. Mosquitos that spread disease, flies that get into your eyes, ears and nose, and of course the ubiquitous cockroach, are all a part of fauna relationships.

A variety of parrots and other birds visit our veranda looking for a handout. If the food tray is empty, the King parrot will come squawking, begging for a hand out. Butcher birds sit on my knee and eat out of my hand. One afternoon one flew in and dropped a present; a baby snake.

My current canine Theo, a fluffy golden twelve-kilo bundle of affection, is a groodle (golden retriever-poodle cross). She loves jumping in the dam, retrieving sticks and chasing hares. She is fast on her feet and has the keenest nose of all the Gods I've had. Intelligence is another matter.

She was a hand-full her first eight months, doing as she pleased regardless of my disciplinary actions. I nicknamed her the blonde belligerent bitch, but she may just be a dumb blonde. On a chain she gets tangled and unable to free herself. By her first birthday she had calmed down and was more trainable. She now knows many tricks and obeys most of the time.

Being a retriever, she has a one-track mind, wanting to retrieve all day long - it is more important than eating. When I go outside she runs up with a stick in her mouth and follows me around as I work in the garden, her big brown eyes staring expectantly at me. If I am not there she will pester someone else. In hot weather she takes frequent breaks to cool off in the dam, promptly returning with her stick.

Her bed is arms-length away on the veranda. First thing every morning she snuggles in my lap while I have juice, tea, watch the wildlife

297

and contemplate the day ahead; this meets some of our physical contact needs. It does not last long as she is eager to say good morning to the other animals and play with someone. She has bonded with everyone in our group. When someone returns after as little as a half hour's absence, she greets them as if she has not seen them for a year.

Over the years I have had several riding horses. The feel of a warm powerful steed between your legs, the snorting, drumming of hooves and wind in the face is exhilarating. Chad, our palomino quarter horse, liked to play fetch with me. When I was working in the corral or pasture, she would nip my hat off, run over and throw it across the fence. If I didn't retrieve the hat, she would eventually sneak up behind me and nip my butt; she obviously liked to get a rise out of me. Somewhere down the road of time when I become old with shaky legs; I'm going to build a cart and get a horse or burro to pull me around the countryside.

Some people have poor relationship skills with people and attempt to correct the situation by relating to animals. Within equestrian circles it is common to find ladies afraid of relating to men; they feel safer investing their emotions in horses. Power personalities often have large dogs. Heaps of people only give their unabashed love to their pet.

Building Relationships - The Hub survival group must have dogs; they provide early warning of approaching enemies, protect Hub members, lift morale and assist in hunting. The survival Hub's food requirements can be more easily met, if a variety of livestock are maintained. Likewise, a new planet colony will need its chickens, pigs, cattle... and maybe fish. Since pets and other animals are so important to humans, it surprises me that they have not been a bigger part of our space missions.

When a newborn infant shares a house with family pets and has domestic livestock out the window, they are well on their way to forming good inter-species bonds. As the child grows, consider giving a pet to each child and some responsibility for the domestic critters. The rural children's 4-H clubs in the United States have good programs teaching the care of domestic and wild animals. The Australian pony clubs are similar.

Teach children at an early age to locate, identify, and understand the uses and habits of the local wild animals. They will enjoy learning to mimic sounds of the wild fauna. Volunteer work at zoos, veterinarian clinics and livestock farms, not only improves a child's relationship with animals, it also helps the child learn to value and respect life. This prepares them for successful relations with humans.

The Canadian author Farley Mowat has written many books that help a person understand nature, primitive peoples and animals. *Never Cry Wolf* is a good one for gaining insight into the canine world. Other writers have given us *The Year of the Gorilla*, *Gorillas in the Mist* and many interesting books on dolphins, birds, insects...

Human Relation Ships

Boats cannot move without water. The isolated hermit or prisoner cannot progress without people. Are those unable to maintain close interpersonal relationships, a lower form of life than a chimpanzee?

If we could go back fifty thousand years and visit hominid clans, I doubt we would comprehend the strength and intensity of their interpersonal relationships. For millions of years they lived in tight-knit communal groups; they were a team facing the dangers, joys and trivia of daily life. Together they hunted, worked, ate, slept and shared sex. Each member was a valuable asset to the group, playing their part in providing food, defence from predators, structure building and all the other survival tasks. The group's bonding and sense of togetherness allowed them to function almost as if they were a 'one.' This connectedness, this closeness may be comparable to what we see in present day soldiers who have endured combat together.

Westerners are big believers in free-will - they have a self-conscious belief that they are the ones in charge of how they think and behave. Recent decades of research decimated this belief system, finding genetic underpinnings for a great deal of homo sapiens behaviour. I further suspect the AM influences relationships. When two sub-conscious minds make contact, possibly sharing AM data, it will naturally result in an alteration of both parties' behaviour. All the while, the conscious mind may be oblivious to what is going on.

Genetically, humans are social creatures requiring lots of physical and emotional intimacy and light-hearted recreation time together. Satisfying interpersonal time involves mutual revelation and sharing of thoughts, emotions, interests and experience. Research shows these connections bring increased joy, energy, mental clarity and sense of self-worth. It facilitates the mating process, the career and obtaining a secure place in the community.

Good relationships are a matter of give and take. Developmental psychology has shown that parental giving to children without requiring something back (reciprocity) tends to produce unmotivated adults who expect the world to take care of them. Likewise, our society brings grievous harm to our children when we hold 'loners' up as models.

Human social skills are an information-processing system in the frontal lobes of the brain and are involved in the emergence of a person's 'self.' This is procedure of understanding who we are and what we are all about. It is most developed in leaders and those in the helping professions, yet its basis exists in all of us. It is vital if we are to value and accept ourselves and others. I will limit coverage to four areas of importance: family, friends, intimate partners and the community. First, let us review inadequate relations.

Poor Interpersonal Skills - The psychological literature suggests that an overemphasis on individuality separates the person from the communal group – the source of their vitality, self-identification and rationale for existence. The resultant aloneness/alienation is a major cause of psychological and physical health problems. It diminishes one's likelihood of a happy, successful life. In the survival Hub or space setting it could mean death.

The problem can begin in the womb as mother engages in detrimental interpersonal interactions, and it may continue after birth as parents, surrounding family, friends and the culture fail to provide good role models and training of interpersonal skills. Thus, the brain filters are improperly set in this regard.

This is represented by those who are shy, lacking friends, anti-social, and by those who are bullied or spend the bulk of their time in loner activities like computers and TV. Some have grown up in a strife-torn nuclear family that had significant problems with relatives, neighbours and little contact with people in the community. Poor relations are evident in the squabbles, conflicts and lack of progressive action within the political entities of the community. News broadcasts and televised parliamentary sessions make matters worse, presenting unbalanced dysfunctional interpersonal relationship role models.

To help those with poor social skills, the therapist must investigate the family and culture of upbringing. The problem's precipitating factors have to be determined and thoroughly understood, eventually leading to a primary, secondary and tertiary diagnosis. All of this is necessary in order to select from all available treatment plans the one most likely to help the client. However, determining causal factors is not a straightforward process; seemingly obvious clues may mislead the clinician to an inaccurate diagnosis.

A common illustration of this is a diagnosis of introversion based on observations and descriptions of behaviour. Introversion may simply be a defence mechanism rather than a diagnosis. For example, Alice came to the office complaining of loneliness, she said her husband Peter was shy and would not go out with her to social functions or community activities.

* * *

'At home he spends his free time with the garden vegetables and fruits or in his workshop. When I call him for dinner, he comes in the house, sits down and gobbles his food down, hardly saying a word. After the meal he plops down in front of the TV and watches science fiction or war movies until he falls asleep. At bed time I wake him so he can get in bed. I have more interaction with our dog.'

'Does he join you when you're out and about town?'

'He rarely goes to town with me to pay bills or do the shopping, and when he does he hurries along looking neither left nor right, I can hardly keep up with him. If we bump into someone I know, he smiles and is polite, but afterword's he has nothing good to say about them. I know better than to bring up issues in the community; he'll just rant and rave about all the bad things in life and say these people should be wiped out, killed or done away with.'

* * *

Somehow, Alice persuaded Peter into my office; he was polite and pleasant. I started with a non-threatening review of his work history. He had completed an apprenticeship in electrical maintenance work and was employed for years in the mines, where he lived by himself in a donga during the week, only coming home to the wife on weekends. His current job was in a manufacturing plant, where the foreman assigned his daily work on the equipment. This was the only human contact he had during the day.

In obtaining his early life history, he revealed a mother who kept herself in the house, rarely venturing into the community; she didn't trust anyone or anything. She was afraid of the dark, mice, insects and dogs. She often expressed fears that the landlord might throw them out of their rented house. As he gave further details of his upbringing and his own life, it became apparent that his introverted behaviour was the result of a paranoid personality. He probably learned most of this from his mother, although there could also be a genetic component. It is common for sons to acquire many of their mother's personality traits and daughters to pick-up personality aspects from their fathers.

His introverted behaviour was his method of coping with a world he saw as frightening. This paranoid based introvert behaviour lies in contrast to the introverted behaviour of others having a different base, Einstein for example.

Einstein's biographers and his own writings reveal a variant of introvert behaviour. His poor interpersonal relationship skills were in evidence in childhood where he refused to join in games with other children. Prior to entering school his parents hired a series of home tutors. He threw a chair at one and she left, never to return. He was rebellious in primary school. His university professors considered him argumentative and antagonistic.

He got his university sweetheart pregnant. She left town to have the baby, which was apparently given up for adoption. Einstein never met nor showed any interest in contacting the child. He married his sweetheart, but in married life he tended to keep to himself and was seen as being distant, confrontational, and harsh with his wife. He showed respect for some scientists, but often showed disdain and disrespect for those not in agreement with his own theories.

Others said you couldn't tell him anything. In his book *The World as I See It* he describes himself as possessing an adamant sense of detachment from people, not needing contact with individuals or communities.

The basis for his behaviour may be a combination of genetics and the impact of his mother. Pauline came from a wealthy family and may have passed on to him a snobbish attitude towards others. She was adamant in pushing her son to become successful and appears to have pampered him. He threw the wild temper tantrums often seen in spoilt children.

Einstein was born with a misshapen head and was slow in learning to speak, saying very little till age three. He remained quiet and uncommunicative till age seven and was not a fluent speaker at the age of nine. This lack of verbal language skills would have severely hampered the learning of interpersonal skills. Whether the verbal problem was the result of family dynamics, genetics, body chemistry or brain dysfunction is unknown. After his death, study of his brain found no significant differences between it and the brains of others.

Introversion may be a secondary diagnosis for Peter and Einstein; however, the primary diagnosis is apt to be a paranoid personality for Peter and narcissistic personality for Einstein. Both are illustrations of poor interpersonal relationship skills, and the use of escapism as a defence mechanism.

Peter escaped by choosing a career removed from people, avoiding social settings, pre-occupation with home chores and watching TV. Some anxious introverts escape into drugs, alcohol, computers and loner activities like fishing and hunting. Einstein escaped into the mental world of his thoughts and calculations, lab work, playing his violin and sexual affairs. Other narcissistic, ego centric personalities may limit their lives to the personal things they enjoy: sports, travel, hobbies...

Introversion is a process of turning off vacuum hoses, limiting incoming data, therefore limiting opportunities for learning experiences. Moreover, it curbs the ability to adapt to circumstances. Peter had experienced difficult times when his employment was terminated for reasons not related to him; introverts are usually dedicated employees. He seemed unable to grasp the idea that a company or the world might change and cause a termination in his employment. As far as he was concerned, he had been a hard worker and therefore should still be on the job. He was angry at 'those bastards' screwing up his life. His life was burdened with bitterness and a host of grudges.

When seeking new employment, he was confused and dis-organized about how to proceed. He had little understanding or interest in other people's needs and motivations. Job hunting for him was an excruciatingly painful and fearful task. If Alice had not been a weak, dependent personality she probably would have bowed out of the marriage early on.

Einstein was obsessional about his work and like Peter failed to learn many facets of daily life. Upon graduation from university he expected a university teaching position; no institution would hire him because of his reputation of being difficult to get along with. He lacked a sense of appropriate attire, and as a consequence his wives selected his clothing and what would be worn in a situation.

Einstein and Peter are part of the multitudinous masses that have inferior interpersonal relationship skills. Many of them attempt to fulfill the need for interpersonal relationships by meeting in the street, sports arenas, shopping malls... J.B. Jackson discusses this in *A Sense of Place, A Sense of Time.* The social sciences make it clear that the individual's social need for understanding, interconnectedness, commonality and togetherness, cannot be met by milling about amidst thousands of people.

My parents were poor models of relationship skills. Dad was an angry, paranoid social misfit who verbally and physically abused us four kids and mom. I didn't dare speak around him, for fear of being backhanded. A cold, aloof, indifferent mother rounded out our happy family. Neither parent had friends; it was rare to have a stranger in the house. Mom would pooh-pooh any concerns I raised; she would not partake in a give and take conversation.

The neighbourhood did not help matters; it was a combination of Jews, Catholics, fundamentalist Christians, university educated, school dropouts, factory rats and businessmen; I spent time in all these families and learnt a breadth of confusing relationship skills.

Moving into adulthood, this confusion was amplified as I became involved in a variety of activities, hobbies and world travel. Nonetheless, there was a positive outcome in that I learned how to be accepted in any social setting. The bad side was that I frequently felt frustrated, isolated and alone. Few of the people around me had personalities compatible with mine. University educated friends came from upper middle-class families; they had little comprehension of what it was like for me as a child living in fear of my brutal father and going to bed hungry. They had been financially supported by their families and had no grasp of what it had been like for me struggling to hold down a job and attend university at the same time.

My reaction to poor interpersonal training was to work doubly hard at getting along with people. Some people take the opposite approach, avoiding human contact if possible. Professionally I have seen countless numbers of them in the form of engineers, accountants, IT specialists…, suffering difficult relationships at home, on the job or in the community. Usually they were pleasant and easy to talk with, but I often got the impression they simply did not like nor trust me or anyone.

Myron Stolaroff, an engineer at a California university, comments on this issue in *Higher Wisdom.* He feels many engineers are sensitive people who early on in life have been so injured by others (generally family) they have chosen a career wherein they won't have to deal with people, only objects. But, of course, on a space mission they are trapped with people. Although, a businessman I know says that's not true; 'they are trapped with other objects.'

A few musicians are unable to emotionally invest in others; they express their emotions through their music. Pub crawling macho men may relate well with their kind, but be hopeless at relating with women or children.

Throughout the western world people are unable to conduct satisfactory face-to-face relations, to have close meaningful relationships; they are desperate to find someone who will listen, someone who cares. Riddled with fear and confusion about relationships, they latch onto electronic communication as it is safer and easier, which it is. Does it work? No.

Physical separation prevents the reading of body language which is an integral element of communication, particularly in intimate and friend relationships. Everyone is overflowing with verbiage, but are others listening? How many times have I seen a mobile phone held to the ear, as the person pivots, gazing at the surroundings and occasionally saying 'Yes!' into the phone. This method of interaction cannot fulfil emotional or social needs.

Social media has a potential to help overcome the social isolation inherent in the nuclear family if initial contacts are followed by regular in-the-flesh meetings where the individuals jointly participate in activities and share intimate personal information. This is how true friendships are built. When several of these friendships join together, they can form mutually satisfying groups and this helps satisfy the longing to belong.

I believe it is safe to say that most of us at one time or another suffered from the effects of difficult interpersonal relationships. It may have been the result of excessive career demands, domestic violence, divorce, idolizing the loner hero, rampant materialism... There is a bright side; we are at birth endowed with a wealth of positive characteristics designed to help us create rich meaningful bonds with others.

Rich Human Relationships – can be the most highly sought after and prized component of life. Their creation begins with the birth of an infant. The mother child relationship is the first and often the strongest interpersonal relationship in life. Next in importance is the family. Sequestered group participants (astronauts, submariners...) list the lack of contact with family (nuclear/extended) as the most difficult part of isolation; little do they know that lack of contact with a Hub group would be an even greater hardship.

The Hub contains a wealth of role model personalities offering a plethora of skills and learning opportunities. Children and adults meld into this communal treasure chest, resulting in interpersonal ties and bonds far stronger than in the nuclear family. Some English homes of the middle ages were similar to a Hub family.

The historians tell us the prevailing English life style during the middle-ages was communal. Houses contained the head of the household their spouse, children and the spouses of their children. In addition, there usually was a set of grandparents, possibly aunts and uncles, plus servants. All spent their free time in the large common room. When the major role models were superb functioning homo-sapiens, the children and other adults could follow suit and develop themselves in a progressive manner. In the homes of weak role models, disharmony and poor relations resulted in stalled evolutionary development, members did not actualize they remained immature.

Communal families also existed in other nations and in the present day it remains the prevalent social structure on the planet. When in Singapore, the locals advised me it was common for four or five generations to live in one accommodation. In North America, Europe and Australia more and more couples are sharing housing with another couple and two generation homes are on the rise.

In the past century there have been hippy communes, communes modelled along the lines of B.F. Skinners novel *Walden Two*, and of course the Kibbutz in Israel. The term 'commune' has partially given way to the term 'intentional communities'. These groups may be founded on various concepts, ecological sustainability, religion, art, communal sharing and other concepts. Some function as a family, others are loose associations. At present there are over two-thousand intentional communities in North America and a hundred or more in Australia.

The diversity of personalities in a vigorous communal family encourages respect, compassion, tolerance, cooperation, and sharing - all necessary prerequisites for vibrant interpersonal relationships. The Hub satisfies the need for belongingness, creating a strong belief in others and in the self. A child's interpersonal skills are fostered; this provides the groundwork for building affiliations with others in the community. The most important of these, particularly for developing children, is friends.

Friendships are often built on commonalities: interests, values, experiences, mutual respect, affection and support. This entails a sharing of emotions and intimate personal concerns, which are handled with empathy, honesty, loyalty and trust. The lack of emotional exchange marks the relationship as an associate or acquaintance, rather than a friendship. An ongoing friendship requires time together, preferably several times a week; time constraints limit the number of friends to probably less than six. Friends geographically separated, may maintain the relationship electronically.

Assigning a difficult task to a pair of Hub children can help them learn to work cooperatively and in so doing form a bond of trust and loyalty. A strong Hub will have a web of interconnected bonds.

Studies have found our brain waves tend to synchronize with that of our friends when we are together; who you associate with does matter.

313

Becoming a friend can be painful; you may have to tear down some of those walls you put up to protect yourself. It could entail talking for hours, talking all night, revealing dark secrets, talk that hurts. Becoming a friend means facing up to things about yourself you would usually try to avoid.

Research reveals that friends have a tremendous impact on our overall functioning. They may act as role models and inspire us to achieve positive goals or direct us down destructive paths of negative behaviours such as crime, substance abuse and so on. Social network studies by Christakis and Fowler found the risk of obesity 45 times higher amongst people who had obese friends.

My experience counselling group marriages, polygamous Mormons and other alternative forms of marriage, found friendship outside the marital group played a crucial role in providing an outsider's perspective and an escape from the home group's tensions.

Learning Relationship Skills - Each person is an expression of the planet's life force and has some intrinsic positive value. Initially it is wise to consider all those you come in contact with as precious and worthy of being cherished, a difficult task at times. It is easy to dismiss someone because they have values and attitudes not in agreement with yours. In so doing, an opportunity for learning and expanding life may be lost. On the other hand, maintaining contact with people who are takers rather than givers, or in some way they denigrate and drag down your existence, is destructive to your life.

Within a community, survival group, Hub family, spaceship, planetary colony..., there may be several languages and cultures represented. Collaborative skills necessitate the learning of another language and the pertinent details of its culture. The Europeans are a good model of this. Whereas, few British speak a second language, or have insight into other cultures. The American are worse.

Contact with your circle of positive affiliations must occur often. If you are keen to sustain these links, consider what you might offer each person. In a sense this involves taking some responsibility for the welfare of others. What needs does this person have that you might help fulfil? How might you be of service to them? What does it take on your part to be a real blessing in this person's life?

As an adolescent, I made my first formal attempt to learn interpersonal skills by reading Dale Carnegie's book *How to win Friends and Influence People.* Since then I have read a multitude of books, research studies, and conducted a research training program- *Programmed Interpersonal Relations Training for Small Groups 1971, m*y Master of Science degree thesis. Additionally, I have studied innumerable multi-media programs and participated in many group learning experiences. There is a wealth of help on the web, like the thirteen-step program at wikihow.com.

I try to incorporate Taoism guidelines when relating with others, such as not being critical, accepting others as they are. I like the comment of the Dalai Lama - he suggested it is more important to find a single fault in oneself, than to find a thousand faults in another person, because you can change your fault whereas you cannot change other people. Taoism posits a peaceful, compassionate approach to get along with even the most difficult personalities and achieve a sense of mutual harmony.

Raising children is life's biggest challenge and has the most far reaching consequences. We need less TV programs on cooking and more on raising children.

Your child's learning of interpersonal skills begins in the womb and continues after birth from family, friends, intimates and the community. When an infant-sleeps with a family member during the first years of life; it facilitates the child's interpersonal relationship PELGAM and a strong, confident, resilient self-concept. Positive continual growth occurs best in a hub (communal) lifestyle, where extensive social/emotional/physical interchanges take place. There are bound to be problems.

The greater number of people under one roof means more interpersonal conflict, which can breed hostility and contempt. Good conflict resolution techniques are necessary. Otherwise a Hub can be more stultifying and damaging than the nuclear family. Any form of alternative life style may be harassed by the prevailing culture, which has been led to believe the 'nuclear' family is the only legitimate family.

If you are unable or unwilling to set up a hub life style; consider spending oodles of time with another couple, or two couples. Upon the birth of your first child appoint one of the couples as surrogate parents. Your second child could have a different couple, as secondary parents. Hence, a child minimally has two fathers and two mothers and belongs to two sibling groups.

Each child should spend a significant amount of time with the surrogate family. This close communal interdependent social time will assist you and your children's brain filter tuning and PELGAM growth. This in turn enhances the child's learning, problems solving, health, stress management and self-esteem.

When children are age 2, form groups of 6 to 8 toddlers from various families; this group can be the training ground for the children as they mature, as well as being the principal identity group throughout life. Sometimes it may be necessary to change a child's primary group.

Children should have a mentor - an adult who has an affinity for the child and who is also admired by the child in turn. Ideally, the mentor is another adult apart from the biological parents - someone from the hub or Circle. It could be a friend, an uncle, grandparent or neighbour. The mentor spends fun time teaching, guiding and helping. This relationship only ends when the mentor dies.

Another approach to creating a communal type life style is to exchange adults for a month or more a year. In the interest of maintaining ongoing stability in the family, exchange one parent at a time. Go be mum in the other family, while that mum comes to your home. Exchange of children will also help. Of course, living communally avoids all this moving about hassle.

Children do not need warriors as models. As long as we worship warriors, we march to our demise. Children need loving, emotionally calm, decisive, cooperative models, if they are to learn how to trust, accept and support others.

To fathom another person's personality, one must understand the interpersonal behaviours common amongst humans, particularly those of the local culture. Likewise, one must comprehend the individual's moods, temperaments, motivations, intentions and behaviours. This information has to be interfaced with ones' own personal characteristics and agenda. Each person and situation, necessitates a unique interpersonal technique. A sensitive grasp of idiosyncratic personalities in each circle of contacts is mandatory.

Children who have grown up in deprived conditions or a disadvantaged culture may have an in-depth understanding of these environments and yet be unable to grasp the expectations of the prevailing middle class. Similarly, the middle-class child will not understand the cultural guidelines of children from other social classes.

Children require training to perceive and comprehend the emotional states, potentials and limitations of those about them. While the greater part of this training may take place in the family; church, school, scout and community camps can offer noteworthy opportunity for the child to learn appreciation of others. A child's free imaginative interactive play with others also helps and makes for a better adjusted, more relaxed and smarter child. This latter part is the focus of an article 'The Serious Need for Play' By M. Wenner, in *Scientific American MIND*; Vol. #1.

Time can be a major stumbling block in the child's learning interpersonal competence. If they are overly occupied in scholastic studies, sports, music lessons… there may be insufficient time to interrelate. Here is a weekly interpersonal time guideline I used with nuclear family parents, suggesting minimal weekly interpersonal involvement for adults:

- 4 hours of recreation with your partner
- 4 hours of recreation with partner and children
- 4 hours of recreation with partner and other couples; sometimes including all the children
- 1 hour or more of privacy time (intra-personal)

An adult must possess good relationship skills if she is to train children. She must be approachable, a good listener, able to put others first, and willing to give others the benefit of doubt. A vital ingredient is revealing one's inner self. Studies have shown the degree of self-revelation determines the depth of the relationship. If you reveal something personal, the other person may reveal something equally as personal in return. If not, the relationship will go no further. If they reveal something as personal or-more-so than your offering, this indicates they want to pursue the relationship.

At this point you give a titbit which is more personal than your first offering. When two or more talk for hours about their weaknesses, fears, hopes dreams…, leaving nothing of personal significance unrevealed then this is true intimacy. It forms the basis of true friendship and the foundation for intimate love. It is important to express care, respect, and gratitude for the others presence and to honour their boundaries and privacy.

In late adolescence or early adulthood individuals expand their family and friend skills to encompass a love relationship with one or more intimates. Love can be a state of rapture; unhappy love is life's greatest turbulence. My heart is strong like my steel yacht; but too many salty tears can rust both. Love can be the ultimate risk, where one is willing to sacrifice their life for another. The basis for a love liaison begins in the individual's vibrant intrapersonal relationship; it is, for the most part, impossible to value or love another, if you do not value and love yourself.

Before entering an intimate love connection, one might consider a period of seclusion. Spending a week isolated and alone, without societies' distractions and pacifiers, is apt to reveal how comfortable one is with one self. If you cannot tolerate yourself for a week, how are you going to handle fifty years with this other person? I have had an annual week solo retreat for most of my life. It helps me appreciate all those in my life circle and life itself.

It would be wise to read about and visit those living in intimate relations. Sample a broad range: newlyweds, old timers, partners of dissimilar age, same sex, polygyny groups, polyandrous groups…The more knowledge you obtain, the more likely you will be able to negotiate the difficulties of intimate relationships which are, with the exception of self- concerns, the longest lasting task of life.

Review the ramifications of a long-term intimate liaison with a given person; what impact will it have on your goals and dreams? Can you accept and fit in with their aspirations? Being the wife of a commercial ship captain entails long periods of time alone. The spouses of medical personnel have to contend with their partners erratic work schedule.

Should you have expectations of others? Some philosophies advocate a no-holds-barred giving of one-self to others. This is a meritorious concept and works well on a level playing field. In our broken world of dysfunctional personalities, it produces drained souls disheartened with life. I believe successful relationships operate best on a give and take basis, embracing mutual benefits.

Are you keen and competent to parent? This is a vital question; most mental and emotional crippling of human beings occurs in their childhood. To grow into well-functioning adults, children have to be wanted, nurtured and properly educated.

Are you aware of how physical attributes impact people? A large person may be viewed as a threat, a small person as insignificant. Are round face people happy and pleasant, those with long narrow faces unhappy and unpleasant? Shortness is interpersonally non-threatening and certainly helps with careers in small confined spaces. Tallness facilitates a basketball career, handling a large musical instrument and may foster a more dominant personality.

In my case being tall caused a lot of brain damage, particularly when touring the UK. In days of old their inhabitants were of short stature; the historic pubs, hotels and houses have low doorways and low-beamed ceilings requiring the modern man to wear a crash helmet.

Are you hirsute? Worldwide research revealed that women with long hair and men with beards are seen as sexier than those with short hair and no beards. I usually have had a moustache, a beard or long hair and sometimes all three. Yet I have not experienced greater than normal interpersonal exchanges with females. I shower frequently, maybe it's my face?

Facial mien, the shape of eyes, nose, lips, and how they are used in facial expressions may bring specific responses from others. Makeup and clothing may help achieve the desired presentation, although clothes hiding an unfit body only fool the wearer.

High pitched or whiney voices grate on people's nerves. Rapid staccato voice patterns wear the listener out, too slow and it creates impatience and boredom. Loud speech is overpowering and too soft strains the listener. Constant verbal chatter suggests self-centeredness and a lack of caring. If you talk very little and listen a lot, people will love you.

Eye contact is similar - too much and people feel intruded upon, too little and the listener feels ignored. Shifty eyes are scary. Sunglasses impede relationships. External factors are important. However, if you wish to improve your rapport with someone, you must look beyond their physical façade and reach within them to their inner person.

As the adult interacts within the community, the very act of participating provides a place to practise relationship skills and learn new ones. A few professors in the arts, social sciences and alternative educational systems may get on the bandwagon and support balanced development. Consider inviting one or more to dinner. Be open and revealing about who you are and what you are all about. Inquire about their interests, probe their minds and offer genuine support. Such activities help one become a valued member of the community with strong interpersonal bonds, all of which leads to greater happiness.

Affectionate interpersonal behaviour like hugging, hand-holding, kissing and so on, are found in all cultures. Spitting on someone is not acceptable anywhere in the world. Staring is not acceptable in England the U.S.A. or Australia; it is common place in Southern Spain and North Africa. If you stare back, they continue to stare at you. I found it slightly annoying. Waving your hands, shaking your fist, and shouting in some ones' face is not acceptable in the U.S.A., but common in Southern Italy. Before you travel abroad, check on the dos and don'ts of the culture you are visiting. Then you will be able to inter-act more successfully with your hosts.

* * *

Mid-morning Salerno Italy, I have come into this ship's chandlery to buy a rubber diaphragm replacement for the boats fresh water foot pump. A guy is being served at the counter and two fellas wait in a queue. 'Buon giorno' I say and take my place in line. Things move quickly, I'm now the only person in the line when the guy at the counter, shifting from foot to foot and waving both arms in the air, lets loose a verbal tirade at the clerk behind the counter. My Italian is too poor to understand what is being said. The clerk with a snarling face hollers back as he grabs the customer's shirt lapel. Like madmen, they are stretched across the counter grasping each other by the lapel, jabbing each-others' chest with pointed finger and shouting. I'm from the States, so I'm thinking one of these guys is going to whip out a knife or gun, I better get the hell out of here.

The shop door opens and a burly guy walks in. 'Buon giorno,' he says, as he gets in line, seemingly oblivious to the fight. I'm torn, not wanting to lose my place in line, but I don't want to get shot either. Then all of a sudden, it's over, they are sweet and smiling to each other, pats on the shoulder and farewell waves as the customer saunters out. I love these crazy Italians.

***

Good interpersonal relationships are an absolute necessity for success at the personal and community level. In any survival setting they are essential. If aliens are able to sense our intolerance of different life forms, human colonization of outer space may be cut short.

Investigate the wealth of online and printed information pertaining to interpersonal skills. These skills start with family structures able to produce children that become good parents, good family members, good friends and good neighbours. Stellar adults build a personality of openness, respect, cooperation, support, conciliation, empathy, compassion, honesty and kindness; they have the capacity to love, learn and think.

Communal groups of such people may over time rekindle dormant genes. In the difficult, hostile environments of societal collapse and alien planets, these groups will temper competition, individualism, property ownership, materialism, conformity and tyranny. Stellar groups will present a unified solidarity against divisive forces in politics, religion, life style and the harshness of the environment. From this, harmonious families/Hubs/circles can evolve and go on to form workable communal societies on earth and on other planets.

Chapter 14 Spiritual Relation Ship PELGAM

I raise my morning glass of juice and toast the gods and powers that may be, offering thanks for letting me live another day. Thanks for my mental, emotional, physical, spiritual, social and financial health. Thanks for the lovely earth, its' elements, botanical wonders, animals, birds and fishes. Thanks for the air I breathe, the water I drink and the life-giving force of the sun; for sending the power of the universe and the energy of mother earth into my being to nourish and inspire me. I wish to emanate that force out to all existence, strengthening those in need and granting blessings to everyone and everything

One-hundred-thousand-year-old stone-age art, purposeful burials and other archaeological finds suggest shamanistic religious spiritual type practices existed amongst the pre-literate communal hominid species. It appears the shaman often was the leader of the primitive group; thus, religion became affiliated with politics.

Early primitives believed there was a spirit dwelling in everything: trees, rocks, water, animals, people and so on. M. Hainer in *The Way of the Shaman*, defines a spirit as an animate soul having varying degrees of power and intelligence. Ancients held reverence for these spirits. We do not know if their beliefs are accurate. Nevertheless, they have value in that they bring a person closer to nature, fostering respect for all existence and they clarify a person's self-perception.

It is difficult to define what spirituality is and is not. It may encompass a variety of feeling states which differ from person to person. Some experience this when they enter a building of worship; others during meditation, prayer, yoga… One contemporary view of the spiritual is as a process of relating to the ethereal values and underpinnings of existence, untainted by material or worldly things. Some refer to this as the religious, sacred, or holy essence of the human spirit found in all people. This stands in contrast to some religions where grasping a sense of the spiritual is seen as the domain of religious scholars, priests and monks.

Spirituality may only speculate about the spirits that inhabit flora, fauna or objects; whereas religion usually contains a creation story and has a belief in a God or Gods. Contemporary societies tend to lump religion and spirituality together; and they do have a lot in common. Some retain the worship of multitudinous spirits or Gods, while others are monotheistic. A significant percentage of United States citizens profess participation in religious activities, the percentage in Australia is low.

I view my spirit as the non-physical me; it's my deepest feelings, thoughts, beliefs, emotions, philosophies and all my PELGAMs. It invokes an all-encompassing wonderment when I am in natural settings. I respond with a sense of joy and freedom. Forests and oceans encourage me to build a framework guiding my life in a natural manner most suited to the person I am.

I view religion as a branch of philosophy offering ideas of how I might deal with existence. Physics postulates existence as a cosmic energy field that appears to have existed forever, may continue forever, and encompasses the entire universe. This interconnection of all, the kinship of all organisms has been superbly detailed by evolutionary biology. This cosmic field is often labelled the 'zero-point field,' and some people hypothesize it as the essence of God. If so, then the individual, who is a part of the field, must also be Godly

The population upsurge and urbanization of humanity dissolved the unity and security of the preliterate Hub life style, leading to confusion and a lack of meaning in life. Amidst the turmoil, the unknown and unfulfilled needs, I suggest the human brain fell into panic mode. Studies have indicated that in such circumstances the brain will create something or latch onto anything that might fill the gap or answer the unresolved questions. Hence, the original simplistic shamanistic pagan spirituality expanded its' political element to become a more highly organized force exerting power over people. This new force leapt in to fill the void of the unknown and unfulfilled needs; offering a more complex elaborate set of theories and possible answers, which helped reinstate a sense of collective unity.

Four thousand years ago organized religion was firmly ensconced in China, Egypt, Greece and the Americas. Its' phenomenal power was recognized and began to be utilized by the power personalities; resulting in a proliferation of Religions some two and a half thousand years ago, including the three major monotheistic philosophies, whose doctrines created a God fashioned in the image of man. Many Religions were and remain political type organizations primarily aimed at controlling people. They became the most effective instrument of subjugating the citizenry the elite power mongers had ever devised.

Poor Spiritual Relations – Early humanity's spirituality fostered his close ties with those around him and nature; whereas, the new force pitted man against himself, others and the natural world. The underlying focus on power tends to be covered by a fraudulent facade of caring for people. This dishonesty is furthered by many of the so-called devout who espouse the doctrines of their faith, but show little understanding of its' tenants. This raises the question, are those claiming to be religious, true representatives of their religion?

When a person claims to be a physicist, carpenter or chef; then I naturally assume they have undergone rigorous training. The Ph.D. physicist would have spent years involved in study, and participated in numerous research projects investigating theories and their practical implications. Similarly, I expect the carpenter has had extensive formal book learning along with years of training as an apprentice. Likewise, the chef has studied the chemistry and nutrition value of innumerable food ingredients and laboured for years as an apprentice cook in different types of restaurants and kitchens. Without the completed training and experience, these people are labelled as student, apprentice and cook.

When a person claims to be a Catholic, Protestant, Hindu, then I am interested to know if they have had training from their faith's scholars, and whether they have read their holy book and other relevant writings, studied the tenants of other faiths, and practised their beliefs every day. If they have not done these things, I feel it is a sham to claim they are Catholic, Protestant, or Hindu. The average person making such claims is in fact only an initiate, not yet worthy of the religious title.

Psychology is concerned with the building and efficient functioning of the individual personality. Hence, belief systems that negatively impact on the human personality are a worry. Studies investigating the amount of clothing that is worn in various cultures has revealed that the less clothing worn, the greater the sense of confidence and self-identity in the individual. I am uneasy about doctrines that dictate the human body should be completely covered (except eyes and possibly face) as it is for Catholic nuns and Muslim women. I cannot help but think such clothing practices would interfere with the healthy development of 'self-identity' – especially when all adherents are wearing the same colour. Are the black herds of nuns simply the beast of burden owned by the church, to carry out the wishes of their owners? Are the shrouded Muslim women a class of enslaved household servants?

Religious leadership in the modern world, like political leadership, has failed to provide humans with adequate answers to the multifaceted problems of life. The citizenry is confused, so they seek answers in other areas. Traditional religion has to compete with contemporary subcultures such as sport, music, art, cults and social groups like the 'trekkies.' The largest group of devotees give fervent dedication to the religion of economics.

The devout attend services in a posh hotel's conference room to hear their priest the motivational speaker. He is bald and bespectacled, holding a red ledger pen in his right hand, the accounting books cradled beneath his left arm, the right-hand thumb motioning off to the side, the left hands index finger is pointing, one cannot tell in which direction. Behind him, sitting on a throne, is a statue of the God of achievement and wealth clothed in a suit and tie. In front of him is a faeces-splattered fountain constructed of minerals, commodities and dollar shop junk which spews forth slimy brown liquid into a pool of oil and alcohol. it is surrounded by incense pots burning industrial waste.

This religion demands endless hours of hard work; instead of sacrificing animals, it sacrifices human health, happiness and family life. Not much different from historical religion which enslaved populations, raped cultures and murdered millions.

Ineffective religious and societal rules have brought about our immature dysfunctional society in which the citizen is unable to design and live a happy, productive and meaningful life. People need a philosophy, a plan and spiritual guidelines to answer life questions and point the way. I believe the lack of this plays a part in the rampant anti-Muslim sentiment.

Most Australians are not church goers, in urban areas they tend to lack a sense of community, a place to meet, to share values and receive caring support. This is less so in rural areas, where the pub often fills these roles.

Average Aussies are confronted by political parties legislating against them, a business sector that overcharges and pays low wages, and organized religion that has sexually abused their children and mistreated elders.

The mosque is the centre of the Muslim community; providing a meeting place, social life, help in daily matters and much more. It gives Muslims a united sense of purpose and meaning, fulfilling the need to belong to something that is bigger than the self.

The non-Muslim population could reclaim this all-important solidarity by forming Hubs and circles. Christians and other Religions could possibly reunite people if they would welcome all with open arms and be less rigid about values and beliefs. They would have to quit painting non-believers as sinners.

Good Spiritual Relations - My religious training commenced when I was a toddler sitting in a pew listening to my mother sing in the Cedarville Ohio church choir. At the age of five mom put me in the youth choir of the Presbyterian church. I had inherited a powerful voice with excellent tonal quality which helped me fit into the group and bolstered my self-esteem. I enjoyed singing. I was fascinated by the older kids furtive passing about of notes and candy during the sermon.

Although mom was no longer involved in church when we moved to Michigan, she required us kids to attend Sunday school. I was in the youth choir again but felt like an outsider. I did not understand why my parents were not at church like the other kids' parents. Have you ever been somewhere where everyone treats you nice, but you still feel like the odd person out? At least I got a book out of the deal - a small New-Testament with a gold-plated steel front cover. It fit in my left shirt pocket, protecting my heart from enemy bullets. I believe these little holy books were designed for and primarily given to our soldiers during World War II.

I learned the church's teachings did not apply at home, but assumed all other families were using them. Consequently, life at school, in the neighbourhood and the world in general was a puzzle. Instead of love I encountered hate and fear. There seemed to be a rule to hit first and hardest. Taking care of your brother was a joke, it was, get all you can from him and take care of yourself. Being taught to turn the other cheek set me up to be a sucker, taken advantage of by many. I reckon my time in Sunday school was one of the most damaging aspects of my development, teaching me values and behaviours that did not work with a cold aloof unloving mother, cruel abusive father and an insane society.

Dad was a printer at the Simplicity pattern printing plant in Niles, Michigan. When I was in the fifth grade the plant was embroiled in work strikes, so we moved back to Ohio. Dad got employment at McCall's printing plant in Dayton.

Mom still sent me to Sunday school at the Trinity Baptist church on Lexington Ave. which you could see from our front porch on Oxford Ave. The church was a member of the northern Baptist organization, a more-easy going and reasonable religion than the fire and brimstone southern Baptists. Reverend Marsh, an effervescent ruddy haired fellow, lived around the corner from us. He was a strict no fooling around kind of guy, yet always warm and accepting. He made up for some of the church dogma that did not add up to me.

I loved walking up the church steps on Sunday morning to be greeted by Mr. Annis. He was a giant of a man with immense warm hands that mine got lost in. I remember thinking how lucky Sally was to have such a nice father. As usual I sang in the youth choir and got into my share of mischief.

Jules my friend that lived on the street behind us told me he too got in trouble in his church for not wearing his cap. I thought that was strange - I got in trouble if I left my hat on in church. I asked him a lot of questions about his church and got some incredible answers. He actually went to Sunday school several nights a week and some of this involved learning a special church language. He showed me his funny little skull cap. I could not see any use in it, as it was too small to keep your head warm and had no bill to keep the sun out of your eyes.

One afternoon, we were in the street tossing a football when this weird guy who lived cattycorner from us came walking down the sidewalk, all dressed in black with a wide brimmed black hat and long black beard. Usually when he appeared I made a fast departure - with all that black he had to be a bad guy. Jules introduced him to me. He shook my hand and was friendly. For all my careful looking, I could not see a gun or knife on him.

One day a week later we were bored and looking for trouble; Jules suggested we visit his church. That made no sense, it wasn't Sunday; it would not be open. He said it would be and was only a half mile away.

A half mile, now that sounds like an adventure; we took off and got there in no time.

It was not a church, it didn't have a steeple. It looked more like a library. We snuck in a side door and up some steps. Not a soul around. The sanctuary was about the same as in my church. We crept about, Jules whispering facts about his religion. I'm sure he made it up as he went along. Like saying the men sat on one side and the women on the other. As we stood on the altar, he showed me a table where they put their special book, not a bible. Abruptly, I was aware of something behind me; I spun around and there looking down on me was my weird neighbour in black. I wanted to run but was paralysed by fear.

He smiled, welcomed us and took over where Jules had left off. He took his time showing us around and explaining things. Eventually we came to the kitchen; he gave us some cookies and got Kool Aid out of the fridge. He had to be a good guy if he is feeding us. I still thought he was a fearful looking minister; I wouldn't want to cross him.

When Jules and I played in the neighbourhood, we would occasionally slip into his house for a snack. Once he pulled a box of 'Matzo' crackers out of the cupboard and we put peanut butter and jam on them. I worried about it, our church said 'Matzo' was special, you only took a little bite at communion with a small glass of grape juice. If his grandmother caught us, she did not scold but offered us more snacks.

She wore a babushka and was bent over with hair growing out of her ears and nose, obviously a couple hundred years old.

Sunday noontime, when us kids got home from Sunday school, our family had their special roast meal of the week. Jules' family had their special meal on Friday evening, which I took part in many times. It was spooky at first, flickering shadows from a candelabra, odd smelling food, Jules, his dad and grandpa wearing those bill-less ball caps. I think the family had allergy problems, which explains the purple noodle soup and other peculiar foods. They explained that they could not eat pork.

They had their own version of the Lord's Prayer and sang a few songs, none of which I recognized. How could they leave out the all-time favourite 'Onward Christian Soldiers?' Their conversation was mostly in their church language. The grandparents spoke little English.

In addition to Jules' Orthodox Synagogue, there was a liberal Reformed Synagogue within walking distance of home. Then and now the Jewish community retains somewhat of a unified communal nature that is centred in the Synagogue. If you are out and about on Friday evening, you can safely assume that the people you see are not Jewish.

Likewise, Monday nights you will not be bumping into many Mormons. Mormon families spend that evening together at home. This type of family and community unity has eroded in most Christian Churches, with the exception of a few ultra-conservative denominations and the occasional Catholic Church.

***

One afternoon I was sitting on the front porch steps, my stomach growling, when I saw red haired Pat coming down the street. I did not like him. Once I had been across the street on Kathy's front porch, when Pat from his nearby front yard shot me with his Daisy BB gun; the pellet came through the porch screen and stuck in my cheek just below my right eye. Kathy's mom was furious. She stomped across the street, grabbed Pat by the ear and dragged him up to his house to see his mother. He was not allowed out of the house for a couple of days. It was nice having an adult concerned about my well-being.

Pat was the type to get angry fast and come on with his fists. I quickly had to get rid of my glasses, if they had gotten broke my old man would have beaten me. Not that it would have mattered much, as I got frequent beatings no matter what I did. Even though Pat was smaller than me, I was no match for that windmill of fists. He used to knock me down, till I learned to grab him. With my larger size I would eventually wrestle him to the ground and sit on him. Once the dog's water dish was within reach, I poured it in his face. From then on, if he started getting riled up I would ask him if he wanted more dog water and he would back off.

'Whatcha doin?' he asked as he sat down next to me, smacking his bubble gum.
'Not doin nothin, just saw Jules' Rabbi walk up the street.'
Yeh! Jules' church is poor people, their priest can't afford a car.'

'He's not a priest, he's a Rabbi.'

'Same thing.'

'Your minister got a car?' I asked.

'The best, a big black caddy.'

'Your church probably doesn't have a kitchen like Jules.'

'Yes, it does. There's a six-burner stove and two fridges with bottom freezers.'

'Hmpf! Two fridges. You expect me to believe that?'

'It's true. We have lots of long tables and chairs. Sometimes we have big dinners.'

'You'd have to show me before I'd believe that.'

'I can't show you.'

'Why not?'

'It's a fur piece away.'

'You too puny to walk?'

'Nah! I ain't allowed to go that far.'

'Didn't know you were such a scaredy cat!'

'I'm not scared of nothin! Come on let's go.'

Pat got us lost a couple of times. After a half hour I began to worry we would never find our way back home. Finally, we found his church.

'There it is, the best church in town.'

'What makes you think it's the best?'

'It's on top the hill, closer to heaven.'

'Ok, that makes sense.'

We traipsed up the hill. With such a tall steeple I knew it was a church; but it had a big factory door, although there were no rail tracks on the stairs leading to the door. We stepped in.

'Why's that dog water dish up so high?'
'That's not for dogs, it's for hands.'

These Catholics took this cleanliness next to godliness thing seriously. We walked across the foyer and peered into the sanctuary.

'Wow! That's a long way up. Any birds up there?'
'I don't think so, only angels.'
'Look! There's several people hunched over, still asleep from Sunday's sermon.'
'Nah! They're praying.'
'Uh-oh! Over in that side room there are a couple witches in front of those candles.'
'Two of them are my teachers.'
'Witches for teachers, that's cool.'
'They aren't witches, they're nuns.'
'Why are teachers called nuns?'
'I don't know. Dad says it's cause, they don't get none.'
We headed towards an alcove just as a tall man in a black dress and a black jewellery box hat stepped out and headed towards us. He didn't appear to have a knife or gun, but on a sash wrapped around his dress hung a cross shaped club.

'Nice to see you here Patrick.' He said as he passed us.
'Thank you, father.'

341

'You got two fathers?'

'No, that's the priest; we call him father.'

'Do you know his kids?'

'He hasn't got any kids.'

'Does his wife wear men's clothes?'

'He hasn't got a wife; priests aren't allowed to have anything to do with women.'

'Well he must have a mother?'

'Nope, priests are born in a monastery of priests and nuns. It's virgin birth like Jesus.'

Pat's religion had my head reeling, my stomach was growling as we entered an alcove full of photographs.

'My church isn't open during the week.' I explained.

'Your minister is poor and can't afford the coal. These are the church's kings.'

Sure enough, the guys in the photos were dressed in white kingly robes, tall bullet shaped hats. They even carried spears - they must be warrior kings.

'So, where's the kitchen?'

We went through another corridor and down a circling flight of steps and came into the grandest kitchen and dining room I had ever seen. Not only did it have two fridges and a big stove, but also a rotisserie. Pat said they put a pig on it. No allergies here. I got bold and opened a fridge.

'Gee whiz it's full of beer and wine.'

'The beer is for the dinners and the wine for communion.'

'We have grape juice for communion.'

'Your church is poor, they can't afford wine.'

We found a bowl of jello fruit salad and some carrot cake in the other fridge. As I scarfed it down, I remembered our minister preaching about the evils of alcohol. These Catholics were clearly caught up in that evil.

I was about twelve years old when Reverend Marsh transferred to a church in another town; I wondered if he did not like us. Our new minister Fred looked impressive in his Homburg hat and bulky overcoat. It was all a front, he was a friendly and jovial character loved by all the kids. During the sermons the older teenage girls in the choir would give the minister a rough time by continually looking at their wrist watches or clearing their throats if he was going over time.

The girls told me about a guy in another church choir who had dropped to all fours during prayer and crawled out the side door. A while later, he returned with a bag of popcorn (only in America) and began crawling back to his seat. Poor guy was on the wrong side of the partition, in sight of the entire congregation.

The church's Sunday night youth fellowship program was a welcome refuge from warring parents and an empty pantry. I had fun and generally was not teased about my thick spectacles as I was everywhere else. They had food like ice cream, soft drinks and potato chips, which we never had at home. Sometimes they had more substantial food like hamburgers. Amongst the kids I had a reputation for being a big eater. Most nights of the week I had trouble falling asleep due to all the loud thunder and rumbling. But on Sunday nights falling asleep was easy.

One summer I spent a week with Aunt Mary and Uncle Thomas in Springfield Ohio; it was a relaxed happy home atmosphere and I enjoyed playing with my cousins. I thought it was cool when we all went to church together. Having guitarists and other musicians up front was neat too. It was a lively session I enjoyed until aunt Mary got in my face. She earnestly looked me in the eye and asked me if I wanted to be saved from my sins. I didn't know what to say. I was not aware of having sins. I thought it would be nice if someone saved me from my family.

In spite of my poor eyesight I was a voracious reader. During the summer months the bookmobile visited our neighbourhood every two weeks and I would take out the ten permitted. The mobile unit did not have a large selection; consequently, I read books I otherwise would not have read. Some were religious and mom was not happy with a few that were Catholic. When I asked what was wrong with Catholics, I got the same unintelligible response as when I asked what the sign on the front of a Michigan resort (Gentiles Only) meant.

At age fifteen I got a part time job at Owens super market and by my sixteenth birthday I had saved enough money to buy a car. A midnight blue 1951 V8 Ford with fender skirts, all leather interior, a spotlight and Hollywood pipes. It was lowered at the rear and would lay rubber in all three gears, very spiritual.

Tommy, a hill-billy kid I worked with in the super market, was a devout holy roller. He invited me to attend a meeting. Well, I had wheels so why not. In an open field on the edge of town was a circus tent surrounded by jalopies, trucks, and shiny Cadillacs, up to their hubcaps in mud. We got drenched running through pouring rain to the entrance, it was happening inside.

We clambered up the bleachers while trombones, guitars, banjos and people sang out 'Onward Christian Soldiers.' There was a lot of heat in that tent and the music was good. It was interspersed with long shouting tirades about being saved from sin. It made me wonder about my masturbation. People were crying, screaming and shouting, 'amen brother, amen!' This was better than the circus.

Disciples roamed through the bleachers exhorting us to come down and be saved. I held tight to my seat while others made their way down to the centre of the tent. The fervour was palpable. People wet with a sweat of frenzy rolled about on the ground wailing, screaming and begging the Lord for mercy. The band played on as others including myself got lost in song. Periodically, the pastor, with one of those light weight useless scarfs around his neck, would go to the centre of the tent with a sick or disabled person. He would exhort the group to beseech the heavens to heal this poor soul. I considered going down to improve my weak eyesight.

I attended several sessions with Tommy till we had a falling out at work. We were on the all-night shift stocking shelves. Henry the German guy in charge got a quart of Pabst Blue Ribbon beer out of the cooler to drink while he worked. He asked if I wanted one and I said no. He said, 'Das is gut vit a stick of pepperoni,' I changed my mind. He was right, it was energizing and refreshing. Tommy took one look at me and said, 'the devil is gonna take you away.' That was the last time he ever spoke to me, so much for Christian forgiveness.

I was in the high school choir till they threw me out for fighting. I was a sensitive kid and would over react when teased. Before that happened, the choir was part of a city-wide singing festival filling the University of Dayton field house. Hearing thousands of trained voices working together was a moving spiritual experience. I was seated on the outside edge of my choir, next to a black church choir. Several of the black kids introduced themselves and we had a good chat. They invited me to visit their church.

'You got any white folk in your church?'
They giggled a bit, 'of course not.'
'Sounds scary, what are your families going to do when this white boy walks in?'
'People gonna treat you good. Besides, we all be there to look after you.'
'I don't know? I'll have to think about it.'

As a child I was under strict orders from my dad not to have anything to do with black kids. Mom supported this. This was also the prevalent attitude in the surrounding culture. I would only obey this when my parents were around. I found different kinds of people interesting, so talking with black kids was like talking with Hungarians or Poles living in the neighbourhood. Sneaking into a Hungarian or Polish wedding feast was a favourite activity. I would eat enough stuffed cabbage rolls to get me through a couple days and farted enough to fill a hot air balloon.

Before I bought my car, I had walked through a black community numerous times on the way to and from various jobs. I never felt particularly comfortable, but it did not worry me either. I think it was pretty safe back then and probably still is.

I suppose one might think my going to a black church was quite a feat because I was stepping out of my comfort zone. The truth was, I did not really have a comfort zone where I felt I belonged. Any foreign place held a possibility of being more amenable than where I was currently. This may be the reason I am widely travelled, I have been searching for my tribe, some place I might fit in.

A month later on a beautiful Sunday morning I found myself parking near this black church. I must have been nervous; I forgot to lock my car. It was a long walk up those church steps; people around me were nodding their heads and greeting me. I shook hands with the men door greeters and stammered out the names of the choir members that had invited me. These greeters were the epitome of being friendly; one bustled away, while the other led me inside the foyer introducing me along the way.

Shortly, familiar grinning faces put me at ease; they could not have been more excited. They were unable to sit with me because they had to sing in the choir. I met their families and one mother put an arm around me and took me in tow. I felt great. This six-foot two skinny white boy sat amongst hundreds of blacks singing his heart out. Although I do not remember what the sermon was about, it caught my interest and impressed me.

During the after-service get-together I met more people and consumed an enormous quantity of baked goods. I had many invites to Sunday dinner. I did not accept as I had had enough stress for one day. As I was saying goodbyes, I desperately wanted to invite them to my church but was afraid to. I was fearful my congregation would come down hard on me for bringing in blacks, and afraid I would be ostracized. I did not think I could cope with that. I left feeling guilty, gutless and ashamed of myself.

I never saw any of them again and never told a soul I had gone to the black church. But for years my weakness haunted me. Every time I saw or met a black, I felt miserable, like a coward, disappointed I had been such a weakling, regretful I had not shown more courage.

I do not know how much impact my church and the others I visited had on me. As a kid with a warped father I had little faith or trust in men. It was men of the church and the fathers of friends that allowed me to slowly realize a grown man could be a good person. Maybe that is spiritual enough.

Unitarianism-Universalism - The UU movement blossomed in Transylvania in the 1400's and spread to England and its' colonies in North America, Australia and New Zealand where it prospered through the 1800s. UUs are keen on everyone thinking for themselves - no one has the right to speak for another. They stress using the power of love to honour and uphold seven guiding principles.

- The inherent worth and dignity of every person
- Justice, equity and compassion in human relations
- Accept one another & encourage spiritual growth
- A free and responsible search for truth and meaning
- The right of conscience and the use of democratic processes
- A goal of world community with peace, liberty & justice for all
- Reverence for the interdependent web of existence

These lofty ideals can be found in other religions and are consistent with my Taoist and Thoreau values. This, along with the absence of dogma and tolerance of differences appeals to me. During my undergraduate days at Ohio State University I could not find a Taoist church or Taoist believers, so I joined the Columbus Ohio 'Unitarian-Universalist Fellowship.'

Through the years I have been to a host of UU churches and fellowships, some you could feel the warmth, communality and acceptance the moment you entered. They are a vital force in their member's lives and the surrounding community. Being part of such a group would be a fantastic enhancement of anyone's life. However, the UU group on the other side of town may be controlled by a handful of power mongers who have their own agenda and ignore UU principles. There are more than a few of these harmful UU groups. Some newly formed UU groups in Africa are adamantly anti-homosexual. You cannot expect consistency in the UU movement.

Today I am a member of the 'Church of the Larger Fellowship' (CLF). This is an international group of UU people who do not reside near a UU church or fellowship. The CLF has monthly newsletters, a quarterly magazine (world@uua.org) and active websites. This helps the maintenance and continued growth of my spiritual existence. The CLF is headquartered and maintained by the American UU association in Boston Mass. Australia, New Zealand and other countries have their own UU headquarters. I was one of the founding fathers of the UU fellowship in Brisbane Australia and represented them in a national conference.

The marketing maxim that says one satisfied customer tells three friends, while a dissatisfied customer tells ten friends, may be a factor in the impending death of the UU movement. I suspect the dysfunctional UU groups are being more successful in destroying the UU movement than the good UU groups are in building it.

Traditionally, about 90% of UU members are university educated, they are thoughts, ideas and words people. This narrow range of membership creates a multitude of problems. Many groups are nothing more than intellectual debating societies, great at discussing pros and cons and making lists but taking no action. A host of members lead busy professional lives and lack time to actively carry forth UU principles with each other or in the community. Others are *'head trippers,'* avoiding the passions of life's emotional issues, thus lacking empathy in controversial areas more so than some of the conservative Christian churches.

A few UU groups are active, but in an unbalanced manner. One group may focus on freedom as many of the members have come from more rigid repressive religions, while another group focuses on Gay rights. They do not seem to realize that diversity of membership and attending to the wider breadth of human existence are necessary to create a vital long-term organization.

The UU movement is not a united group of churches led by a centralized administrative office; it is only a loose association of independent churches and groups. The lack of an organizational structure requiring the meeting of basic standards is another contributor to the demise of the UU movement. The declining percentage of the national population belonging to the UU movement means it will most likely cease to exist by the end of this century. Current North American membership is quite low.

Mormons - After I received my B.S. from Ohio State University, I worked as a testing psychologist for six months in the Ohio state penitentiary, before moving on to grad school at Utah State University Logan, Utah - a Mormon community. Once a month a Mormon bishop and his aide would come knocking. They gave me their holy book and would explain their faith. I listened politely, and in the intervals detailed UU principles. There were no converts either way, but I adopted some of their practices.

Mormons expect the end of the known world in the near future. In preparation, families are expected to keep a years' food supply at home and university students a month supply in their dorm rooms. Shopping in Mormon community super markets is a unique experience. The aisles are much wider, down its' centre are the shelf items in bulk quantity; one hundred -pound bags of flour, sugar, rice... and cases of canned vegetables, fruits, condiments... I adopted their strategy of storing large amounts of food, it helped rid me of my paranoia of not having enough to eat. I also like their idea of Monday home evening, where the family stays home and spends the time with each other.

After I returned to Michigan and set up my clinical practise, the Mormons opened their regional headquarters in the same building as my office. It was like old times talking with the young missionaries working the mid-Michigan area. My young vivacious secretary mercilessly teased the young fellows, regularly dropping in their office and standing up close to them, patting them on the shoulder and so on. Rules for the missionaries forbid physical contact of any kind with females and under no circumstances are they allowed to be alone with a female. The young fellows daily dropped into my office complex to visit my secretary.

These young virile males are dispatched in pairs around the globe for a two-year stint. The church provides intensive counselling when they return to help them merge back into the ongoing life of the community. A sizable percentage of the returnees are sexually involved with each other, the counselling and ready access to females straightens it all out. I found Mormons less sexually hung up than members of other Christian groups. This makes sense given the original Mormons were communal.

The original Mormon family was a male with numerous wives. Under political pressure, the church rescinded its bigamist policy. When I was in graduate school there were three separate groups of approximately two hundred thousand people maintaining the bigamist life. I hope these groups are still flourishing. They certainly have their problems, but I view then as a better option than the nuclear family.

After grad school, part of my clinical work included a university led program assisting clergy to cope with problems. Since religious organizations have an open-door policy, there usually are a few troubled and problematic people in the congregation; some are there for other than spiritual reasons. Some aim to enhance their career, others use it to meet their social needs, a few are looking for victims.

There is a high proportion of female to male members. A few of these women have had unsatisfactory relationships with their fathers or men in general, and look for a male surrogate in God or the minister. I do not know how God handles it, but the male ministry has a devil of a time coping with the plethora of fluttering butterflies. Some are seductive, while others quite deviously attempt to knock the minister off his leadership perch.

There is a male counterpart, men too afraid of women to permanently invest in a relationship; a female clergy may serve as a mother figure for him. She will be kind, supportive and not threaten him. Some men are so alienated from the opposite sex they seek the refuge of a church under male leadership.

Building Relations - Spirituality poses many questions but few concrete answers. Literature overflows with lucid, flowery descriptions of the heightened states of ecstasy attained by the devout (joy, peace, strength, fame, money and so on). Are these a correlate of enlightenment? Or is it a defence mechanism bringing welcome relief from attempting to cope with the immensity and complexity of the world?

Are the creationists on the right track? Has our species been created by a design office and laboratory somewhere out there in the unknown? Maybe the half dozen or so different hominoid species were trial models? Are we currently the updated and improved model? If so, when will the present model be superseded? Or has the home office written us off as a failed experiment and installed a better model on another planet?

Numerous scholars stress that neither words nor beliefs can bring one into the ecstasy, mystical union, pure consciousness, the void, or satori of spiritual awareness. First-hand experience is required. Spinoza felt the only way to find God was via a close relationship with nature. Einstein also believed this. Thoreau suggested one needed a contemplative meditation of nature. Others suggest the way to achieve this is through some form of yoga, sensory deprivation or entheogen substances. (Rabbi Zolman Schachter-Shalomi, Aldous Huxley, Albert Hofman…). These experiences initiate a heightened state of awareness which many contemplative traditions cite as necessary for spiritual growth.

I identify with Gnosticism's non-attachment, non-conformity, no egotism, which melds with my Thoreau, Taoist and U.U. leanings. All require one to step aside from selfish concerns to become aware of the larger picture, reverence for all that exists, a sense that all things are connected and sacred.

One aspect of this is expressing gratitude for all existence. I have a need to regularly give thanks; it makes me feel better and more a part of the world. I do this in part following Pascal's idea, to cover myself in case deities do exist. An important part of expressing gratitude is to include myself. I try to recognize myself as a manifestation of the universe, a wonderful creature of infinite possibilities. One of the most holy activities is to honour, respect and care for oneself; to do otherwise is to denigrate the very existence of the universe.

Not giving thanks for all the good about us can lead to an obsession with the ubiquitous bad (a problem I have). Forgiveness and acceptance of the world as it is, is an essential element of spirituality and personal growth; it can help curtail your mental preoccupation with the bad in the world, allowing you to enjoy the good and get on with life's tasks.

While I am not a resentful or revengeful person, I have always questioned forgiveness and todays' over emphasis on positivity. Turning the other cheek, giving forgiveness is not natural. A serious mistake at sea can bring death, get too close to a grizzly and you may be eaten, if you are improperly prepared the amazon jungle will smoother you.

I tend to see forgiveness and positivism as manipulations to get people's minds off our corrupt society and our leader's questionable behaviour. If I give love and forgiveness to those that abuse me, what do I have left to give those that treat me well? This dilemma plagues me. I evolved from a Christian upbringing to a liberal, agnostic Taoist framework incorporating the inter-connectedness of the universe. All of this suggests that when I fail to forgive someone or treat them badly, I am also failing to forgive my failures and am treating myself badly.

'I am good to good people

I am good to not good people

Because Virtue is goodness

I have faith in faithful people

I have faith in unfaithful people

Because Virtue is faithfulness'

Tao Te Ching

It all sounds good but trying to live up to these concepts remains a struggle for me.

I have extensively studied and spent time with various religious disciplines. The prolific writings of Joseph Campbell have been particularly helpful; they compare and contrast the planet's vast belief systems. He posits the 'monomyth' theory, the idea that all religions/myths/spiritual movements are variations on the same theme, the great story of life. He was certainly ahead of his time when he spoke of an eternal source of energy binding all humanity together. This is a thesis of the ZPF. Campbell's works are a treasure trove for building an understanding of spiritual relationships.

'The mass of mankind live in quiet desperation due to materialism and a lack of a sincere, authentic spirituality.' Thoreau.

CONCLUSION OF RELATIONSHIPS

Ancient humans lived communally amongst nature for millions of years; hence they possessed relationship skills far surpassing modern man. Our recent separation from nature and breakdown of communal life has been a disaster which has led to the loss of many human abilities and the withering of relationship skills. Your relationship PELGAM is in dire need of strengthening; increase your relationship contacts and give them more time and care.

Again, we find balance is important. Meaningful relationships are a balance of give and take. Would you maintain a relationship with a person who took from you, but instead of giving back, only abused you? How much do you give back to the natural world that makes your existence possible? What do you do for the sun that lights your day and the constellations that provide you twinkling beauty at night? What people do you receive benefits from and yet you give little in return?

History and science, makes it clear that it is impossible to be a loner; all things are inter-connected. You are related to all that exists, and life is enriched when you maintain quality give and take relationships within yourself, with nature and all life.

Chapter 15 Philosophy PELGAM

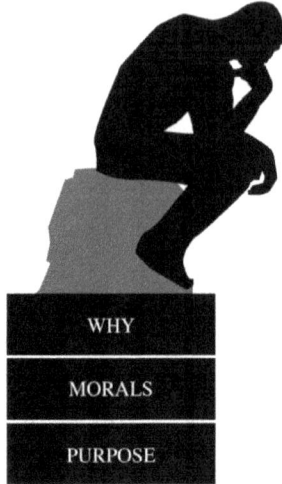

The morning sunlight warms my skin and sets the deciduous trees ablaze with gold, yellows and reds; a myriad of dew drops sparkle like diamonds. As I walk the deer path my muscles and bones feel the gravity of the earth beneath my feet. The crisp air is alive with the flutter of birds, scampering of squirrels and the scent of autumn. I, like the other animals, merge with the kaleidoscope of luxuriant earthly experience.

The thinking mind is dependent on experience fully received through awareness, not screened out or distorted by brain filters. This cognizance followed by responsiveness, are integral features of my personal philosophy, my viewpoint of life. For me, the essence of life is the collection of experiences from the vast complexity of our biosphere; this also involves understanding these encounters and acting on them in an appropriate manner. I cram in as much diverse experience as possible within the time I have.

Philosophy studies human thinking, knowledge and existence; aesthetics, math, ethics, logic... It encompasses the entire range of existence, including the psychological aspect of cognitive functioning, which traditionally looks at thinking, conceiving, reasoning, problem solving and so forth.

The 'problems of living' is the proper subject of philosophy according to Lin Yutang. Indeed, philosophy posits questions about how we should live and behave, what is the meaning of life, the value of knowledge, whether there is a God, infinitude, and how we are to confront the unknown and death. How can one plan life given that permanence, certainty, and reliable answers do not exist? How do you greet each new day in spite of the depressing awareness that there may be no hope? How does one keep going once they have recognized their terrible aloneness and their spirit is crying?

I have failed to find answers for many of my questions about life Therefore I have learnt to live with not knowing. Bill Plotkin suggests, if I found the answers I might not comprehend or be able to apply the knowledge.

Freud and others have postulated work as the main theme of life. I do not agree. Work is only one thread in the fabric of life. A meaningful life entails involvement with people, animals, elements, nature, science, art.

And we must not forget play. Yes, it is good to say we have achieved, we have contributed, we have accomplished - but only if we can also say it has been fun, it has been exciting, that we have felt the all-encompassing joy of life in the universe. At this point in history human survival is dependent upon the attention we give to these factors.

Philosophers have prescribed the path to a democratic society, the way to economic success, formulas to become enlightened, how to find inner peace, heaven, and so on. Despite cultural differences the theories are often similar. Aldous Huxley's, *Perennial Philosophy* details similarities, as does Roger Walsh, in *Essentials of Spirituality*. Research suggests the mind has an innate tendency to synthesize and organize the development of its potentials. This facilitates our problem solving and future planning; It also permits our creator PELGAM to devise an enjoyable, productive, safe and predictable existence.

In 1958, prior to my high school graduation I happened upon a new publication. *Taoism the Parting of the Way* authored by Holmes Welch and published by Beacon Press - the publishing house of the Unitarian Universalist Association (UU). Taoism is about negotiating one's life through the labyrinth of life experiences, with emphasis on compassion, nature, simplicity, polarity, reduction of desires and balance. I found it a natural progression from Thoreau.

The fundamentals of Taoism can be found in ancient mysticism and an endless list of religions and philosophies, including Thoreau and

Emerson, which stress the importance of living in harmony with nature. Taoism believes humans are a part of the universe much as our limbs are a part of our body. We must flow gracefully with the driving natural force pulsing through and around us. Failure to live in accord with this natural force results in a disintegration of the life spirit. It would be as if your left foot strode off in one direction and your right foot another painfully tearing you apart.

According to Lin Yutang, the spirituality of China is a blend of Taoism and Confucianism. Taoism has its share of confusing concepts. Chinese culture has been around longer than most; yet by the twentieth century they were far behind the achievements of other cultures. I wonder if the concept of non-action put forth by Lao Tsu may be a partial cause:

Tao abides in non-action
Yet nothing is left undone

It is a keep your hands off and let things follow their natural course concept. What goes up must come down. Human behaviour should be effortless spontaneity, non-action *(wu-wei)*. Sure, there is always more that can be done; but, not striving, not always trying to fill the time, allows one to relax and become aware of the natural reality about them. One flourishes not by adding more, but by stripping off the trappings of culture.

I have difficulty agreeing with withdrawal from the world; to paraphrase,

A small country has fewer people

Machines for doing work are not needed

Because people fear death, they do not travel

They do not us vehicles or weapons

They give up reading and writing

Food, clothing and housing are simple

They do not visit their neighbours

Happy in their ways they grow old and die.

How is that for a withdrawn isolationist philosophy? Perhaps this attitude was fostered by the power elite. It would be easy to control such a population.

I have included Buddhism and Taoism in this 'Philosophy' chapter rather than the 'Spiritual Relations' chapter, because neither in their earliest form postulated the existence of a God.

Transcendentalism and Buddha - Thoreau's emphasis on independence, self-sufficiency and getting back to nature, is obvious in the Transcendentalists approach to life. In a 1937 reprint of Thoreau's major works *Walden and Other Writings*, the prominent critic Brooks Atkinson described the Transcendentalists as renouncing the collection of knowledge and material possessions; they preferred to draw their inspiration from living in harmony with nature and human nature.

In contrast, Buddhist philosophy seeks to exclude a key element of human nature (emotion). Siddhartha Gautama offers us the 'middle path' to a meaningful life. The approach decries human emotions as an evil to be dispensed with. What kind of intelligent personality would suggest this? It is true emotions are problematic, yet they also enrich life.

Siddhartha had been a prince in a wealthy family and his father was the raja, the leader of the local principality. As a young man he married, had a son, and continued living in his father's palace - all normal behaviour for his cultural group. During his twenties he rarely set foot outside the family palace; this is strange behaviour in a culture that is made up of emotionally inter-dependent, close-knit extended families and villages. He could not have been in tune with nature, nor the world of humankind.

Some suggest his father kept him on the property to protect him from the harshness of life. Shortly before turning thirty he abandons everything - wife, son, parents, relatives, friends and villagers. He wanders about the nation for many years, living in deprivation and hardship, and eventually creates his own philosophy of life. Today it is known and practised world-wide.

Is his theory the product of an emotionally undeveloped and cold personality? Or is it an example of secure wealth moving on to strive for power? Whatever the case, I find many of his teachings helpful.

Over time followers may alter a philosophy and make improvements. At other times the opposite can be the case - teachings can be distorted in such a way as to make them meaningless or harmful. All too often founders cultivate a following of disciples who worship them as Gods. Around the world the faithful followers take-action to cope with the vicissitudes of life. They invest in materialism, cast their votes, bow on bended knee, lay prostrate on the ground, spin prayer wheels, chant mantras, sit in meditation and so on. It is debatable as to whether this is better than what non-believers do.

At the societal level there often is a wide variance between philosophical tenets and what is practiced. Look up the definition of democracy, capitalism, security, happiness and compare what you perceive going on around you. The disparity suggests a schizophrenic society. The philosophy stressing hard work and specialization produces socially inept workaholics, who stay in the workforce till they drop. This is an example of carrying beliefs to the extreme. I am aware of professionals in their nineties, who still work fulltime.

Mathematics is included in philosophy, which is not surprising given that many philosophers were also mathematicians. I include it with trepidation, because I always loved philosophy, but struggled with maths.

* * *

Math and the Troll - It is a cold November morning 1946, in Springfield, Ohio. Light snow lazily drifts down from a dull grey sky. My parents are asleep, because dad works second shift at Crowell Collier's printing plant and mom waits up for his coming home at 11:00pm. I too am sound asleep, as yet not adjusted to rise early for the first grade of school.

At the last-minute mom rushes in and wakes me. She hastily thrusts me into my clothes and shoves me out the door. Bundled up in a thick coat with cords attached to my mittens, heavy rubber boots and a hat with ear tabs, I trudge along the sidewalk towards school one and a half miles distant. My six-year-old legs are up to the task. As instructed, I look both ways at every intersection. Vision blurry through snow wetted glasses I finally see the dirty brick school building in the misty gloom ahead.

I remove my boots and hang my coat and hat in the cloakroom that runs across the rear of the classroom. I walk down the aisle past the adult European immigrant sitting at his desk near the back wall and go to my desk at the front, this desk has been allotted to me because of my poor eyesight. From this position I can just barely read the teacher's blackboard writing.

The bosomy broad shouldered, heavy boned, stout faced troll (I didn't know there were caves nearby?) paces around in a rustling floor length dress, wielding a yardstick. It is broad daylight, why isn't she rigid stone? As I try to learn the numbers my wrong answers are rewarded with a whack on my hands as she towers over me. Repeated mistakes make my knuckles sorer and she screams at me, 'Did you eat your breakfast?' 'No,' I reply meekly. She yanks me out of my seat, whacks my butt, drags me to the cloakroom and screams, 'Go home and eat breakfast!'

Lots of snow coming down, the wind is stronger and the snow deeper with drifts as high as my waist. I slip and fall a couple of times. It's difficult to see through my frosted glasses. My raw knuckles sting from the cold, I enter the sleeping household.

Ear lobes burning and fingers tingling, I quietly slide a kitchen chair to the cupboards, stand on it, open the door, grasp a bowl, climb back down and place the bowl on the table. I repeat the process at another cupboard to retrieve the cornflakes. I scoot the chair back to the table and pour the cereal. I forego milk, as I am not sure my numb hands can handle it without spilling, for which I would get into big trouble. Just as I sit down, mother shuffles in closely followed by dad; 'Why are you home?' I tell them, and all hell erupts.

They holler, shake and terrorize me because people might think they were bad parents. I kept protesting that I had been honest! - Mom always stressed honesty, but it did not help. Having vented their anger, they poured cereal down my throat, crammed me into my coat, hat, and boots, and pushed me out into the blizzard.

Slipping and sliding through the snowdrifts, I was relieved to have escaped home, yet terrified of returning to the troll. With all this snow I wondered if there were any of those white bears around? I considered sitting in a drift till I froze, but then I would miss the morning cookies and milk.

* * *

Historically, schools presented maths in a confusing manner. Vast numbers of people fear and hate maths. Current math teaching utilizes more understandable approaches, making it possible for the average person to master basic algebra, geometry and statistics. These skills enable them to handle their tax return, understand their mortgage payment plan, their insurance statistics and design the lines of their new home. Plus, they are much less likely to be led astray by manipulative politicians or corporations.

***

Logic - is another branch of philosophy, a systematic method of reasoning, requiring the collection of the relevant data and organizing it into a seamless flow. The nitty-gritty details are processed in the brain's left hemisphere and synthesized in the right hemisphere to produce a useable answer or plan.

Like math, logic can have word problems, statements and abstractions that confound the best of scholars. At the more negotiable end, logic merges into common sense (whatever that is), which is what most of us are referring to when we claim to be logical. If you want to scare yourself, create a diary of your behaviours and determine how many are logical and what ones are kneejerk emotional reactions.

Western society provides piecemeal logic training, some at school, some on the job and some in the community. Consequently, many citizens do not know how to go about the collection, organisation and analysis of data upon which they will make decisions. Thus, it is difficult for them to create workable plans, directions and actions for their life.

Ethics - are the moral principles guiding our determination of what is right and wrong, good and bad. Stoicism stresses the tranquil mind, having a sense of peace and contentment as the right or ultimate good. This along with freedom from material attachments appeals to me. When the theory advocates abstinence from sex, they lose me.

Having grown up in the United States I am thoroughly indoctrinated with the work ethic that asserts it is good to work hard and be productive. This moral belief plagues me to this day. I have worked hard and accomplished much; now in old age it is time to relax and have fun. Joe Campbell stressed the goodness of 'hedonism'; the seeking of pleasure.

During my working years I participated in many fun and pleasurable pastimes; now I cannot find light hearted activities that interest me.

Some hedonism stresses striving for pleasure in the present; this is in line with meditation, stressing focus on the here and now. I agree, our focus should be on today. However, society does not include some peoples in its concerns, and has a calloused disregard for the well-being of future generations.

We maintain an exploitive economical system creating poverty and crime. Our educational system fails to provide those with low IQ, physical disabilities or mental problems a means to build a successful life. Programmed destruction of the environment and the extinction of species are direct consequences of our present behaviour. Would you accept these behaviours in the family living next door?

Imagine a nuclear family of four children; one is slightly darker skinned, and another is a slow learner. The parents (perhaps embarrassed) shunt these two aside and ignore them. The best of everything is provided for their two preferred children. They purchase chemistry sets so they can experiment with things, elaborate telescopes, radio receivers, musical instruments, art lessons, and all manner of things. Enormous sums are spent on high stone walls around the property, video and audio surveillance systems and private police are hired to protect the favoured kids from the world's riff-raff.

The 'undesirable' offspring are only given meagre food and clothing, live isolated in a chicken coop and given no guidance. They barely survive and are crippled as they enter adulthood, only able to subsist on the margins of society. Are these parents acting morally?

Sometimes it is almost impossible to determine what is right or wrong. This is made worse by governments, religions, institutions, private interest groups and individuals who attempt to sell their version of what is right and wrong. Often this only benefits them and no one else. The killing of blacks is acceptable in many United States communities; Christians are fair game in some countries, and a particular group of Muslims are currently being slaughtered in Miramar.

I view the societal slippage into immorality as another facet of stunting that began with the population explosion and other dysfunctions. It is yet another signpost indicating we, as the last upright walking hominid species, are on the road to extinction.

A full investigation of ethics' three main areas, meta, normative and applied, is beyond the scope of this document; it is something you can pursue on your own. It would help if high schools required in-depth study of values within the culture and those of adjacent cultures. In the meantime, try to keep your behaviours in accord with the natural world and not too much in conflict with the local culture.

Philosophy PELGAM

You as Philosopher - You are a philosopher if you have ideas about the meaning of existence and how to solve problems. However, the majority of people have not thought about it, or cannot verbalize their philosophy. This fits with Bertrand Russel saying – 'most people hate to think'. You cannot expect a successful life, when you do not know your own guiding principles, or whether they are valid? Each person needs to place their life philosophy, beliefs and values into black and white. Where did yours come from? Did you choose them, or were you born into them? Are you following a crowd or charismatic character? Again, you need a plan, a map, rules orchestrating your thinking and problem solving for today and the future.

The brain likes structure, I schedule weekly work and all my diverse activities in a daily diary; future work, goals and commitments are placed on a computer document. Thus, I increase my efficiency and remove the pressure of trying to remember things.

If you are single or a couple, then your philosophy will be somewhat individualistic; however, it should pave the way for an eventual transition into a group. Hub living minimizes individual philosophy and emphasizes group philosophy, which facilitates the well - being of members for all time. It encompasses science and the hard facts of life, as well as the intangibles - sentimentality, humor, beauty…. It promotes a sense of joy and gratitude for the blessings of life and a determination to make the best of what the Hub offers. It incorporates methodologies

373

for coping successfully with the vicissitudes of life, whether in present day society, a survivalist world, or in space.

Laboratories have been unable to determine the optimal process your brain should follow to efficiently solve problems. Women and men do not use the same method. Studies have shown ten brains may each use a different technique to solve the same problem. This is to be expected given societies' failure to standardize the tuning of brain filters, and its failure to teach formal thought processing skills. This may be on the verge of changing. Some UK schools have embarked upon teaching students how to think.

Industry, business and government often use the think tank approach for problem solving. You too can use it. Write down a problem confronting you; then write down as many solutions as you can think of, no matter how silly they may seem. You will be amused by some of the ridiculous ones and surprised at how many good solutions you think up. There is a downside - random, unconnected and useless thoughts may flood in and result in confusion and inaction. It is important to learn how to channel your thoughts into productive action or slow down and stop thought processes.

Life's journey is similar to a journey over the world's oceans, both are dangerous adventures. Let us suppose you come down to the bay and I show you six attractive boats tied to the dock. You may choose for yourself the one you prefer. The land beneath your feet, stricken by earthquakes, is beginning to sink beneath the sea. Shortly, you will have to sail out upon the ocean. The nearest safe land is thousands of nautical miles across tumultuous, reef strewn, pirate - infested seas. Although all the boats look good, one has internal keel rot, another an unreliable engine, a third has weak poorly fashioned planks that leak and the fourth is not designed to handle rough water. Only two boats are seaworthy.

Do you have enough time left to climb in and assess each vessel, time for philosophical inquiry? The evolutionary unfolding of life requires a sound philosophy as the back bone of a life plan; it must account for all possible scenarios. Remember, some people have accidents and die at the age of twenty; others are killed by chronic health problems by age fifty, and only a few live to one hundred.

Swapping vessels mid-ocean can be hazardous or impossible. Each philosophy you investigate could have viable aspects to enhance your life. The philosophy you construct for yourself will determine the quality of your life journey (or what's left of it); will your life be safe and successful or full of stress and hardship, possibly ended prematurely by a gruesome death.

Yes! Philosophy is a deep subject and often difficult to grasp. It is like a new software program - incomprehensible at first, but after sufficient time and effort it becomes more doable.

Daily casual thoughts tend to become our life intentions. Have a look at *theintentionexperiment.com*. You may learn successful strategies by watching other animals or people, and by keeping tab on your own wins and losses.

Life's purpose may be beyond our comprehension, yet we dare not dismiss the issue; to do so could entrap our family line into a culture that is stagnate and invalid. We are part of a jigsaw puzzle. Our thoughts and intentions impact everyone around us, as well as future generations and societies. Will your great, great, great grandchildren look back upon you and wonder why you made so many poor decisions, why you failed to act, why you left them a burden? If you are to avoid these negatives, you must investigate many philosophies and give the matter a great deal of thought.

'As a single footstep will not make a path on the earth, so a single thought will not make a pathway in the mind. To make a deep physical path, we walk again and again. To make a deep mental path, we must think over and over the kind of thoughts we wish to dominate our lives'.
Henry David Thoreau

Have a read of Bertrand Russell; the past century's greatest philosopher and brilliant mathematician. His publications are short in length, easy to understand and tackle problems we all face.

Chapter 16 Destroyer PELGAM

The young smiling boy's fingers grasp the hair of the severed head, a patient swallows the antibiotic capsule, the employee bursts into tears from the boss's tirade, the swinging ball renders the historic building to dust and the baby tooth is pushed out – examples of the destroyer PELGAM at work. It has genetic and learned components, some have positive impact on life, while others are negative. First, we will examine the negative aspects.

Negative Aspects –I suggest distortion and misuse of this PELGAM began before written history; one of the causes may have been the population explosion which strained the food supply. Clan members having an obsessive destroyer PELGAM led the clan's subjugation of rival clans to claim their food resources. This triggered the demise of cooperative behaviour, replacing it with destructive action and aggressive rivalry.

Hence the warrior concept emerged, the glorified and romanticized individual or group focused on destroying the psyche, the property and lives of others. Japan had the 'samurai', the 'warrior monks' were prominent in medieval Europe, and Vikings had a warrior centred social structure. Sadistic religious groups eradicated foes and non-believers; the Spanish inquisition slaughtered one hundred million. In the past several decades, ethnic cleansing has become the vogue.

Proliferation of destroyer behaviour laid the groundwork for contemporary society's preoccupation with competition. Competition is so entrenched in the modern psyche that people think it is normal. They search for ways to compete, giving no thought to what might be accomplished by cooperation.

Destroyers are a stain on the path of human evolution. They are like young children with a box of matches, enthralled with devastation. Ever seeking to eliminate opposition, drunk with the power of smashing others into submission, determined to prove they can subjugate everyone and even the very planet they live on. They serve as models for the stunted masses and are held in high esteem as warriors and conquerors. Many leaders have assumed this celebrated roll: prime ministers, Queens, presidents…

Destroyer models dominate literature, music, theatre, movies, and television. People of all ages weekly spend hours viewing violent mayhem and playing explicitly violent video games. Emotional abuse, intimidation, bullying, physical attack, rape, murder, financial deprivation, sexism, racism, social stratification... are in part activated by the destroyer drive. It's all about denigration of a person's self-concept. These behaviours could in part result from the voluminous storehouse of frustration, resentment and anger citizens have from trying to survive in a system that oppresses and enslaves them.

The daily news reveals large scale destroyers at work, genocide, species extinction, environmental destruction and war. Modern day nations expend huge efforts and monies for their war machine. Legislative policies destroy any effort to improve the meeting of basic human needs. Legislators often hide behind the word 'progress', as their justification for demolishing historic buildings. Political parties push legislation for law and order and use this to infiltrate every level of personal life, seeking out and eliminating those who might rock the boat. Political campaigns fervently attack the character of adversaries. In the most advanced nations, contrarians, those attempting to alter destructive actions, are often exterminated or imprisoned.

In the business world millions of advertising dollars are spent attempting to destroy the reputations of competitors. Drug corporations spend fortunes to destroy natural aid and self-help movements. Oil, timber and mining companies conduct wholesale slaughter of animal species and the natural environment.

Freud used the term Thanatos, the Greek God of death, to describe an instinctive destructive death wish present in humans. Masochism is a moderate form of this, those who seem hell bent to make their lives difficult and miserable. Perhaps addiction, dangerous sports and high debt levels are masochism in disguise. When the average person's personality contains too much destroyer intent, domestic and civil violence ensue.

Social commentators predict we are approaching civilian unrest and international war over food and water. In the impending calamity a government might use its destroyer capabilities to poison the air, water or food of a rebellious group, the poor, or an ethnic group. Chemical or biological measures might be used to curtail a group's ability to propagate. A country might then blame the catastrophe on neighbouring nations and use this as an excuse for a military attack to decimate the population of a rival country. While history is littered with the wreckage of destroyers and the future looks grim, we need to acknowledge the benefits of the destroyer PELGAM.

Positive Destruction - Apoptosis is programmed cell death in the immature brain. Another program destroys old skin cells. White blood cells act as soldiers destroying invading pathogens, the eosinophil is one example. It secretes chemicals that consume parasites, such as hook worms and tapeworms. The human mind contains functions to rid the system of outmoded physical, mental and behavioural elements, as well as external threats. Humans use the destroyer function to overcome dependence on parents and exorcize incorrect learning. In many ways it can be life supporting and finds a natural and positive expression in the work done by timber cutters, demolition crews, butchers, surgeons, heavy equipment operators and so on.

When adversity threatens your destroyer PELGAM kicks in, goading you to run away, or fight and destroy the antagonist. We are genetically primed to obliterate anything or anyone that interferes with our access to food, sex or shelter. Some of the resulting actions are questionable. The farmer burns off underbrush to kill noxious weeds and pests, but this also results in the destruction of natural wildlife habitat and the ecosystem. In contact sports some athletes seek to injure the opponent, destroying their ability to compete. Boxing speaks for itself.

Is rampant destruction perchance society's saving grace? Humanity has chosen to ignore the overpopulated status of the globe; consequently, it will not be long before most people will be living on the precarious edge of survival in a daily state of misery. Is war the answer? World II two cost eighty million lives. If the coming chaos exterminates a couple billion people, it could buy time for the human species to evolve, to mature, to delete the negative aspects of the destroyer PELGAM.

Learning Positive Destruction - A proper diet, physical and emotional fitness and superb cognitive functioning provide the ground work for positive utilisation of the destroyer trait. Those not employed in a destroyer role can learn to vent frustrations in a non-harmful fashion. Back in the sixties when I was an undergraduate at Ohio State University, I witnessed an exorcising of torment via the destroyer PELGAM.

Each fall a fraternity held a fund-raising event; they placed a junk car on the front lawn of the fraternity house near the curb. People would pull up in their automobiles or get off the bus from the city and gleefully donate money. For five dollars they could pick up the sledgehammer and have one bash on the car.

One twilight evening a flashy Cadillac pulled up; out stepped an executive impeccably dressed in his Botany 500 suit. He slipped off his suit jacket and loosened his tie. Donning protective goggles and heavy gloves, he literally went berserk with nine powerful blows. With a relaxed smile on his face he gave them a fifty-dollar bill, said keep the change and calmly departed.

Some years later at the Idaho Falls mental health centre, I and several staff took groups of patients for weekend therapy sessions at a private lodge in the wilderness adjacent to Yellow Stone National Park. Harry, our recreational therapist would bring along boxes of pottery left over from his weekly pottery classes. I set up an exercise wherein each patient would pick several pieces of pottery as symbols of a person or issue that was problematic. They then lined up outside, six meters from a stonewall. Taking turns, they screamed and hurled the pottery, smashing it to smithereens against the wall. The release of tension, frustration and resulting joy was amazing to witness. Even more amazing and sad were the one or two individuals who were too emotionally tied up in knots and full of fear to throw pottery.

During each stage of life, a person must remove thinking and behaviour which is no longer appropriate. This could be done in rites of passage wherein a child or adult destroys and frees themselves from some pattern of dysfunctional behaviour, moving on to a more mature, effective lifestyle. The Hub may use various hobbies to help members constructively employ the destroyer PELGAM, such as clay bird shooting and ten pin bowling.

My whipper-snipper is a great outlet. I don my battle gear of goggles, long pants, boots, long sleeved shirt, hat, breathing mask and go to war.

I wade into the tall grasses, swinging my weapon back and forth, chopping them down with a vengeance, destroying the opposition.

Dressing for a destroyer session can be helpful. For instance, people don a swimming suit when swimming, pads and a helmet when roller blading and special clothing for a party. A person might imagine themselves in suitable attire, such as a suit of armour, or it could be an impressive business suit to address a hostile board meeting. On alien worlds a space suit and ray gun may be needed to drive back the stinking, slimy aliens which spit fire and acid.

Are you in control of your destroyer PELGAM or is it controlling you? You do not always have to obliterate roadblocks in your life's path; sometimes it is easier, safer and quicker to go around obstacles.

Optimal human existence relies on destroying and discarding the old to allow room for the new.

Chapter 17 Power PELGAM

I crouch astride the beast and hang on, feeling the tremor of her strength. Her bellowing roar is resonating in my ears as we hurtle through the mountain conifer forest; the passing trees are but a blur. We rocket up steep slopes and down winding rocky creek beds; every fibre of my being is intensely alert. My body leans in synchronized alignment with her every move. With a sense of exhilaration, I use my power to control her power to catapult me into freedom.

Power is to have command, to be the dominant force in your existence; self-determination is the ability to move in the direction you wish to go, to significantly influence your destiny. Power is having the strength and fortitude to overcome adversity, break free of entrapments, and possessing the resources to meet and surpass survival needs.

Vacuum nozzle training establishes a person's power orientation; this starts in the womb and continues via environmental learning through adulthood. Detrimental exercising of power is a typical trait of narcissists. Whereas an insufficient wielding of power is often found in shy or fearful personalities.

There are numerous personality classifications having a touch of the power monger. The authoritarian desires the status, the obsessive compulsive is fascinated with the systematic ordering of things. The antisocial and the histrionic are masterful manipulators using coercive control for their own benefit, with little or no empathy for the well-being of those about them. Deceitfulness is a given in this group, who at any time may push your button simply because they enjoy watching you jump.

Inadequate Power –A long time ago some of the power wielders in a clan (chief, priest, prominent warrior, merchant...) began to usurp the personal power of the average person. Like present day predator power wielders, they manipulated the variables to enhance their personal status and power. This evolved into the absurd; a person claiming to be a God or a representative (King) of God.

A consortium, as detailed in the current affairs chapter, wields power within most nations; one of its goals is to insure the citizen has insufficient power to threaten those in the seat of power. Many governments are for the most part puppets, carrying out the mandates of the consortium. Nevertheless, they do have power over the masses in areas that are of no concern to the consortium.

The French Revolution upset the power of the aristocrats, big land owners and church, leading to a more egalitarian sharing of resources and power. Over the ensuing years this progress has been eroded for the average Western citizen. Today the general public has little voice in fundamental questions such as education, where they live, their vocation, or how their society functions.

The majority of U.S citizens do not vote, as they know politicians, regardless of party, pander to the elitist and ignore the masses. In

Australia voting is mandatory, implying voters are in control, nothing could be further from the truth. In the last decade or so, prime ministers voted into office by the public, have routinely been sacked and replaced by the political party in power.

In contemporary western nations approximately 95% of assets – and thus also power - is held by less than 1% of the population. The election of a multi-millionaire as Australia's prime minister (and more recently a billionaire snatching the U. S. presidency) suggests society has regressed into the aristocrat era not unlike what existed in pre-revolutionary France. Many citizens feel robbed and have an air of hopelessness. Their frustrations can be seen in the social problems of the community.

Modern life *'has produced alienation, powerlessness and the subordination of all aspects of life to economic and bureaucratic requirements of control and efficiency. Modern man does not seem to have any firm guidelines on how to behave towards others; he feels estranged from the world in which he lives and has the impression that his life is run by impersonal forces over which he has no control.'*

With permission from Philosophy Now magazine, March 2010.
'Political Philosophy After Metaphysics' by A. Aoujit.

Can a windfall of money from lotto, inheritance… inspire reclamation of personal power? More often than not, newly wealthy people buy the mansion, yacht, fancy automobile with the aim of imitating the life of

387

the super wealthy; not realizing they are still trapped in cultural myths which undermine their personal autonomy. For the ruling class, material possessions are only frivolous status symbols. The elite do not have the time nor interest to mess about in boats or laze about the pool; they derive their pleasure from wielding power.

I doubt power mongers and destroyers possess the comprehensive flexible cognitive abilities necessary for good leadership. Nor do they have a grass roots understanding of the populace. Their puppets, the politicians, are only interested in themselves. The public is well aware of political faulty decision making, incompetent management and poorly conceived ventures which waste public dollars, resulting in faltering infra-structure and excessive debt.

Many of those in power have been successful because they have no qualms about being unscrupulous, nor any concern for the well-being of the community. Countless others in possession of natural leadership ability have avoided taking leadership as they were unwilling to lead dishonest unbalanced lives. Aldous Huxley in his book *Perennial Philosophy* suggests democratic government is only achievable in small populations. Hence, large communities are apt to be governed by oligarchies of people covetous of power.

Kleptocracy and Gun Slingers - When power is held by a few it results in kleptocracy, transferring wealth and power from the masses to the

388

ruling class. In reading reviews of Jared Diamond's *Guns, germs and Steel,* and other political analysts, numerous writers suggest most governments are a kleptocracy. The intellectuals (10%) and the workers (60%) may succumb to this arrangement, rationalizing that they have more power and status than the poor (15%) and the disaffected (10%). Society keeps these latter two groups buried, out of sight; they are viewed as unavoidable costs of the system. Protecting the kleptocracy from foreign nations is the military's responsibility. Protection from the local population is the most important task of the local politicians and police.

The abusive power of an openly coercive political regime is perhaps not as dangerous as a government that pretends to put forth positive options for the citizenry. The French philosopher Michael Foucault cites an example of this when he described the 'disciplinary power' arising in 18th century European administrative and social service systems. The ruling elite vocally supported and created myths that on the surface appeared to be in the best interest of the people. The contemporary western society citizen is quite familiar with the smiling, benevolent appearing politician who presents a new legislation, touted as a benefit for the public, but in practise, the law will undermine the power and well-being of the citizen.

Oligarchies, kleptocracy and misuse of power occur regardless of the political system - socialism, communism, democracy, monarchy... *Terror in the Name of God* by Jessica Stern details how the Indian government in its administration of the Kashmir province, used local compliant politicians to monopolize business, both legal and illegal. Present day governments of first world nations typically administer a multitude of taxes on the average citizen, while taking little or no taxes from the elite. The 2015 publication of *Putin's Kleptocracy* by Karen Dawisha probes the billions of dollars looted from Russian citizens by the Russian elite.

Those in power often live grandiose lifestyles that ignore the laws and mores of the community. When they make mistakes, like the GFC, they recoup their losses from the masses. If the multitudes were functioning maturely and had power, they would not have tolerated this.

When power holders become excessively focused on self-concerns and fail to maintain adequate positive living conditions for the populace, the society collapses. Civil conflict ensues between groups and between the masses and power holders. Historically, the abusive use of power has led to terrorism, revolution and warfare. Whether it is a new social order on earth or a planetary colony, society must devise a system to circumvent kleptocracy.

I got nailed by tradesman power when building the cottage. Political parties promise benefits in return for votes. In our state the plumbing lobby has successfully ensnared the lawmakers to enact legislation which limits the number of plumbers to be trained and outlaws plumbing by homeowners. Hence, the demand for plumbers exceeds the availability. Which means they only do work that is convenient, do it their way rather than the customers and charge exorbitant rates.

My plumber left me with no hot water in the bathroom sink and a grey water tank that floated up out of the ground with the first big rain. This latter calamity cost me hundreds of dollars and he denied any responsibility.

I filed a complaint with the state plumbing regulatory agency; they claimed they had no means of making the plumber pay my costs. Many consumer laws and agencies are in fact just means of collecting more taxes and/or protecting the workers who voted them into office. Sometimes you win and sometimes you lose.

Sufficient Power – I believe the original human was genetically endowed with a loving cooperative nature. He lived in a group amidst a naturally productive uncrowded environment allowing him to quickly and easily meet food, shelter and clothing needs. Group members having a high degree of skill, such as the best hunter, toolmaker and so on, had some power to lead in their area of expertise. Otherwise, I suspect power was shared; the individual always had the freedom to follow his own path.

This individual power was still evident in the North American Nez Pierce tribe when Europeans encountered them. Today this power over one's destiny continues in a few remote indigenous clusters and some urban groups. But for the most part, small groups like the Australian aboriginals, American Indians, European Kurds… are among the most powerless and disenfranchised people on the planet.

As a youngster I lived in a neighbourhood populated by Jews; the majority worked for themselves. They owned junkyards, pawn shops, furniture stores and other businesses. Some were employed in positions where they tended to be leaders and almost operated independently, such as teachers, professors, lawyers and medical practitioners. It seems the Jewish sub-culture is aware of the importance of maintaining personal power.

Bertrand Russel in his book *Power* suggests power and glory are major goals for a human. Bertie states that each of us would like to have the ultimate power of being a God who everyone worships. I wonder if this infinite need for adoration and attention is a result of the destruction of communal life; would the communal child awash in the love of many parents, receiving constant attention from many Hub members, have an infinite need for power?

Bertie goes on to posit that once the individual, group, or community has achieved a modicum of comfort they will then pursue power rather than wealth. Continued focus on wealth accumulation only occurs if it increases the accumulation of power. The correctness of his statement is readily observable. People successful in media, sports, and business often go on to become board members of organizations, enter politics or seek power in some other fashion.

Levels of Power - Each personality has a genetic need for power that involves the basics of survival - the power to find food, shelter, protection and propagation. The learned need for power is the result of early brain filter training and may be weak or strong. A person with a high need for power will spend an inordinate amount of time and energy to gain power and avoid the attempts of other power wielders. Let us look at the negatives and positives of power wielders.

High Need for Power– Hypothetically, the average person might devote ten percent of their brain filter hoses to power concerns while the high-power person may allot forty percent. Having thirty percent less nozzles to receive valuable non-power related incoming information, is essentially a learning disability. As children they may be belligerent at school and run afoul of the law; others become 'passive aggressive' personalities always smiling and pleasant, but undercover doing what they want.

As adults it is often said of them, 'you can't get through to them,' 'they don't listen,' 'they are naive.' Generally, high power people avoid positions of authority as they cannot tolerate criticism, nor cope with large numbers of people who might challenge their power. They are unable to maintain close interpersonal relationships, as they have no interest in, nor concern for the well-being of others.

This confines them to small, simple, low populated settings. They generally only maintain control over their family and sometimes only over their spouse. The stay at home control freak mother who dominates her husband and wields an iron fist over her children is a well-known character in literature. Within this cloistered life some live a contented happy life; others suffer. Friends do not exist unless they are more dysfunctional than the power wielder.

Obsessed with controlling others, self-control is lacking. Some women spend their way to bankruptcy via expensive makeup and clothing; obesity, alcoholism and drug abuse are common. The dominance obsession clouds thinking making daily life a struggle. With little success in marriage, child rearing or other pursuits, they plod through one misery after another. They can be extremely brutal, vengeful and antisocial, and may follow a scorched earth policy. If they cannot have their way, they obliterate everything to stop others from winning. A few become depressed and suicidal.

Moderate Need for Power – Perhaps 30 percent of nozzles are devoted to power. These people are more in contact with reality and are better at learning how to use power in a constructive manner; they are capable of taking on power positions in their career and the community as long as the demands are not too severe. Moderate power wielders can often be found in community organizations such as dog obedience, sport and service clubs.

Some inhabit entry level and middle management positions at work. When conditions are problematic their inefficient thinking processes often lead to poor decisions and cold hearted, ruthless, combative, dictatorial behaviour. In private business they are quickly moved out of decision-making positions. In the public sector they are usually left in their position or are promoted.

They tend to be lenient with their family and usually have friends. Have you ever had someone ask you a question and as you give the answer you notice they are not really listening to you? Or maybe you will ask them if they want a drink or some food and they decline, saying they will just share yours? In both cases they are exercising their power over you, they do not really care what answer you give; they are only wanting you to respond to their command.

Pets are often vehicles for their need to control, which is far easier for them than dealing with people. Life is fairly satisfying, but hectic; many just keeping their heads above water. Again, self-control can be an issue.

Above Average Need for Power – Twenty per cent or so of nozzles are devoted to power issues, resulting in fairly good contact with reality. Threats to power are sought and sucked in, the data used to refine power techniques. They may be drawn to causes and conflicts to satisfy their power cravings. These are the leaders in a culture, confident, self-assertive, decisive, action oriented. They have little or no concern of power over family and all too often ignore them. Friends are sought that can match or enhance their power. Self-control is usually good.

Average Need for Power – Only 10 percent of nozzles are used for power issues. Thus, there is a good grasp of reality, given there are no other significant problems. They usually have meaningful interpersonal relations, can take care of themselves, take risks and act independently. Those low in neuroticism and having strong balanced PELGAMS are capable of leadership roles if provided sufficient training.

Below Average Need for Power - Less than ten percent of brain filter nozzles are involved in power matters; they have little interest in wielding power, occasionally taking power stances when they should not and failing to exert power when they should.

Low Need for Power - Less than five percent of hoses are employed for power and tend to draw in useless or harmful data and reject rich stimulus, resulting in widespread dysfunction across personal, career and community issues. They may lurch from calamity to calamity. Unable to lead, they often stay in the background and can be good followers.

All power levels are inexorably linked to all PELGAMs and are not necessarily good or bad, it is all in the application. The dictator uses power to subjugate, the cave monk uses power for self-control. The administration of power by chosen representatives can produce a good girl-scout group, viable nation or a centre for torture.

Claiming Personal Power - The French philosopher Camus claimed the only true success in life was spending your time doing what you want to do. This is personal power. I have known numerous executives and professionals who were considered very powerful. They often work sixty hours or more a week, their afterhours being devoted to making the right contacts and being seen in the right places. In retirement they continue the same pattern sitting on boards. I view them as having little meaningful power and leading grossly unbalanced unsatisfactory lives. They may see me as powerless and irresponsible.

Be careful of the term 'buying power.' Buying things reduces your assets, requiring you to work more hours to meet needs. This is a loss of free time, a loss of power. Instead of focusing on the acquisition of money, learn how to avoid financial expenditure. The less spent, the more available for basic needs, thus the less you have to work. As a result, you have more free time to do as you wish. This is a common trait amongst cruising boaties, farmers, some poor people and a few wealthy.

A low level of personal power and the feeling of impotency; brings many people in for psychotherapy. They complain of having little say about issues at their place of employment, within their community and sometimes in their marriage or child rearing roles. Some are aware they have allowed themselves to become ensnared in cultural traps - materialism, wealth, fame... A therapist can help them build the courage and perseverance necessary to accept responsibility for their lives, to exercise self-control, eradicate bad habits and stand firm against the power wielders.

Therapy encourages and trains them to experiment with leadership roles at work, and to become involved politically or in a social organization. Group therapy is very effective in expanding their awareness of their moral obligations and responsibilities to those about them. It also provides one-to-one practise in confronting power wielders. Such experiences help an individual develop their power potential and steer clear of other's power entrapments.

As a rule, the communal family assists the individual to have more personal power. This may not be the case for the Hindu population of

398

India where power is wielded over relationships via the caste system. One has to give credit to the genius of the power mongers that copied the barnyard pecking order of chickens to create the caste system. It is a magnificent way to keep the population divided and thus easier to control. India is not the only culprit; the divide and conquer approach infects the entire globe; the British class system, the slave commoners of Singapore, the United States lower, middle and upper classes...

Currently space flights utilize a military hierarchal rank system with an identified leader as the mission commander. The lines of authority are clear, as are the work activities for each astronaut's position. On long-term missions and during colonization, periods of unstructured time and the stress of isolation and confinement call for leadership that is both task-oriented and supportive. A strict military approach is likely to breed destructive resentment.

Many space exploration crew problems can be avoided by using Hub families as crew. A Hub's cooperative operation involving diverse personalities and skills makes them ideal candidates for the complex hazards of stellar voyaging, and planetary colonization.

Hub members share power; thus, the Hub is well suited to teach proper use of power and curtail improper use. A major deterrent to the abuse of power is learning to form emotionally close interpersonal bonds. This is facilitated in the Hub family. The individual learns how the smallest act of personal affirmation given to others, the tiniest thought of faith or the simplest word of praise may have immeasurable power to positively benefit a group member.

Teaching children skills (work, hobby, sport…) increases their self-confidence; thus, they are more likely to be resourceful, assertive, to stand up for themselves, and decisive in their thinking and acting.

Your power will be obvious when you maintain a meaningful balance of all your PELGAMs and assist your group in its pursuits. The ultimate power is the ability to give it to others, to give love and commendation, to instil togetherness and cooperation. If these qualities were adopted by 10% of those who currently sit in the consortium's seat of power, it might stem humanities slide into chaos and allow us to find our destiny in the stars.

I believe humans are a loving cooperative species who have the capability to avoid the abuse of power and create a unified, meaningful life style here on earth and the planets of the universe.

Chapter 18 Hub Elements

Philosophy, Administrative structure, Goals

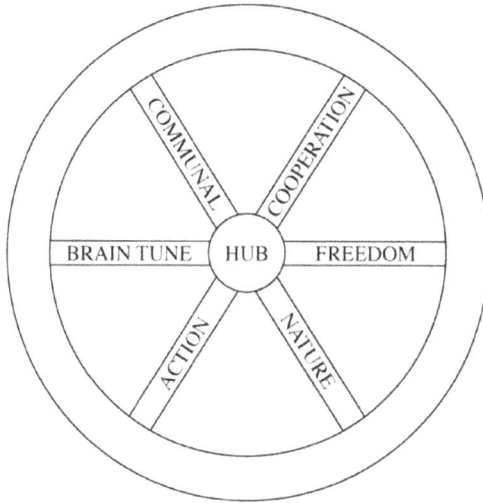

Philosophy – 6 Principles

1 Brain - Tuning of brain filters and maximization of key potentials are prerequisites for successful human evolution. This entails keeping equilibrium among all facets of life.

2 Communal - The Hub extended communal family of up to fifty people is the foundation of human life. It provides an ambience in which the human's intellectual, emotional, social and spiritual growth can fully blossom. Allowing each person to realize their intrinsic capabilities and fully develop them. A Hub of such individuals produces members who possess keen awareness, proficient skills to pull people together and

establish effective daily living systems. The Hub's collective intelligence facilitates the building of an integrated, socially cohesive community which can serve as a model for building the new society on earth and the far-flung planets.

Building a communal family structure will not be difficult, as it is already in the human genetic makeup. It will be easiest in those societies that retain some communal structure - the Italians, Indians, Indonesians, Chinese.... The multigenerational makeup of the traditional extended family is also a part of the Hub. Both share a focus on family rather than economics and always have at least one male and one female on hand to guide children and meet the daily needs of all present in the household

The foundation for Hubs in western society can also be seen in those citizens currently living alternative life styles, families of three or more adults, two adult couples, group marriages, couples living with parents and siblings...

Eight Hubs in close proximity form a Circle containing less than four hundred individuals. Research suggests dysfunction begins when a community exceeds this sum and gets worse as the numbers grow. Next in size is a Constellation; four circles located within walking distance of each other.

In communal living, clothing, bedding, and personal accoutrements are for the most part the only belongings personally possessed by a member. Generally, the majority of material items, such as property, housing, equipment, and tools are owned by the Hub and in some cases by the Circle or Constellation.

The interconnected families of the Circle and Constellation are a self-sufficient network, supplying food, water, energy and meeting human needs from birth to death. The diversity of people is a key element, differing ages, background, education, innate abilities, personalities, physique, interests... Communality is emphasized as more vital than leadership and individualism. These units reduce the need for consumer goods, thus lowering the drain on resources and negative impact on the environment.

Communal families have been the dominant lifestyle throughout history and remains so today. Plato spoke of communal life and in more recent times the Englishman Thomas More.

Traditional communal members lived in one dwelling or several closely aligned structures. Monasteries, although single sexed, are an example of this. The Neolithic long houses of 5000 BC, the Germanic long houses and the Wharenui of the New Zealand Maoris' are other examples. When Europeans explored the North and South America they found indigenous people living in communal structures, such as the Iroquois log structures in North America and similar structures of the Tucano people in South America.

During my visit to the island of Bali in Indonesia, a fifty-year old man invited me into his family compound. As we passed through the gate I noticed a government plaque on the fence stating there were eleven occupants within. A vegetable patch and fruit trees took up much of the plot of land, with a small dwelling in each of the four corners. He and his wife occupied one, his parents another and the other two were his number one and number two married sons, spouses and children.

We walked to a three-sided structure and sat at a table next to a gas stove and grill arrangement, introductions were carried out. Number two son's wife brought cups of tea and a platter of rice cakes; two big eyed children came up and gently ran their fingers over my arm. An electric washing machine and laundry sink were along the back wall. The extended family shared appliances and one motorcycle.

Africa and Asia contain farming villages similar to a Circle or Constellation, wherein a strong alliance exists between families in part because they have intermarried. These units fulfil human needs for love, recognition, socialization, emotional and physical support, and also provide a wealth of learning resources. The resulting internal strength and flexibility of these groups not only increase the likelihood of survival, but also enhance the quality of life. You can read more about communal societies in anthropological studies. The Great Courses

Company has a course on African villages presented by Professor Scott M. Lacy.

I have read histories of communal societies like the Oneida communes and the Brook Farm experiment in the states and I have visited Shaker, Amish and Hutterite groups. These groups do not have long history; thus, I was impressed when I wandered into a North African Berber encampment.

***

In the early morning light, the coolness from the surrounding Atlas peaks envelopes me as I walk into an assortment of tents. The air is full of strange cooking odours along with the familiar scent of donkey, horses, camels, goats, sheep and straw. Soft whispering and the crackle of cooking fires greet the new day.

Walking between tents I stumble and come up face to face with fierce black eyes gazing from beneath the hood of a dark purple djellaba. A white bearded jaw smiles as I draw back, he offers his hand, I shake it. He is my height and looks like me; I feel like I have found a long-lost brother. He motions for us to sit in his tent entrance on a carpet of exquisite designs. A female appears in a colourful fringed and sequined robe. She places a small round wooden tray on the carpet between us; it contains two clear glass cups, into which she crushes mint leaves and pours steaming water. We clink our cups together as he says, 'a la votre!'

We converse in a blend of French and Spanish, with the occasional English word. I will translate our talk into English.

He introduces himself with four or five names, but says, 'Call me Ali.'

'I am Roberto, tis a pleasure to meet you.'

'Why are you in Morocco?'

'I am traveling about Europe and North Africa in my caravan.'

'Ah! you are a traveller as we are. In the winter we graze our herds in a valley such as this one; each winter a different valley. The rest of the year we have stone houses in the mountains.'

'You use donkey drawn wagons to haul your tents and belongings?'

He quietly chuckles. 'No, too much work and old fashioned.' He points to the far side of the camp. 'We use that old Mercedes truck for the heavy hauling during camp moving. It's also used to transport our livestock and produce to market.'

'So, you have some modern conveniences.'

'Si, we are adaptable. If something will help us, we use it. It is one of the reasons we have persevered over time.'

The woman returns with two plates containing hot pancake-like pastries covered with honey.

He says, 'This is baghrir; a common Berber food.'

'How long have you lived in this area?'

'Forever, throughout history our tribes have roamed this area now called Morocco and Tunisia. Some have gone as far East as the Nile and I have ancestors that took part in the invasion of Spain. Many of them remained in Spain, but a few returned to their homeland here in the Atlas.'

Archaeology has found the Berber occupation of North Africa going back to the last ice age and persisting in spite of invasions by the Phoenicians, Greeks, Romans, Arabs and more recently the Germans.

'How many people are there in this village?'

'About eighty, we are one of many sub-groups making up the (unintelligible to me) tribe, scattered about these mountains.'

As we talk, children and adults come and go from the tent and I see an old woman in the corner weaving on a kilim. Nearby, a herd-of-horses graze.

***

Berber tribes reveal how a tightly knit faction can provide a sense of belonging, meaning and security - a life style that persists under threat over thousands of years. I found similar examples in Europe.

Driving through the hilly rural country of south eastern France, we met a young couple living in a picturesque stone cottage. He was a carpenter and she was a beekeeper. They were self-contained with an orchard, vegetable garden, pigs, chickens, a cow and the bees. It was obvious from their talk that they owned this place of many acres; I wondered how a young couple could afford this? She advised me it was an inheritance from her grandmother, who got it from her grandmother and so on. Four hundred years ago her ancestors built the cottage and worked the land.

Quite a few of the surrounding properties and those in the petite village had similarly been handed down through the generations. This community operated like a family, cooperatively helping each other meet needs, only rarely having to venture out into the wider world. They were reality oriented, living in unison with nature, ensuring the long-term viability of the clan.

During graduate school I sat in on counselling sessions with people from polygamous Mormon families living in southern Utah. One distraught twelfth grade girl was to become a second wife upon graduating from high school. She was a firm believer in her faith, but felt a need to experience some freedom prior to marriage. After consultation with the family and the husband to be we arrived at a satisfactory solution. Upon graduation she went to Salt Lake City and worked as a secretary for a year. She lived in a house of wives from other polygamous families who also worked in the city. Two years later, I heard through the grape vine that she was happy and functioning well in her marriage.

The original Mormons held plural marriage as sacred, usually a man and two or more wives. Groupings of these families shared the responsibilities and resources of the community. When the majority of Mormons rescinded plural marriage, three factions representing a couple hundred thousand people, remained polygamous. Mormon culture, whether polygamous or not, provides benefits found in communal societies. Consequently, they probably offer the average citizen a better way of living than the isolated disconnectedness of contemporary western culture. The 2011 book *Love Times Three* by the Darger polygamous family provides insight into this contemporary group life.

A fraternal polyandry family, wherein brothers share the same wife, is the norm in rural Tibet. In this cold harsh environment, it takes the labour of two or more men to feed, clothe and house a family. Fewer offspring are another benefit of this family system.

During the seventies I met five middle aged American couples who lived together. They shared a mansion on ten acres near a major city where all were employed as professionals or in business. In addition to their mansion they owned a yacht, an A frame ski retreat in Sun-valley, and a condo in the Virgin Islands. Lower cost of living and greater economic freedom are benefits of the Hub lifestyle.

The group seemed ensconced in the American work ethic, its members often working long daily hours. In general, they did not work weekends and only worked about forty weeks a year. They had been together eight years and could see no reason why they could not successfully continue. A variety of conflict resolving systems were employed to keep things running smoothly. As a young psychologist I was amazed at how such a group of go-getters could possibly maintain peace and harmony.

Most of us have met or known of a multigenerational extended family consisting of a dozen or so blood related relatives. Similarly, Hub structures of up to twenty similar aged adults have always existed and can be seen today as young people cut their expenses by living together. Likewise, there are increasing numbers of young couples with children, sharing accommodation with other couples.

Contemporary gated communities and retirement villages closely resemble human housing of old. Counselling retirement village seniors has been an enjoyable and sometimes humorous task; they often are game to try new activities, new ways of thinking and behaving. The women customarily out-number the men by five-to-one or more and show no scruples as they try to outwit each other for the attention of the men. The men enjoy the sexual access to so many women but struggle to keep up with the demand.

Strength and survivability of the strongly committed group can be seen world-wide in criminal organizations that have a long history (Mafia) and more recent innovations such as 'bikie gangs.' Many of the wealthy have close ties and work together for their own benefit. Political parties do the same. In western culture the closest the average person gets to this type of solidarity is the labour union.

In building a Hub, the pressure to conform and the fear of exclusion could be major problems. It is impossible to know beforehand what problems may crop up. The group will have to feel its way along via experimentation.

3 Cooperation - United cooperative relationships are more productive and satisfying than the adversarial and competitive relationships that have plagued human history. Hub members accept diverse philosophical, cultural and religious beliefs, as long as the tenants do not place humans in conflict with each other or nature. Hence, members flow with the changes in life and the environment, using their creative collective ingenuity to optimize life.

4 Freedom - Primates genetically demand the freedom to be nomadic, to openly express themselves, to be active physically, emotionally, mentally and socially. Their insatiable curiosity is a mandate to break free of fetters and venture into the unknown. They detest walls and cages. The mental functioning of animals deteriorates when they are caged; many go psychotic.

Morning dove's ancestors spent several hours, several days a week, foraging for food and other supplies. Maintaining their abode and tools took less time. There was ample free time to socialize, play, explore, think, satisfy their curiosity and develop potentials.

The survivalist Sylvan Hart described life as a 'jumble' for the constantly busy city dweller; whereas, he could understand and cope with anything because he had free time to think about it. In contemporary life we need plentiful free time to investigate world happenings, new research findings and study means of improvement.

***

Herb – 'My personal cubicle in the office is a better cage than some; I have a window view over the city. Big deal eh! I took this job because it offered more freedom; I no longer take paperwork home. Sue and I continue to lower our cost of living, allowing us to take more time off without pay.'

'You have more time to socialize with your neighbours?'

Herb – 'We try, but both members of the couples around us work full time; after work they're busy trying to take care of the kids, house and car. They do not have time to relax, socialize and just live.'

'Over time your family as a model may have beneficial impact on them.'

Herb – 'Maybe so, it's like you say, their brain filters were set up wrong, they don't know any better. Plus, there is the fear of the unknown; they think they are safe in the cage.'

***

Self-imposed restrictions can be the most difficult chains to shake off; they often stem from a persons' lack of self-understanding. Take a look at the ape in the mirror; how much do you really know about this character? Do you own up to your flaws? What secrets do you keep from yourself and those around you? You are a sucker when it comes to what? Is there ever a time when you don't consider yourself first? Why should anyone love you? Are you ever going to accept responsibility for your talents so you and others may benefit from them?

5 Nature - Humans have lived amidst nature for 99% of their history; it is their home, where they thrive. I cannot over stress the importance of living within a natural setting. It fosters physical, mental and emotional health and vitality. More and more people are beginning to accept that we do not own the environment; we are only short-term tenants sharing it with other species and we have a responsibility to maintain the planet's viability. As diverse groups join hands, bonding together into stronger communities, they will create more feasible beliefs and customs which acknowledge the sanctity of the wilderness realm.

To accomplish this, future human settlements will be limited to one third of the planet, while another third of the planet will be entirely devoted to other species. The final third could be acknowledged as a joint use area. Planetary population could be kept below 4 billion. Population guidelines for Mars and other planets, awaits assessment of resources.

6 Action - Life is in the living, the experiencing, involvement and participation that provide happiness and emotional satisfaction. Hub life demonstrates that love relationships are a greater force than power, and maintenance of operating systems is more important than progress.

Administrative Structure

Society currently requires the meeting of certain standards if one is to drive a vehicle, practise a trade...; why are there no such criteria for parents or politicians? The formulation of guidelines for the rearing of children will be one of the first tasks for a newly formed Hub. In the long run associations of Constellations will take up this role. I suggest some rearing components in other sections.

Hub participants have input into the communal functioning and devise methods for assigning leadership and other responsibilities which avoid the common pitfalls of too much power in too few hands - corruption, incompetence... Outstanding Hub or Circle members who demonstrate the importance of self-cultivation, brotherhood, and the sacredness of all life would be possible candidates. Leadership and roles of responsibility should probably be of short duration and routinely rotated to maintain the strength and flexibility of the communal unit.

ADMINISTRATIVE SERVICES MAY INCLUDE

PLANNING, CONFLICT RESOLUTION, EDUCATION, PSYCHOSOCIAL, MEDICAL, TRANSPORT, COMMERCE, COMMUNICATION.

Planning –A Hub is the centre of life and therefore needs planning to ensure proper construction and maintenance. Genome sequencing may be used to select Hub members having the widest diversity of healthy genes. This method along with individual assessment of intelligence, emotionality, and physical abilities could be used to guide the selection of males and females to begat children. Child bearing may be restricted to those between the ages of twenty to thirty.

Planning will require research of needs, desires, evolving changes and an in-depth assessment of each member's potentials and personality. From this data, responsibility, occupational and educational decisions are made. It also assists in the allocation of resources to members.

Food production, building construction, maintenance programs, service provision, and social milieu are some of the areas needing planning.

Conflict Resolution – Hub emphasis on cooperation will help keep conflicts to a minimum; however, some conflict is inevitable. Consequently, Hubs will research, devise and implement methods of conflict resolution and means for existing with irresolvable problems. Plentiful media materials are available to help with this. The current adversarial legal system is often damaging to both parties and therefore should generally be avoided.

Education – The prolific science fiction writer Isaac Asimov commented that the accumulation of knowledge by science has out-paced mankind's development of wisdom. I believe this is true in large part due to society's failure to apply what has been learned. In the formation of a stellar society,

415

application of existing knowledge takes precedence over the search for new knowledge. Assessment of community needs and citizen feedback are used to build viable educational programs for the individual, family and community. These programs must blend in a mutually profitable manner with nature, beneficially facilitate the ongoing life of the communal group (Hub) and complement the innate characteristics of humans.

Innovative Hub home schooling could assume education in values, cultural traditions, socialization, use of the senses, survival... Physical training and the arts could be a part of Hub and Circle life. Individuals are encouraged to engage in new activities that are the opposite of their usual undertakings, practise speaking from a differing viewpoint and so on.

Consider alternative educational programs like Montessori, and Steiner (Waldorf) schools The Steiner programs view humans as a part of nature and stress balancing physical, behavioural, emotional, cognitive, social, creative and analytical attributes of the student; there is much in agreement here with Hub standards.

Circles might provide primary school classrooms in math, language, history, science, propagation of plants and livestock with classrooms arranged according to ability level Rather than simply age. Adults will monitor and limit media - TV, movies, video games, radio, internet, printed material. Consider a year of part time employment between primary and secondary education.

Secondary school could utilize Circle, Constellation and online resources as well as visits from educators and trips to organisations and businesses. It could entail intensive study of social, political and environmental science; along with international culture and history.

For a period of one year after secondary school, students could live and work in two foreign cultures (six months in each). Upon completion of the foreign work they may return to their Hub or another to begin career training or tertiary schooling. They should be encouraged to enrol in a one-year intensive political science course which is a prerequisite to obtaining voting rights.

An altered form of tertiary education could be conducted in universities, and on-site work locations. It would draw upon individuals and resources available throughout the Constellations. University is open to all students who have completed secondary school and employment requirements and have had at least one year of world travel. Course work would intensify the teaching of social sciences, of expanded awareness, emotional wellbeing, quality interpersonal relationships and collective unity. These are fundamental for the successful continuation of the human species.

As Einstein has suggested, the acquisition of specialized knowledge is not the goal of education. In the Stellar society education will include hands on experience and focus on creating a student capable of independent thinking, judgment and action. It will foster emotionally stable personalities who are able to accept the responsibilities inherent in a cooperative, socially intertwined life style.

Throughout society, people need to acknowledge the responsibility they have to everyone and everything in the world. This is necessary for Western culture to transcend the great harm that arises when food processors put sugar or other detrimental substance in their product, manufacturers use inferior elements in merchandise - or build-in obsolescence, marketing makes false claims, politicians/governments distort/mislead the public and so on.

Most forms of competition will be avoided, as it is detrimental to the forming of the personality and the community.

Currently exorbitant resources are funded for power organizations (military, police) resulting in a funding shortfall for community infra-structure, environment, health and education services. Universities are forced to focus on generating revenue rather than providing education and leadership.

Psychosocial – A trained counsellor within each Circle will be backed up by a psychologist, social worker or psychiatrist from the Constellation.

Medical – Circles have a trained paramedic or nurse and each Constellation will have a medical physician who has extensive training in medicine and the social sciences.

Transport – Circles have transport vehicles for individuals and cargoes; which link the Circle with other Circles. Ground based transport is likely to be replaced by air transport.

Commerce – In the stellar age, exchange of goods and services within and between Hubs and Circles will likely involve some form of sharing and bartering. Commercial entities required in a society, such as manufacturing and distribution are kept small and maintain a quality work environment for all employees. Every effort is made to produce superior, long lasting products and services that meet the needs of the community without harming people or nature.

There will be an amalgamation of generalist/ jack-of-all-trades workers and university liberal arts graduates. When the vast breadth of this group's knowledge is applied to research, development and systems application, it will enhance and help secure a comprehensive, progressive evolution of the society.

419

Communication – Regularly scheduled Hub meetings will address current concerns. A member may request feedback on their functioning within the group. Video and sound equipment will be available for self-monitoring. Access to world news and events will be accompanied by analysis, labelling items as trash, not significant, untrue/inaccurate, questionable, manipulative, significant...

HUB GOALS

1 Quality Life - knowledge, wisdom and effort, is dedicated to the well-being and happiness of members and the vitality and security of offspring in the present and the generations to come. Hubs have superior food, clothing, housing, medical care, education. They are the initiating force striving to bring humanity's ship back onto its' evolutionary course.

2 Alliance - Hubs liaise with local, national and international Hub societies and share an empathic, reasoned unity of core values and beliefs that accepts the rights of all societies to exist, no matter how different they may be (transpersonal consciousness). Hence, a vast array of customs and practices peacefully coexist.

These connections ensure offspring are able to marry into other Hubs for a continuation of Hub benefits. Plus, it paves the way for Hub individuals wishing to join another Hub.

3 Planetary Maintenance - Protect and enhance the earth's life forms and elements. This includes the biosphere of space surrounding earth.

CONCLUSION

The guidelines offered in this chapter are only starting points for consideration. It remains for the Hub builders to delete and/or add to the list. The final listing can serve as an introductory explanatory document for prospective new Hub members and those interested in supporting Hub development. Hubs will keep detailed journals and records of all procedures. The information is assembled into an operation manual guiding Hub building, functioning and maintenance. Thus, future generations can profit from the experiences and learning of the past to constantly improve efficiency and avoid making the same mistakes as their predecessors.

Chapter 19 Golden Ambience for Growth

Issues - Finding members, Social structure, Personality development

The initial individuals embarking on the journey of Hub building will customize chapter 18's guidelines and keep copies as they seek to enlist members and support for their adventure. It may be easiest to start the search close to home. Parents have a vested interest in their offspring and might be willing to help. Siblings are probably facing many of the same life issues, thus they will be interested in the procedures and may be supportive. It is particularly important to be supportive and caring of brothers and sisters; a lifetime close relationship with siblings is priceless.

Other relatives may be empathic; enlisting their support could require persistence and patience. Older people may believe their numerous years give them more wisdom; frequently this is not the case. However, loosening of filter restrictions during the senior years often results in a clearer perception of reality and the ability to rise above cultural myths. Seniors often surprise others.

Friends and acquaintances are the next line of support. You do not have to agree with their ideas and behaviours; they still deserve your support and you never know when you will need theirs. Do not become disillusioned when some people appear keen about your different-ness but remain closed to real conversation or input. They have the right to choose their own course through life. You may learn something from them.

A nifty trick for learning from others is to make a list of ten acquaintances. The person most agreeable to you would be number one, least agreeable number ten. Now endeavour to be close friends to the three people on the bottom of the list; you will learn tolerance if nothing else.

When the circle of known people is exhausted, it is time to visit social groups and clubs (hiking, astronomy, science...) Create activities pulling people together - a dinner party, ball game or weekend outing. Include varying ages, socioeconomic and educational level.

Be on the lookout for someone that stands out in the community as innovative or different - a businessperson, activist, religious leader or societal dropout. Seek consultation from social scientists. Locate farmers, cruising sailors, foresters... they spend their lives in the natural elements and their career demands they be actively involved in a wide array of challenges. They have to be mechanics, electricians, carpenters, metallurgists, meteorologists, horticulturalists, biologists, - the list is endless; they tend to function in a more balanced manner than the average person. In catastrophic times these are the people that survive and go on to rebuild.

Usually there is a maverick or two in any group. If you can locate a wealthy maverick, they might provide leadership, motivation, political clout and financial assistance. Look for those that shun fancy cars, palatial mansions, elaborate holidays and lives of leisure. They might expend energy helping various community charities and institutions. You have to be careful here as the predators also use such activities to reduce personal taxes and buy the support of locals.

Investigate innovative leaders in the business sector; not all of them are predators, a few are conscientious. They know balanced development not only helps humanity, it lowers business costs, increases profits and establishes strong adaptable organizations. Check out 'B' (benefit) corporations, in their practices they seek to protect the individual, society and the environment.

In 2015, Forbes magazine in its 'Change the World' competition for social entrepreneurs under the age of 30 awarded $100,000 U.S.to the Unitarian Universalist Community Cooperatives (UUCC). This UU group seeks to set up houses containing elders, single parents with children, young professionals and others under one roof; striving for sustainability and social change. The initial house has 13 residents ranging from age 12 to 70.

Visit religious groups; some retain communal characteristics and could again be a leading force for humanity. Monasteries could become the headquarters of communal families. Churches led by families of clergy could pull together cohesive neighbourhood groups including agnostics and atheists.

Buddhist organizations may be supportive of your growth efforts and contain members of your ilk. Our nearby Buddhist forest retreat offers guests meditative peace. Some of my clients have found the open acceptance beneficial, although not without problems.

***

Cheryl: 'I had a wonderfully relaxing weekend. As requested, I kept the toilet lid down so innocent insects would not drown. But, when a mozzie lands on me, I smack it!'

***

Professional associations, particularly those in the helping professions, have a breadth of talent. Offering your services, perhaps as a volunteer, will expand your knowledge and increase your ability to tap into association resources. You might help two diverse associations step aside from differences and unite.

Look for politicians and government departments that support diversity, human rights and the environment. Small nations and small sub-cultures are most likely to have the flexibility and interest in furthering progress. Minimally, learn how you might use the legal system to protect yourself.

Fortunately, the nuclear family only exists in a small proportion of the world and is on the wane. Current economics are forcing western cultures into a group style of living. Young adults leaving home rarely live by themselves; households of four or more young people are common. Young marrieds in increasing numbers are remaining under their parent's roof after marriage. It has become more acceptable for two married couples to share a dwelling.

If your family lacks accessible relatives, consider inviting single adults or other couples to be aunts and uncles. There are organizations that line up retirees to serve as grandparents for youngsters in families that have no grandparents. Investigate all of these living arrangements; they are a gold mine of information.

Aligning human support and finding soul mates may take a while, do not give up. The natural environment is always there to support you; but you cannot hide in the forest, you must venture out amidst the smoky warped societal mind to find like-minded people and possibly a few helping hands. There are a multitude of books and audio/video programs detailing society's history.

Understanding the past helps to clarify the present and plan for the future. What we need now are depictions of a possible future where communities of balanced fully mature people confront the rigors of life. A weekly television series of this type could lead the way, informing and teaching us how to endow people with stellar qualities?

SOCIAL STRUCTURE

The potential of a fully mature human is so great that it would require many volumes to detail it. When a group of such individuals bonds and enlists further support from like-minded souls in the surrounding social milieu, they can create an organizational structure of phenomenal strength and flexibility. The diversity of talents and resources within provides members protection from life's hardships and an infinite array of growth pathways.

Governments often fail to provide adequate assistance when someone loses their job. On the other hand, the small community is always there to support and assist members through trauma. In the coming civil upheaval, the Hub is more likely to survive than the nuclear family; particularly, if the nuclear family is in a large town removed from nature.

In one of Brian Aldis's science fictions stories an elder from another planet sets a goal for an earth man to demonstrate his self-discipline. The fellow is instructed to leave a specific item on the dining room table and never move it. The earthling says, 'no problem', and advises his wife of the arrangement and she agrees to honour his wishes. On returning many years later, the elder sees the item sitting on the table, 'yes, it is there, but it has been moved many times as your wife cleaned the table.'

This is an example of one of the many pitfalls of a nuclear family. In a communal family there is great veracity, members make sure each person maintains their commitments to each other and the family. Hence, ongoing deceptive, abusive and other forms of damaging behaviour are kept to a minimum.

A Hub building group does not have to reinvent the wheel; they can study the history of communal groups in the past and learn from the first-hand experiences of existing communal family groups. Agrarian, religious, artistic, political and offbeat cultural groups exist world-wide. People generally are friendly and delight in sharing the features of their life style. When you find a group or movement that appeals to you, live with them for a period. Make note of their good attributes and their shortcomings. Are they able to match the positive offerings of the prevailing culture? Some groups have been created upon sound principles, but lose the plot and ferment into a deadly brew.

Employment –plays an integral role in building personal self-confidence and helps cement the relationships within the Hub. This expedites a united social structure in which each member has a sense of place, a sense of belonging and being valued by others.

Stellar age work tasks will be designed to be fun, exciting, challenging, an opportunity to express creativity, and will complement human functioning, not degrade it. When possible, debilitating odious work tasks will be done by computers or machines. Otherwise Hub work teams may negotiate amongst themselves so an individual may be able to completely avoid those chores they detest. Work is more pleasant if shared. Work assignments in the future will be chosen by the worker who has a passionate interest in that work and the work is compatible with their personality.

At present there are numerous jobs that do not add value to the society, and many of them actually increase the cost of living for everyone. Advertising, selling, financial manipulation and so on, need to be eliminated.

A lack of work decimates the ability to function. This has been borne out by research of the unemployed and the occasional time an ISS member did not receive items necessary for conducting their work. Hence, work skills training would be available to all citizens of the constellations. This will produce diversely educated and trained groups, who will have the skills to meet all the work demands of the Constellation.

Contemporary Hubs forming near or within cities will benefit from the wide range of employment opportunities; although the rural Hubs' greater access to free resources results in a lower cost of living. In both scenarios plentiful free time and diversity of skills results in better maintenance, so equipment lasts longer and a greater degree of self-sufficiency and profit making becomes possible.

Employment provides income for life's necessities, but, does not guarantee life will be a bowl of cherries - wisdom and self-control are needed. I remember primate experiments where food was placed near a caged monkey; he had to straighten and narrow his hand, to reach through the hole and grasp the treat. But, he can't pull his clenched fist back through the hole; he sits immobilized, trapped by his greed. How many citizens are imprisoned at their work site, unable to escape due to the house mortgage, car loan, and credit card bills?

Hub members and Stellar voyagers have multiple skills, insuring their self-sufficiency. A few voyagers will be space transportation experts; however, the majority will have abilities needed for colonization: construction, engineering, mining, agriculture, creation and maintenance of atmosphere and water, system designers, social and educational planners, psychological and medical services, food services...

Play - Work must be balanced with play; some type of diversion, amusement or recreation which may foster excitement and joy. Such activities lubricate social interactions, leading to better adjusted, relaxed people. Play fosters intellectual use of cognitive abilities and encourages creativity. The emphasis should be on cooperative endeavours, with an avoidance of strongly competitive enterprises.

Stellar communities provide venues and occasions for members to socialize - such as cafes, dance floors, hobby groups, group retreats, concerts, plays, parties... Likewise, there will be places for intrapersonal contemplation and introspection - seats beneath the trees, next to the water, on mountain peaks, mirrors...

Customs - Festive occasions will be organized to celebrate momentous Hub happenings, such as, the Hub's anniversary, group achievements, a day in tribute to mother-nature and one for the spirit of cooperation. Births, birthdays and deaths will be honoured. Some events will be commemorated throughout the Constellation.

PERSONALITY

The structure trembles in the onslaught of horrific destructive forces. The facial veneer fractures in places and fragments of the personality are ripped away, leaving the individual feeling incomplete, un-whole and vulnerable to the Machiavellian demons. Just as the universe is in perpetual motion, your personality is always on the move. The question is; is it moving in a positive or negative direction? Or is it madly dashing about, yet going nowhere, floundering ever closer to the abyss of nothingness?

Developmental psychology and personality theory are essential learning areas when one attempts to grasp the complexity of the human personality. A group's ethnic and cultural heritage, religious practices, ethics and numerous other factors also have a bearing. The home milieu is crucial in the formation and nurturance of personality. Since family members share responsibility for offspring, and indeed for each other; it means everyone's actions have a bearing on numerous personalities. Each person is a model.

Models - Hub members are immersed in a lifestyle of mutual support, loving and sharing, that is sustainable within the wildness of nature. This engenders a sense of peace with oneself and others providing a sense of contentment in each day. They possess the internal fortitude to successfully negotiate the difficulties of life and to do so in a casual happy manner. They are aware of their assets and liabilities and nurture their unique traits and characteristics. Furthermore, they are always learning and developing their potentials while maintaining the nuances and relationships inherent in life on mother earth. They have risen above the myths and shortcomings of the prevailing society. Their daily lives portray principles that will ensure that those around them can learn emotional strength and all the facets and talents of a well-rounded personality.

Training - From birth onward praise, affection and training are daily staples. Personality may be likened to a muscle; training and active use of a muscle creates a skill - throwing a ball, operating a key board, ice skating... In the same manner, training in social skills, work skills, life planning, how to cope with stress and so on strengthens the personality.

Belonging - Children born into this optimal developmental setting will be able to draw upon an extensive range of resources and thrive amidst the love, support and values of a communal family. This highlights the great intrinsic qualities of the natural homo sapiens, such as the naked infant's need for skin to skin contact which will be met by extensive bare skin handling by carers. This imbues the infant with a ground level sense of acceptance, belonging and self-confidence.

Self-Identity - Minimal use of clothing throughout life is advisable; studies have shown a stronger sense of self-identity and security amongst groups wearing little or no clothing. Historically, some clothing has denoted career, family or tribe. This may once again gain prominence within Constellations. At present, ancient forms of physical adornment have come back into vogue; face painting for children is common in contemporary festivals and many adults now sport tattoos.

Responsibility - As the infant progresses the learning of self-control and responsibility can begin. Non-threatening toilet training procedures are employed; evacuation control is an early step in acquiring self-discipline. Adults may devise a variety of didactic approaches helping children to be responsible; to accept their obligations to make the correct decisions, take appropriate actions, be culpable for their mistakes and do so without supervision.

A five-year old is capable of maintaining personal hygiene, laundering their clothes, caring for pets and maintaining the cleanliness and order of specific areas within and outside of the housing complex.

Confidence - Training children in simple skills (shoe string tying, dressing, setting the table…) enhances their sense of capability and helps them understand that they are valued by the family. Maximization of potentials and learning how to cope with adversity further solidifies an unshakable confidence. This produces Stellar souls who possess firm confidence in their ability to cope with all situations, including their failures and death.

A child is bound to have some inherited traits from a distant ancestor that differentiate them from their parents; adults must be observant to ferret out what those qualities are, so they can organize appropriate training and experiences which will capitalize on the child's unique traits and potentials.

Honesty - is the natural state of the youngster and should always be praised. As long as Hub members practise a forthright caring honesty, it will reinforce the child's honest nature. Such children become stellar adults who are honest and forthright; they can be taken at their word; if they say they will do something, they do it. When asked for information, they provide it clearly and accurately. They can be trusted. Children are quick to pick up discrepancies between what is said and what is practised.

Flexibility - is a hallmark of survival; rigidity is a sign of death. Many elements of life are transitory, good in the initial stage but bad later on. A Stellar soul is flexible; they learn from each life experience, then move on, not getting bogged down.

Consider children's debating groups wherein they research and then defend a position the child does not actually believe in. This fosters acceptance of other people's ideas and beliefs.

Assign a task and when it is half completed, place the child on another task. As the brain does not like unfinished business, this procedure creates anxiety. Therefore, it helps the child learn to flow with the changes in our real world where it can be difficult to finish things and get closure. It also builds resilience and help form a disposition that is able to accept defeat and disappointment.

Assign tasks and problems in which the structure, contradictions and unknowns make resolution impossible. Require the child to put forth and defend what they view as the best possible plan of action; it strengthens their capacity for coping with ambiguity and hardship. This, in combination with diverse life experiences, is a prime builder of flexibility.

A twelve-year old could be responsible for the preparation and delivery of common meals, tending food crops, care of livestock, looking after young children (not infants), upkeep of records and so on. Consider having a child serve as a 'gofer' for a specific adult and changing the adult every 6 months; this assists the learning of cooperation; plus, the child may absorb positive characteristics from each adult.

The 16-year old could be involved in administrative and planning meetings, care of infants, teaching youngsters, operation and maintenance of machinery... From this point on group consultation can help the individual strengthen self-discipline and responsibility throughout the life span.

Adult - training and activities help members keep an open mind, to be accepting of change and new information, to probe contradictions, the unknown, the perplexing, the repugnant and life's ambiguities; always searching out alternative routes of action. They learn to accept and appreciate differences in individuals and groups, aware that a singular political, educational, economical or religious system stifles optimal development. Similarly, they avoid becoming preoccupied in a singular activity and have the flexibility to strive for beautiful action across a diversity of pursuits - painting, carpentry, sports and so on.

The Chinese philosopher Lin Yutang praised the benefits of diversification often found in amateur activities. He states he enjoys the musical playing or magic tricks of a friend as much as attending a professional concert or magic show and points out how parents enjoy the amateur dramatics of their own children more than career actors in a Shakespearean play.

Hub members have the elasticity to maintain a balance in the time they allot for themselves, the Hub, friends and the community. They keep a balance in work and play, mental and physical activity, social time and solitude, reading and hands on learning, frivolity and seriousness.

Such balancing of polarities fosters excellent physical functioning, mental alertness (they observe everything), intellectual curiosity and emotional stability.

Hub members act with gentleness, compassion, love and generosity; are noble in attitude and move with pride and dignity through the humdrums, joys and battles of life. They are loyal and dedicated to each other, the Hub, society and world.

Courage and perseverance - the will to live, to survive, is an observable quality in the stellar citizen. Originally this fortitude was built up during millions of years of physical hardships and the more recent fifteen thousand years of mental/emotional instability inherent in the world's debased societies. The Hub continues the strengthening of these traits via assigning difficult tasks and teaching strategic coping and resolution methods. In the face of hardship, the stellar individual may pause to regroup, reconnoitre, alter direction, change strategy or gather new forces, but they never give up.

In this way they courageously carry forward the strength of the ancestral lineage; allowing them to live ardently, tackle the seemingly impossible, to keep going in spite of fears, odds stacked against them and condemnation from others. This generates new learning which further strengthens the sense of self and self-confidence.

CONCLUSION

Personality development creates a new self; a being that lives in a new dimension. This brings forth facets of the individual and the world, about which the person has no awareness. Confusion looms large. Over time the mists dissipate revealing with clarity a new comprehension, a heightened awareness of ubiquitous beauty. Therein one becomes grateful and gracious, emanating a colour and fragrance that warmly draws in the life about them.

When a group of these superlative functioning people link up with similar groups, they form the solid core of a society blossoming into maturity. Global unity must first be preceded by family unity in the Hub, unity in the neighbourhood and unity in the local region.

Hubs provide the means for the species to survive the coming chaos and are the genesis of humanity's future that will steer the evolutionary ship back on course. The future lifestyle specifics of this evolved human cannot be foretold with accuracy, but we can imagine some of its characteristics.

Chapter 20 Stellar Life

LIFE POST CHAOS

In the predawn twilight a smoky haze hangs over the Queensland hillside. Atop the knoll a lone sentinel sits concealed amidst the brush, her senses super alert, the woman's canine assistant sniffs the breeze. The acrid stench of death comes and goes with the wind shifts. Here and there around the countryside fires continue to burn. No birdsong or mammal sounds interrupt the low drone of insects.

Mid-slope, fingers of sunlight filter down through the dead and dying canopy of trees falling upon a series of dug out caves and make-shift shelters harboring the 34 sleeping members of the Ognam Hub. As a result of their being united and fully functioning, these remnants of humanity survived the bombing, gassing and spraying, the shooting and looting.

Being reality oriented and having an accurate unbiased perception and comprehension of the surrounding world, gives these scraps of humanity superlative logic, meticulous analytical thinking and rapid, decision making skills. Hence, they are systematic in all endeavours and deftly handle complex, abstract data; all of this assisted by superb memory skills. These qualities are in full use now as homo-sapiens reclaim their place in the bounty of nature, re-establish their place in the animal kingdom and set their sights on fulfilling their evolutionary return journey to the stars.

As the sun rises the red, orange and yellows of vegetables flicker amongst the low-lying vegetation. A 12-year old boy crawls out of a shelter and strides down the hill to a series of pens. Opening the first, a flock of chickens swoops out. From the second, a dozen goats scamper free and spread out into the shrub growth.

Mostly naked hominids are popping out everywhere; an old man carries an infant on his back as he sets about lighting a cooking fire. Two teenage girls open a hatch in the ground and remove several sealed containers of cereal grains and nuts, which they place on the rough-hewn table. A woman begins milking the goats. A lady tacks a notice on a bulletin board.

NOTICE FOR ALL HUBS

February Update - World-wide communication channels are in full operation and indicate all violence has ceased. Head counts reveal approximately 100 million planetary humans remaining. This number is constantly changing as most of those who underwent toxication are slowly succumbing. On the positive side, isolated individuals, as well as, hidden pockets of people are being discovered almost daily.

Hubs representatives are working together to consolidate methodology for the daily functioning of a Hub based society. In the meantime, they suggest survivors join or form living groups utilizing the guidelines of the existing Hub and Circle groups. All efforts must be made to avoid the old hierarchal systems of ranking people by their economic usefulness and degree of compliance with governmental dictates. Within your family units, weed out detrimental practices, and incorporate the salient attributes from nature, ancient learning and modern innovation to construct community living patterns of political and social equality which foster stable, emotionally sound cooperative groups.

Intl. Hub Assc.

***

15 thousand years of human history makes it clear homo-sapiens future will not come from faith in a God or Gods, warfare, increasing the gross national product, global business unity, scientific research, technology, or education. Nor will the reestablishment of the natural human be initiated by governments, the wealthy or corporations.

Too many corporate boards, company officers, politicians, community leaders... are males; society needs a more feminine perspective. Although these men may possess high calibre technical abilities; some are heartless-emotionally cold, never having had a friend, lover or partner. Others deny responsibility to anyone or anything other than themselves. Many of these men simply don't understand the human qualities of honesty, respect, honour...

Their inhumanity is not their fault; they have been moulded by a pathological society of immature dysfunctional beings. Bestowing upon them an inability to give to others, to care, to have an aesthetic appreciation of beauty, of life, of the world about them. You cannot expect these automatons to lead our species forward; for they are the harbingers of death and destruction.

Humanity's future lies in the hands of each and every one of you having the bravery to abandon our previous society's highly acclaimed, but pathological, life style and reinvesting in each other. Via the association of Hubs, Circles and Constellations, we shall pull together to set up a nature-based lifestyle. It is up to us to show courage and serve as exemplary models of unified human behaviour helping our species to rekindle faith in itself and move as an indomitable force into the future of a truly meaningful life, and eventually into the infinity of the Stellar realms.

A DECADE PASSES

In a remote northern temperate forest, a Circle is being established to harvest timber, strengthen wildlife populations, and research methods of adapting plants to severe cold. The botanical work is aimed at crafting food plants that can flourish on the colder planets.

***

Beneath the snow laden grey clouds, the Hover Truck flits across the tree tops as the buffeting winds threaten catastrophe. Kapaluch deftly manipulates the controls to keep the heavily laden platform upright and level, as her thoughts ponder the impending crisis. *If I don't get this prefab unloaded and setup before this blizzard sets in, this communal family of 25 will have to suffer yet another night of cold and misery in their tents. Not good for the ailing grandmother.* She activates the deicer to slough off the ice building up on the vehicles leading edges and begins the descent to the well-lit platform below, her face intent with concentration.

***

Far to the south, next to a grove of mountain ash, a thin metal rectangular contraption hisses and hums as it forms a bed room, windows, doors and all, within minutes. A light crane lifts the room into place alongside the other two rooms already in place. The home is completed by mid-afternoon.

Throughout the Feather Circle, the Hub dwellings reflect the persona of its members. Some modular units are partially sunk in the ground, while others are stacked into the trees. All Hub housing is amenable to expansion, modification, and blends harmoniously into the environment. One kitchen, dining room, shower room, laundry, pantry and recreation room serve the entire Hub. Compost toilets are numerous. There are dormitories as well as single rooms for sleeping.

Strolling about the parks, shopping areas and social venues, Sheila, the Circle's psychologist is keenly aware of a throbbing vitality alongside a sense of peace, contentment and tranquillity; an atmosphere that welcomes all and makes a person cognisant that they belong here. The place is entwined within their inner being. The citizens are jovial and relaxed, in all manner of dress and undress and while their individuality is obvious, there is no sense of separation, isolation or loneliness. No one in this community is better dressed, housed, fed, or educated than anyone else.

Sheila passes a fly fisherman wading in the bend of an idyllic stream, the waters calm surface dimpled by trout feeding on a new hatch of mayflies. Further along the stream flows into a lake where a group of artists with their easels dot the sandy beach. Several wave, she goes over to meet them.

'Gday Sheila!'

'Hola Felipe, Annette, Bill, Karen, Klaus and Roger, being creative and soaking up some rays eh!

Roger chimes in, 'It's really more about socializing and gossip.'

Steve questions - 'What are all the changes in the Constellation's brain filtering and PELGAM growth program about?'

Sheila responds – 'It is hoped it will further strengthen the Hub's atmosphere of sincere honesty and trust, because it is that atmosphere that primes the person to be emotionally, socially and intellectually mature enough to pursue truth, meaning and unity in daily life.'

After more conversation Sheila moseys along to a garden café for a mid-morning cuppa. While sipping she scans a newspaper. A research study reported it was on the verge of producing a drug capable of stimulating the growth of the 'creativity' PELGAM. Another article detailed research on the manipulation of genes. Progress was being made on reactivating genes that had been turned off during humanities post agricultural revolution stagnation. Deactivation of problematic genes was meeting with mixed success.

There are numerous Hub notices seeking members who have a specified skill. Scientists from the Global Association of Constellations predict that the planet's space program will be up and running within the year.

***

It was a close call, but human extinction was avoided and the population growth has ceased, allowing ample room for other species, and making it easy for humans to thrive with the available resources. The species has a bright future. The return to the balanced communal life in nature reignited his vision for an ideal existence that savours the good qualities of his species and abandons the bad. It produced a flowering of potential that made previous human advances seem miniscule. The advances in life quality are amazing,

A CENTURY PASSES

Strapped in my seat, the commuter cabin is suspended mid-air; awaiting the shute. Below the regional orb Cariopolis is barely visible amongst the luxuriant tropical foliage extending uninterrupted twenty kilometres to the coast. The seventy passengers relaxed, after five minutes the shute zipped up. It took 45 seconds for our cabin to replace a cabin on the larger craft. The four-level shute was

Rongolian and elaborately decorated in the snow horse and sand theme.

I was looking forward to my assignment in sub-tropical/ Jacarpolis. My duties are to assess the ongoing functioning of the aldea Constellation with their two thousand members and some of the smaller four hundred-member Circles near the mountains. Several stops have significant personal meanings. In Circle Arbol I always borrow a guitar to play along with their famous instrumental group. I've known Leif, the noted organist all my life. Carleta of the Wigwam Hub is a long-term lover and soul mate always capable of diverting my mind from work.

A circle of seventeen hydromatic wigwams adorn a meadow midway up the mountain slope. I sit with several hunters around a fire; while out hunting they found an injured fawn in a ravine. With loving care, they cleaned the fawn's wounds, closing lacerations with the telesuture.

Being an avid fan of the American continents indigenous cultures, I loved visiting the people of the wigwams. Their wigwams were the epitome of simplicity and efficiency. Solar collecting hydromatic panels were supported by alloy temperature beams; all set upon a firm waterproof insulated sandwich.

Conversation shifted to recent technological improvements in their stun gun. I listened intently but failed to grasp the physics behind the nebelizer's ability to painlessly kill their prey. Odella was the most knowledgeable about the improvements. Slight of build, with tight ringlets of brown hair framing her oval face, she, like all the wigwam members, had expertise in many vocations. I have not heard her sing, but they tell me she has a voice as clear and pure as a ringing bell.

On extended hunts, the hunters spend nights in one of many shelters scattered throughout the bosque. These abodes also serve as retreats for individuals or small groups needing a break from the Hub's main group and as maturational training sites for the young people. From age ten each child spends one week alone each year focusing on life skills and learning how to relate to nature. At age fourteen a month is spent alone as part of being welcomed into the adult community.

Standing and stretching, I walk over and gaze down the slope; my binoculars spot the silver dome covering the Hub's anti-gravity generator in the valley forty kilometres away. It is the only visible evidence of the hunter gatherer Hub.

A prism powered Hover pickup came up the slope skimming across the treetops and settled on the parking zone beneath a gnarled beech. Carleta and Tryon stepped down onto the lush grass and began to unload supplies as I and several others rushed to help.

**

'Hola! Roberto. Como esta?'

'Muy bien Carleta, y tu?'

'Oh! Glad to be home and it is so good to see you. Give me un abrazo y un beso.'

It felt good to hold her. 'Hi Tryon, you must have had a hard day, there is enough powder on you to insulate ten trans pods.'

'Welcome my friend. Yeah! One of the oscillating fabricators broke down; I spent the last four hours in its guts. Leon from Jacar will be on tomorrow, he'll complete the repairs.'

Pickup unloaded, I stripped and spent an hour with others chanting in the sweat lodge; then cooled off in their fish farm pond. Finally, we all moved to the hot spa beneath the cliff face; sipping their local brew we conversed as the sun slowly sank into the misty western peaks.

***

Turs - 'Is this the first time you have been to our mountain retreat?'

'Yes. I've been to your riverside Hub twice, but never here.'

Turs - 'Many of us spend the summer months up here where it's cooler; a few linger on in the fall collecting maple syrup, but the place is empty January through March, too cold.'

'Anyone come up for a white Christmas?'

Hannah responds 'Oh yes! Over half of us spend Christmas through New Year here, skiing, sledding and skating.'

'Must be a lot of work tearing down and reassembling the wigwams for a couple weeks use?'

Turs says, 'See that shack built into the hillside, with some pipes coming out of the ground further up the slope?'

'Yes. I noticed that earlier and wondered what it was?'

Turs - We've constructed all necessary facilities into eleven rooms built back into the hillside, which we occupy Christmas holidays. During our summer stay it is used for storage and guests. One room is used for Trylac assembly, we are part of the Pacific basin Trylac suppliers'

***

The wigwam Hub has failed to develop the mountain chains mineral resources. None of their members has the interest or expertise to do so. They have posted an advertisement for a metallurgist on the international light wave advertisements.

Prior to my visit, I reviewed their life style functioning records. They maintained good birth control and balanced the numbers of incoming new members with the exodus of members to other Hubs, always keeping their population below the 400 allowed. Their child rearing practices for tuning brain filters and balanced PELGAMs were well within acceptable parameters as they had been for the past hundred years. The results were obvious in the Hub's general demeanour.

They are relaxed, full of adventure and fun; with a lot of chuckling, whistling, humming and singing. They display many evocative facial expressions; smiles, exuberance, curiosity, tenderness. Sensory handicaps are almost non-existent. Even the members over 100 years of age retain excellent vision, hearing, memory and physical agility.

They have a lanky young fellow of eighteen who has exceptional wave sense. He can detect, pinpoint and diagnose energy wave transmission disturbances from ten kilometres. He is able to sense what insects are present within a one-hundred-meter radius and can locate and name life form waves from a kilometre distance. Although, he admits a few birds confuse him.

Since last year's evaluation, the group continues to struggle with a young male's aggressive power behaviour. However, they have become so adept at dealing with a coy manipulative member, that she has shown tremendous growth benefiting herself and the entire group.

The Hub's free, yet highly supportive lifestyle has seen the young adults group break free of negative acting out or damaging rebellious behaviour. It is amazing to witness how they keenly soak up all they can from their elders.

After a week of mountain air, I joined Mark and caught a local beam for the flight into Jacar, where he is employed as a chemist several days a week. Currently they are breaking down and analysing unknown compounds recently brought back from the habitable planet Illian that lies within Alpha Centauri A. I asked him how many hours he spent in the lab.

***

I work the twenty hours maximum allowable per week; but, only work seven of the permissible nine months a year.'

'How do you spend your off hours in Jacar?'

'I participate in the wider range of musical outlets available, attend classes in sculpting and volunteer teach chemistry. The rest of my time is in the Hub playing with the children, cooking, socializing and just loafing.'

I told him about my return to music. 'I have recently gotten back to music, playing my guitar in a jazz group composed of members from several hubs. It is the first I have played with others since completing the mandatory prenatal to age ten music training. I'm finding it quite enjoyable.'

'Did auditory discrimination deteriorate during your absence from playing?'

'Minimally, I can still hear a flowing river or waves on a beach at a distance of five kilometres. I think the vibratory nature of sound waves is so tied in with the tactile sense that you would almost have to undergo long-term sensory deprivation to seriously impair hearing. I can put my hand on the ground and feel the river or waves from double the distance that I can hear it. I sensed three minor quake tremors on the mountainside last evening.'

He said, 'did you sense the wind shift out on the plains this morning?

'Sure did.' Marc asked me if I used the lingual drug to get back into music?'

'No, I didn't think it was necessary. I did use it four years ago to help me learn the lutvidron dialect.'

'It is fascinating how the drugs chemical properties allow an adult to process music and language in much the same manner as children.'

'Well it worked for me and I'm not particularly good at languages. It was still a struggle that took a lot of time, but I finally mastered the dialect after about six months. You enjoy your time in Jacar.'

'Yes! it's great. I prefer the climate at the Hub, as I enjoy experiencing the four seasons. I find the year-round warmth of Jacar a little boring; although, I would not want to live in one of those stadts in the frigid-zone. Are there many of them left?'

'I believe there are twenty world-wide. Last year I participated in a team review of Norburg two hundred kilometres south of the artic-circle. They use solar focalizers for energy.'

'Did you get a chance to see the woolly mammoths?'

"Yes, I spent some of my free time out on the tundra plateau observing them, they are impressive.'

'I was impressed by the dodo birds when I visited Chiloe island, off South America. Next year a group of us plan to spend time in central Africa. I've read interesting studies on ancient birds, mammals and reptiles regenerated and placed in the area between Lake Victoria and Mount Kilimanjaro.'

***

We arrived in Jacar and said farewells. I had two hours to spare before the carrier shute was due. I walked about the dozen commercial ventures forming this regional centre. Walls were generally frescoed or covered with colourful murals. Sculptures and fountains were scattered about the forested areas between buildings.

All manner of wild life was present on the ground and in the trees. Only a few of the buildings were left over from the destroyer era.

Walking in the shade beneath a huge Banyan tree, its arms spread fifty meters in every direction; I came upon a media screen. A Balmanian university research team reported they had been successful converging time and space at the micro-level in twenty subjects. Eventually this could lead to exploration much further into infinity.

The 'Memory Institute' reports current human memory ability to be 3 times greater than it was a century ago. Recently developed techniques are giving more complete access to a person's ancient memories. This has led to the discovery of ancient civilizations not listed in the history books, populated by our species, plus two others. So far, they have been unable to determine if the other two species developed on our planet or another.

CONCLUSION

A long time ago in the vast void of the universe, mother nature constructed a round space ship, 25,000 miles in circumference; crewed it with a variety of species and innumerable other elements, and sent the ship hurtling through space. Homo sapiens have begun to imitate mother nature's actions, throwing a few bits and pieces into the vast darkness. So far, we have only gotten humans as far as earth's moon and he may reach Mars in a decade or so.

Intergalactic ships capable of leaving our milky-way to traverse the vastness of unknown space are but a dream at this time. It may take centuries, but eventually humanity will launch itself beyond our solar system. We can imagine an epileptically shaped vessel 100 meters high and the length of 2 football fields with a corrugated surface. The ship might pull itself along on the universe's dark energy flowing along the corrugations. Or the ships may have gravity controllers that reverse gravity, thus ejecting the ship from a planet and then intensifying gravity so the vessel is pulled to other planets. Such vessels possibly will have a capacity for almost constant acceleration, speeds approaching half the speed of light may be possible. Research may discover methods for collapsing and converging time and space. Relativistic time dilation could play a role.

Interstellar ships will establish bases on those rock bodies most amenable to setting up a terrestrial type environment. Cold tolerant plants that emit huge quantities of oxygen, space energy that creates a protective halo and robotic space probes that retrieve ice, could facilitate a habitable environment.

Alien life forms will be found that force us to revise our definition of life. A non- tangible gaseous life form that procreates may exist. There could be beings that are like thoughts yet can fabricate and handle material items. Wouldn't it be mind boggling to come upon a system of planets inhabited by a species the size of a grape that walks on all fours, resembles an armadillo, and are much further advanced than earthlings.

Hub families could be the most efficient ship crews and excellent ambassadors to the universe, yet they face a high prospect of death. They may be captured or annihilated by another civilization; although, their demise is more likely to come from small things. If an interstellar ship encounters an undetected cloud of snow flakes, it would vaporise the vessel in less than the blink of an eye. A foreign planet virus could do the same.

It remains to be seen if space warps, the zero-point field, black holes, unknown wave fields, unique chemistry or expanded biological systems will have positive benefits for homo sapiens? Are we going to find multiple universes, confirm the existence of an omnipotent force, or find the limits of the universe? Outer space and the inner mind of man contain infinite possibilities for the fully functioning Stellar voyager to discover and utilize for the achievement of an exemplary existence for all inhabitants of the universe.

I wish you Bon Voyage on your journey of discovery.

Roberto

Bibliography

Amen, D. G., "Making a Good Brain Great," Harmony, 2005.

Arieti, S., "Creativity," Basic Books, 1976.

Armstrong, T., "7 Kinds of Smart," Plume, New American Library, 1993.

Attwater, Helen; "The Gorilla Journey," Sidgwick & Jackson, 1999

Auel, Jean. 'The Clan of the Cave Bear' Hodder & Stoughton, 1980.

Babcock, C. "The Imprinted Brain" Jessica Kingsley Publishers, 2009.

Bandler, R., Grinder, J., Satir, V., "Changing with Families" Science and Behaviour Books Inc. 1976

Barrow, R., "Language, Intelligence and Thought," Edward Elgar, 1993

Boldt, L. G., "Zen," Penquin, 1992

Boll, T. & Bryant, B. (Editors), "Clinical Neuropsychology and Brain Functions," APA, 1988.

Bookchin, Murray. 'The Ecology Of Freedom.' AK Press, 2005

Brown, K., Grunberg, N. E., "Physiology & Behavior." Vol.56, Issue 6, 1995

Brown, L. R., Gardner, G., Halwel, B., "Beyond Malthus," Worldwatch Paper 143, 1998

Buscalglia, L., "Living, Loving, & Learning," Slack, 1982

Constantine, L., J., "Group Marriage" MacMillan 1973

Carter, R., "Mapping the Mind," Weidenfeld & Nicolson, 1998.

Cayce, E., "Health Anthology", A.R.E. press, 1979.

Coontz, Stephanie. Marriage, A History. New York: Viking 2005

Csikszentmihalyi, M., "Flow", Harper, 1991.

Dale, C., "The Subtle Body." Sounds True Inc. 2009

Darger, Joe-Alina-Vicki-Val and Adams, B. Love Times Three. Harper 2011

Dawkins, Richard, 'The Ancestor's Tale'. Phoenix 2005

Diamond, Jared, "Guns, Germs and Steel" Vintage 1998

Edwards, E. & Bhaumil, K., (Editors), "Visual Sense," Berg. 2010

Einstein, A. "Ideas and Opinions" Three Rivers Press 1954

Einstein, A. "The World As I See It" Snowball 2014

Flora, C; 'Friendfluence' Short Books, 2013.

Fox; K. C. & Keck; A., "Einstein A to Z" John Wiley & Sons INC. 2004

Franklin, B., "The Means and Manner of Obtaining Virtue, 1780"

Human Stellar Voyagers
Bibliography

Gardner, Howard., "Frames of Mind" Fontana 1983.

Goleman, D., "Emotional Intelligence," Bantam, 1995.

Gribbin, J., & Cherfas, J., 'The First Chimpazee'. Penguin Books, 2001

Grof. S., "When the Impossible Happens," Sounds True, Inc. 2006

Guilford, J.P., "The Analysis of Intelligence" N. Y. McGraw Hill 1971

Haisch, B., "God Theory." Red Wheel/Weiser 2006

Harner, M., "The Way of the Shaman."

Horowitz, F. D., & O'Brien, M., (Editors), "The Gifted and Talented," APA, 1985.

Houtz, John, "The Educational Psychology of Creativity," Hampton Press 2002

Howard, P. J. "The Owners Manual For The Brain," Leornian Press, 1994.

Jung, C.G. "Man and his Symbols," Doubleday Windfall, 1964.

Kahn, Lloyd, "Homework," Shelter Publications, 2004

King, Barbara J; "Roots of Human Behavior." The Teaching Co. 2001

Knox, D., "Marriage Happiness" Research Press 1971

Koestler, A., Janus: "A Summing Up," Picador, 1978

Lacy, Scott, "Anthropology and the Study of Humanity," The Great Courses, 2017

Lame Deer, John; Erdoes, Richard. Lame Deer, Seeker of Visions. New York: Simon & Schuster, 1994

Laszlo, I., "Quantum Shift in the Global Brain." Inner Traditions 2008

Lezak, M. D., "Neuropsychological Assessment," Oxford, 1976.

Maslow, A., "Religious Values And Peak-Experiences, "Viking, 1964.

Maslow, A., "Toward a Psychology of Being," Van Nostrand Reinhold, 1968.

Mayeroff, M., "On Caring," Harper & Row, 1971

Mc Taggart, L., "The Field," Harper Collins 2008

Mc Taggart, L., "The Intention Experiment," Free Press 2008

Merton, T., "The Way Of Chuang Tzu," New Directions, 1969

Montagu, A; "Touching," Columbia University Press, 1971

Moore, T., "Soul Mates," Harper Collins, 1994.

Moustakas, C. E., "Loneliness," Prentice-Hall, 1961.

Nearing, H. & S., "Living the Good Life," Schocken, 1954.

458

Human Stellar Voyagers
Bibliography

Neufeld, G., Mate, G., "Hold On to Your Kids' Ballantine Books N.Y. 2006

O'neill, N. & G. "Open Marriage" M. Evans & Co. 1971

Patton, J. R., Kauffman, J. M., Blackbourn, J., Brown, G. B., "Exceptional Children In Focus" 5th Ed. Maxwell MacMillan, 1991

Peterson, H., "The Last of The Mountain Men," Tower,

Peterson, J. B., '12 Rules For Life' Random House Canada, 2018

Plotkin, B., "Nature and the Human Soul" New World Library, 2008

Plotkin, B., "Wild Mind" New World Library, 2013

Pyle, R. M., "The Thunder Tree' Oregon State Univ Pr; 2011

Restak, R. M., "The Brain," Doubleday, 1979.

Robinson, K. S. "Red Mars,"Bantam, 1991

Rogers, Carl, "Becoming Partners" Delacorte Press 1972

Russell, B., "Power," Routledge, 1938.

Russell, B., "Authority and the Individual," Unwin Hyman, 1949.

Russell, B., "In Praise of Idleness," Unwin Hyman, 1935.

Russell, B., "The Conquest of Happiness," Unwin Hyman, 1930

Sapolsky, Robert M. "Monkeyluv" Scribner 2005

Schofield, W., "Psychotherapy," Prentice-Hall, 1964

Sheldrake, Rupert. 'The Sense of Being Stared At'. Park St. Press, 2003

Shermer, Michael, "The Believing Brain," Holt 2011

Siegel, R., "The Science of Mindfulness," The Great Courses 2014

Skinner, B. F., "Beyond Freedom & Dignity," Alfred A. Knopf 1971

St. James, Elaine., "Living the Simple Life," Hyperion, 1996

Sternberg, R.J., "Beyond IQ," Cambridge University Press 1985.

Streznewski, M. K., "Gifted Grown Ups," Wiley, 1999.

Sturges, T., "Every Idea Is a Good Idea' Tarcherperigree. 2014

Suzuki, D., "The Sacred Balance." Allen & Unwin, 1997.

Tammet, D., "Born on a Blue Day" Hodder & Stoughton, 2006

Tammet, D., "Embracing the Wide Sky" Hodder & Stoughton, 2009

Thoreau, H. D., "Walden," Modern Library, 1854. Mentor

Tocqueville, Alexis de, "Democracy in America," 1835.

Tsu, Lao., "Tao Te Ching," Vintage.

Ungerer, T., "Far Out Isn't Far Enough,"
Methuen, 1984.

Waal, Frans De, Lanting, Frans; Bonobo;
University of California press, 1997

Waal, Frans De; "The Age of Empathy;"
Three Rivers Press, 2009

Waal, Frans De; "The Bonobo and the
Atheist." W.W. Norton & Co. 2014

Walsh, A., "The Science of Love,"
Prometheus Books, 1996.

Walsh, R., "Essentials of Spirituality"
John Wiley, 1999.

Walsh, R., Grob, S., "Higher Wisdom."
SUNY Press 2005

Wambach, Helen, "Life Before Life,"
Bantam, 1979

Wambach, Helen, "Reliving Past Lives,"
Harper & Row, 1978

Wechsler, D., "The Measurement and
Appraisal of Adult Intelligence,"
Williams & Wilkins, 1966.

Wei, Wu., "I Ching Life," Power Press.

Young, J. Z., "Programs of the Brain,"
Oxford, 1978.

Magazines

American Scientific

Cosmos

Philosophy Now.

Australian Geographic

National Geographic

Films

Reggio, Godfrey, Qatsi Trilogy
Koyaanisqatsi – Life out of Balance
Powaqqatsi – Life in transformation
Naqoyqatsi – Civilized violence
Anima Mundi –

www.ingramcontent.com/pod-product-compliance
Lightning Source LLC
Chambersburg PA
CBHW060018030426
42334CB00019B/2085